A History of Chorley

A History of Chorley

Jim Heyes

Lancashire County Books, 1994

A History of Chorley
Jim Heyes

Published by Lancashire County Books, 1994

Typeset in 10/12 Monotype Ehrhardt by Carnegie Publishing Ltd,
18 Maynard St, Preston, Lancs.
Printed and bound in the UK by Cambridge University Press

British Library Cataloguing in Publication Data
A CIP record for this book is available from the British Library

ISBN 1-871236-31-2

Contents

Acknowledgements

Some seventy years ago Canon Porteus opened a lecture with the question 'Can anything interesting be said about Chorley?' It was a rhetorical question from an antiquarian who firmly believed that the answer was yes. I share his opinion and during the past few years the research for this book has taught me more about Chorley's history than I had known before.

I received generous help from a great many individuals and organizations, amongst which I must highlight the libraries and their staff of Accrington, Blackburn, Bolton, Chorley, Derby, Preston, Manchester and Toronto Public Libraries; the archivists of the Lancashire Record Office, Wigan Record Office, Mrs Kathryn Murton of the British Library, and the Public Record Office. To all of them I tender my thanks. The Crompton extract plan on page 67 is reproduced by the kind permission of Napthen, Houghton, Craven, Solicitors, Preston.

Chris Aspin, David Hunt and Bill Turner each gave valuable encouragement, and a special word of appreciation is due to Denise Westbury-Haines who led the Historical Interpretation Team for the Community Programme. Her tireless research into archives of all kinds revealed a wealth of 'new' information about Chorley's past.

My thanks are also due to Mr A Green of New Jersey, USA, Ms Felicity Goodall, for BBC South and West, Mr Gordon Haworth, Mr Alistair Hodge, Mr Ken Hodkinson, Mrs Zoë Lawson, Mr J. S. Miller and Miss Diana Winterbotham, MBE.

This book is dedicated to my wife Elizabeth with much love. Her support and encouragement were with me every step of the way.

CHAPTER ONE

The Early Period

Introduction

AT THE CLOSE of the twentieth century Chorley faces a future in which the traditional industries which fuelled its growth and prosperity have receded and died. Industry transformed a sleepy market town into a thriving centre of manufacturing and commerce but exacted a heavy price on the environment. Strangers were frequently shocked by what seemed a harsh, industrial landscape – but many revised their opinions when they had time to appreciate the community. Sidney Campion arrived in 1913 to work as a journalist and wrote his first impression in a letter home.

> I came here last week but I shall not stay a minute longer than I can manage. The people are very rough in their ways and speech. The town is small and depressing and without an impressive building, except the Parish Church, and Astley Hall. I don't like the cobbled pavements, and I don't like the clatter of the clogs before six in the morning. All the men wear caps and all the women wear shawls. I am in lodgings where I am given rice pudding every day. I have met only two men who have read books – one a reporter, and the other an accountant at the colliery.[1]

An even less favourable picture comes from the diary of Richard Crossman, the Labour minister responsible for the Central Lancashire New Town, in 1965.

> I arrived in Preston to find all the Lancashire people delighted with the news about the New Town, and I spent the morning in a bus with them, taking a look at that dreary Lancashire plain . . . I found [that] I had designated the New Town in an area with at one end a really ghastly town called Chorley and at the other end a slightly less ghastly expanded village called Leyland . . .[2]

Crossman came in February, the least congenial time of year; Bishop Nicholson, however, travelling from Carlisle to Manchester in 1704, wrote of Chorley,

> October 17, Tuesday. From Garstang to handsome and proud Preston, 10 short miles, and thence to Chorley, six, as long in riding

> as the other ten. Twas Mercate Day here; and I could not but take notice of the generally fair countenance of both sexes.

Despite the defects noted by some outsiders, a fierce local pride has endured in Chorley over the centuries, equally evident in the writing of observers. One such, James O. Halliwell-Phillips (1820–1889) was a noted Shakespearean scholar and critic, whose father had left Chorley, penniless, in 1795. The son recalled,

> My father was very fond of his native county – used to talk the old Lancashire dialect to perfection to the dismay sometimes of his hearers; used to breakfast on porridge he got from Lancashire.

In total Chorley's history spans perhaps a thousand years, from its earliest settlement to the modern day. During that period of time the character and nature of the community was shaped, as a small market town evolved into a nucleus for a sub-region of neighbouring communities, among them Euxton, Coppull, Adlington, Whittle-le-Woods and more. This clustering was as much for economic and historical reasons as for administrative convenience, and during the last two hundred years, moreover, the network of roads, canals and railways has strengthened the role of Chorley within the county of Lancashire.

Chorley's history is linked inextricably with its location astride the great highway, now the A6, which links Manchester with Preston and the North. In war and in peace travellers using this road have passed through Market Street and out over Red Bank to the south. During the Jacobite Rebellion of 1745 Chorley was a mustering point for Sir Henry Hoghton's two companies of volunteers to fight the Scots; fortunately, his scantily armed men were not put to the test. The Jacobites, however, were still recalled in folklore down to 1924 when Sir Henry Hibbert retold his family's story of the retreating Scots passing through the streets of Chorley on their way north.[3]

Leland's summary of Chorley in the sixteenth century was 'a wonderful poore or rather no market'. Four centuries later a piece on Astley Hall for *Country Life* magazine (1922) reported, 'Today, with its colours dimmed by smoke and coal pits martialled like an encircling regiment of Colossi upon the horizon, it strikes the stranger as a depressing place.'[4]

This book will therefore trace an industrial community from its origins, up to the point when it could be said to have reached the summit of its prosperity and success, in the early years of this century.

Regional setting

In this area the land rises gradually to the east, to Heapey and Anglezarke from 300 feet (91 m) at Chorley to the moorland tops, Winter Hill (south) 1498 feet (456 m) and Great Hill 906 feet (276 m), while to the west the land falls away to the coast at Banks.

A section from Yates's map of Lancashire, published in 1786, notable as being the first modern map of the county and for the inclusion of sites of industry such as coal mines and mills. [Lancashire County Library]

In geological terms the area is called the Chorley Platform, occupying land on the 200- to 250-foot range, with a thin layer of boulder clay over rock. During the Ice Age much of Lancashire, including the Rivington, Anglezarke and Darwen moors, was covered by the ice sheet. When climatic change melted the glaciers immense new lakes were formed and dammed at certain places. Water escaped through meltwater channels: one example extends from Chorley towards Bolton, another through the Douglas Valley. Another meltwater lake covered Gale Moss (now under the M61) – this drained away through Botany Bay, Cowling and into the Yarrow Valley. In the 1790s the Leeds and Liverpool Canal exploited an old meltwater channel of this type. After the Ice Age a moraine deposit left a ridge of boulder clay, sand and gravel called the Chorley Moraine, running north from the Yarrow to Whittle-le-Woods. A bonus for early settlers came from outcrops of sandstone which provided quarries at Charnock Richard, the Whittle Hills and at Brindle, the stones from Whittle being especially valued for millstones.

Documentary and soil evidence support the impression that, with peaty moorland to the east and wet marshland to the west, an ancient tract of woodland cloaked the district in early times. Domesday Book records a wood running from Leyland to Horwich while many placenames suggest that woodland was once plentiful.

Prehistory and the Roman period

Lancashire is not as rich as other regions of Britain in known prehistoric remains, though what clues there are help experts to piece together stages of human habitation. In the Chorley area the best-known sites are found on the high moorland to the east. The region's climate changed markedly after the Ice Age, becoming warmer and wetter, encouraging plant growth to flourish – forests covered all of these high moors, the slopes being swathed with oak, alder and hazel, birch and elm in some pockets.[5]

Firm evidence of early settlers came in 1957 when a burial mound was identified on Winter Hill. The mound dated from about 1500 BC and was built of stones and turves in the form of an outer circle 63 feet in diameter and an inner ring enclosing a burial site. The contents of the grave had long since been plundered but pollen analysis showed that the burial was made in a woodland clearing surrounded by hazel, alder and oak. Heather, ferns and forest-grass clothed the forest floor.[6]

Several other burial sites are known from the Rivington area. One burial mound was investigated at Noon Hill in 1959 – its site still housed flint arrowheads, a small flint knife and traces of three separate bodies, buried here about 1100 BC. Similar burials were made at Round Loaf and Anglezarke, the Twa Lads at Horwich and the Pikestones long cairn. Pottery urns were found at some sites, often containing the occupant's cremated remains.

In later centuries these places were regarded by the locals with deep suspicion – some were haunted, it was said, and should be avoided. The legend of the Spectre Horseman of Rivington, quoted by Roby (*Traditions of Lancashire*) shows the fear still associated with the moors. Their very names show the folk belief – in Devil's Ditch for instance, near Round Loaf. By the Victorian era antiquarians were taking more interest in the earthworks. Some believed Round Loaf to be an Anglo-Saxon creation, others dreamed up a picture of Druids engaged in gory rituals. One Chorley antiquarian, writing in 1840, said of the Pike Stones, 'I measured the circles and looked with awe upon the cromlech or altar of sacrifice.' He recorded that the local farmers, disregarding any superstition, had carted away any uniform-looking stones for walls and sheepfolds a few years earlier.

By contrast a discovery was made in 1963 which revised all previous knowledge of Chorley's earliest settlement. At Astley Hall Farm the farmer was uprooting a sycamore before erecting a Dutch barn. Tangled in the tree roots he found a pottery urn (later dated to the Bronze Age). Inside the urn were fragments of bone, identified as coming from a woman

Gorse Hall formerly stood on the east side of the old Blackburn highway, close to the boundary of the manor and at a spot where a roadside cross was recorded up to a century ago. [Lancashire County Library]

who had suffered from osteo-arthritis. Eleven years later the site was acquired by the Central Lancashire Development Corporation and archaeologists were able to carry out a detailed excavation of the area. Their work showed that six people, both adults and children, were buried here between 1400 and 1000 BC. A second burial urn, and pit burials of four cremated bodies, were found together, in a rough circle; signs, perhaps, of a large homestead. This find from Astley Hall Farm is the oldest known site of settlement in Chorley to date.[7]

After the Romans had conquered the North West they built military bases to control the region at Chester, Manchester, Walton-le-Dale (a supply base), Ribchester and Lancaster. Chorley has no known Roman settlement, although parts of the road network have been found nearby.

Lancashire's first Roman road ran north from Manchester to Ribchester, then north to Burrow in Lonsdale. A second arterial highway ran from Wilderspool on the Mersey, then to Wigan (given the Roman name of *Coccium*), and on to Walton-le-Dale on the Ribble. D. C. A. Shotter has pointed out that Wigan Road (the A49) at Charnock Green follows the line of this Roman road and sections of it have been excavated in the past near Coppull. A number of finds of Roman material have been made in the Chorley area, and some have speculated that other roads, as yet undiscovered, may have passed through the district.

Heapey was the location of a much-publicised find in January 1835, when a group of workmen, engaged in removing earth from the top of a stone quarry near Heapey Church, came across a cache of coins. At a depth of one foot they found a hoard of Roman coins and a silver chain. The coins, reportedly eighty-one in number, sixty of brass, twenty-one of silver, and all said to be in good condition, were probably put in their hiding-place at a date no later than AD 140. They were from the reigns of the Emperors Nero, Galba, Vitellius, Vespasian, Domitian, Trajan and Hadrian. The chain, which is now in the British Museum, consisted of two brooches, linked by a chain of silver, the whole weighing about four ounces.[8]

In the year after the find at Heapey Church another hoard was discovered in the Chorley area, in this instance in the quarry at Whittle Hills. A chance find turned up a group of a thousand coins, apparently deposited much later than the Heapey cache. Most of the Whittle Hills hoard can be dated to the period between AD 253 and 273, though a few coins date from the reign of the Emperor Philip (AD 244–9). In addition to the coin find there is a long-held tradition that the Whittle quarries were worked by the Romans.

During the last century a significant cluster of finds was made; an interest in antiquarian matters was fashionable and the likelihood of finding Roman remains seems to have stimulated more interest. Two finds were made at Leyland, the first in 1836, the next in 1850. In 1833 a large gold coin of Nero's reign was reportedly found at Euxton and in 1884 at Croston workmen found an earthenware dish, buried with 200 to 300 coins of the third century AD, on the site of Littlewood Brick and Tile Works. At Brindle, too, a hoard of twenty-one late fourth-century coins buried in a pot was found in 1934. Chorley town's contribution is slight; during the building of Fosterfield Mill in the 1870s a Roman amphora was turned up in the diggings.

Place-names

For the period after the Roman withdrawal in the early fifth century, there is a dearth of archaeological and written evidence. Historians have therefore turned to the study of place-names to supplement their knowledge. They conclude that the area was settled by Angles moving west through the Pennines. From the tenth century Norse settlers migrated from the west, enriching the cultural mixture still further. Ekwall argued that local place-names show the diversity, British settlements named, for example, in Ulnes Walton and Walton-le-Dale, while Limbrick and Rangletts have a Norse origin. Margaret Gelling has also dated a name such as Chorley itself to the pre-Conquest period, being Saxon in origin.

In 1246 it appeared in a court record as 'Cherleg' and on one occasion local people testified that the correct form was 'Chorley'. It is not an uncommon name – the Ordnance Survey's index of modern place-names has twenty-two Chorleys, from Sussex to Lancashire.

Expert opinion argues that 'Chorley' is formed from two Saxon words, *leah* and *ceorl*. *Leah*, *Ley* or *leigh* is a very common place-name element, originally denoting a woodland glade and later used to mean a clearing from woodland. *Ceorl*, however, has seen a change in meaning. It is now only used in the modern form *churlish*, yet its original meaning was very different – a *ceorl* had the status of a freeman, akin to the yeoman of the Middle Ages. Combining the two words denotes a clearing in the woodland made by a freeman. The Domesday Survey for Leyland Hundred tells of twelve berewicks (manor farms), held by twelve freemen for as many manors, of which Chorley is assumed to be one.

An alternative theory interprets the name as the 'clearing on the River Chor', but Canon Porteus argued that, so far as records go, the River Chor was known as the Main (or mesne) Brook until 1577, implying a boundary division. Porteus also offered the theory that 'char' might simply be a name for the district around Chorley, suggesting that Charnock might have the same derivation. His argument is supported by the tendency in

Botany Bay Wharf on the Leeds and Liverpool Canal, 1987. The canal navvies gave this name to an area known as Knowley Wharf during the cutting of the canal in the 1790s. [Author]

local dialect to pronounce the town's name as 'Charley', a fact recorded by travellers in the seventeenth and eighteenth centuries.

The suffix *ley*, frequently found in local place-names, implies that there was an extensive tract of woodland from Leyland roughly to Bolton. Locally, leys are found in *Hea*ley (high . . .), *Baggan*ley (boggy . . .), *Kings*ley (King's . . .), *Ast*ley (east . . .) and *Know*ley (. . . on the brow). In one case, *Wymunds*ley (in Astley Park), the first element could be a personal name Wigmund, as a similar form is at Wymundshouses in the Ribble Valley. Well into the seventeenth century Chorley's parish register records an area called the 'Leigh', yet the only clue to its location comes in the Duchess of Norfolk's estate plan of 1734, placing the 'Lee' approximately between Harpers Lane and the River Chor. Around Chorley a group of names with the suffix *-ton* denote Saxon settlement: examples are Euxton, Croston, Wheelton, Adlington, Anderton and Ollerton.

Bretter's Farm, just outside Duxbury, was once Brettargh, a Saxon name for a British farm. Names which include British elements are few: Charnock is probably one, Heskin, Douglas and Yarrow others, while Eccleston marks the site of a pre-Saxon church.

Linguistically, the dominant surviving place-names have Saxon origins – *Eaves*, as in Eaves Lane and Eaves Green, meant 'land at the edge of a wood', and Crosse Hall was originally Eaves Hall. Nearby the name *Burgh* denoted a fortified farm holding, echoed in the name Duxbury. Close by two place-names, now largely forgotten, were Culmerley and Culmariclough, next to Birkacre and Plock Wood, each of the names containing the element *maire* (a boundary).

Relatively few Norse place-names occur in Chorley; examples include the Rangletts on Chorley Moor (from *Vrangr* = crooked, perhaps describing the stream), Northgate on Knowley (including *gata* = road), Carr Lane (*kiarr* = a marsh overgrown with bushes), and Gale Moss (*galla* = barren, wet land), significantly all on the periphery. From the Tatton papers comes one medieval reference to a field named Hefstanisfeld, incorporating what seems to be the personal name Hafstan.

Medieval names

The Domesday Survey (1086), carefully recording lands and tenures, has no entry for Chorley in Leyland Hundred (nor, in fact, for many local villages) – *Lailand* itself is included and a mention of the twelve berewicks. However, a number of documents survive from the Middle Ages, quoting local placenames, many of which are no longer in use.

The occurrence of 'greens', as in Chapter Two, is linked to early farming practices, as in Hartwood, Baldwin's or Fool's Green. Lidyate Lane was a medieval lane giving access to Astley Wood, made redundant by the demise of the town fields and then built over in the last century. Juffars Croft is no longer identifiable, while Judeland, on the Astley lands, is a puzzling name, perhaps meaning Jew's Land. The Charnock estate extended well beyond Astley itself and much of the east side of Bolton Street down to Duxbury was Charnock land. Merefield occurs in 1304, Merelane in 1417 and Maire fields at other times, recalling the boundary concept. By the 1770s the name had become corrupted to Mermaid! Until the last century Brownsfield lay near the entrance to Astley Park, though the name is given as early as 1417: it is apparently derived from the Brown family.

Fellery Street is older than it seems. Originally a field named Fallow ley, Fallelley or Falloway was here; in 1417, as the Faleley, a path led from the Stump and Steeley Lane to Chorley Bottoms. At Healey the Twitchills has been interpreted as the witch hills (Porteus), but in 1324 *le Twecheles* meant a crossroads.

Other survivors from this period include Plymouth Bridge, a name debased via Plummers and Plimmers from Thomas le Plumber of Charnock Richard, living in 1441. At Cowling, Butcher's Ridding is notable, both for illustrating the site of a woodland clearing for farming (a ridding) and for the mangled version of the name Bourchier, one of the lords of the manor in 1381. Close to this spot, on the boundary of Duxbury, lies Riddings farm, now almost fallen into decay, an abandoned homestead hacked from the wild perhaps seven hundred years ago. The name Hartwood occurs at least six hundred years ago and may be older, a reminder of the once extensive woodland where deer were hunted for sport. Medieval assarting (or woodland clearance) is seldom confirmed, yet intakes are found in several places, one near Moor Road being evidenced from old plans.

During the Middle Ages a group of names reflected wildlife habitats:

Brockholeclough (the cleft with a badger's sett) from 1252; Foxholes and Catclough (for the wild cat); Burrage Bank, Red (or reed) Bank, and Pease Croft were all derived from plants, while Birkacre, Lighthurst and Blackshaw indicate copses or woods. Ackhurst has the same suffix as other examples, the prefix being Les Acres (from the 1300s) and often called Ackers, Accus or Haccust. A deed from 1252 mentions Harestan in Hartwood, on the edge of Euxton Lane. This name began as Hoar Stone, a prominent boundary stone – later maps alter this to Horse Stone Farm.

Up to the last century an old farmstead stood alongside Water Street (at the bottom of modern Commercial Road), named Trigg Hall after a Wheelton family who lived here five hundred years earlier. The Haydocks were later owners of this house. A relic of the past still found in Chorley until 1864 was the pinfold (used for penning strayed livestock), near the modern entrance to Astley Park. Examples of names associated with early industry include the 'bark houses', found at Common Bank and Cowling: these were adjacent to oak woodlands, whose bark was processed for use in the tanning of leather. The township papers of the 1720s provide a name lost in later centuries; Bellybuttlane was a farm lane leading through the Gillibrand estate, possibly along the line of modern Ashfield Road.

Eighteenth-century names

At the beginning of the century Union Street came into being, its name celebrating the union of the kingdoms in 1707. Relatively few new streets were laid out before the latter half of the century, one of the first being Hollinshead Street, named after John Hollinshead. Weld Bank came into use as a borrowing from the Weld family who had inherited the Shireburne lands. As the eighteenth century drew to a close some patriotically-minded townsman conferred the curiously exotic name of Bengal Square upon a group of newly-built cottages, just off the top of Hollinshead Street in honour of the future Lord Wellington's series of military victories in India.

One example of the shift in Chorley's economy from agriculture to embryonic industry lies in the abandonment of 'personalised' farm names in favour of 'locational' names during this century. Thurston Hodson's, and Kingsley's Tenement, for instance, two examples of many long-established and clearly identified farms, had lost their relevance to later generations. In a few cases the farmer's name was adopted permanently, as in Pilling Lane, named after Oswald Pilling.

Two examples of names which probably date from earlier centuries, first enter records in the eighteenth century: Peter Wink, often called Peter Weind, uses the medieval term 'weind' found in Preston and Wigan for a narrow lane leading to fields, while Fosterfield, off Eaves Lane, is found on the 1734 Norfolk estate plan and may derive from *fauster*, a link with church lands allotted for the upkeep of the parish priest.

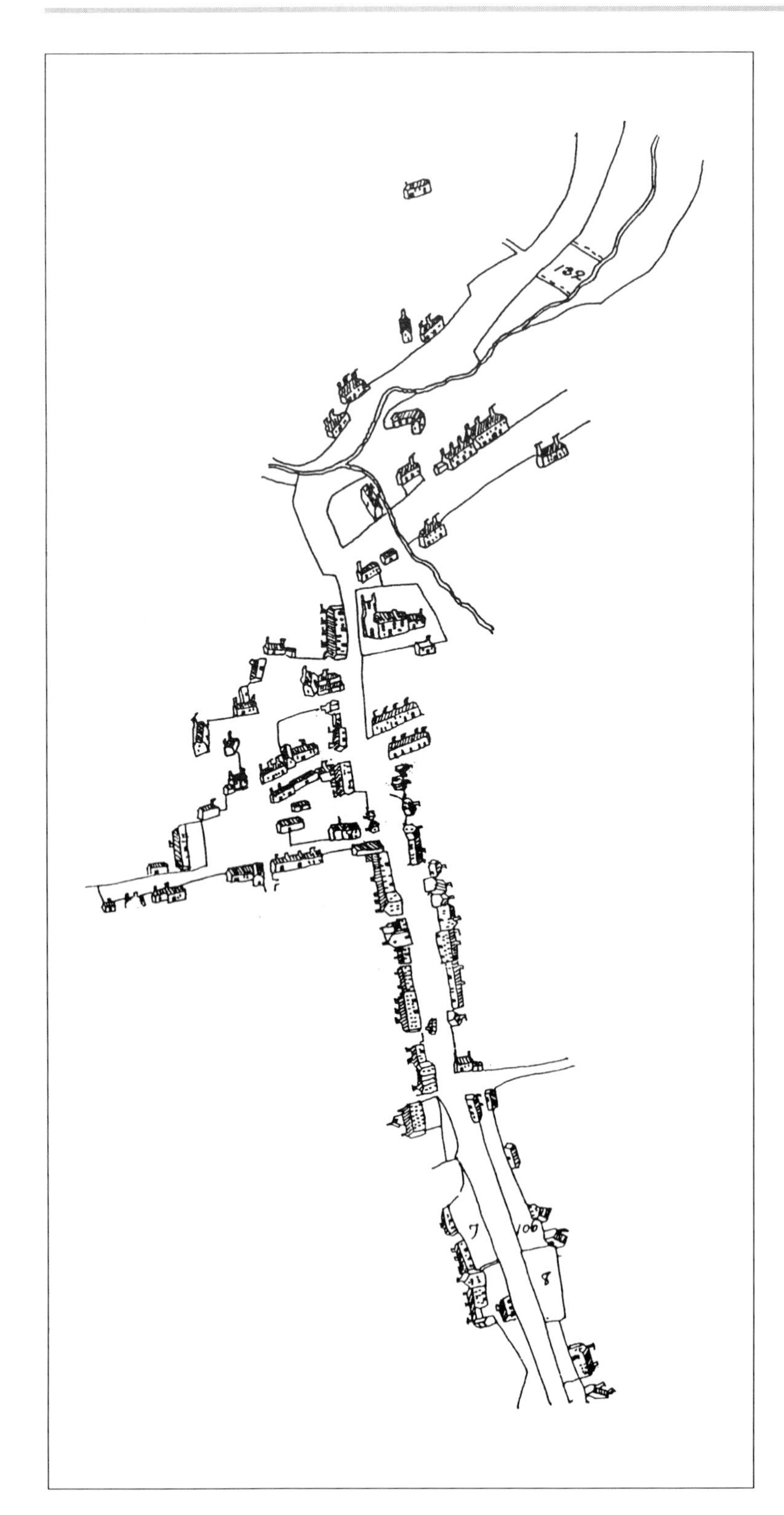

Chorley Town, 1766, from the Commons Enclosure Plan. Until the last century Chorley was a 'linear' town: Market Street formed most of the urban centre. At upper right the parish church is identifiable and the River Chor crosses Water Street at the top right. [Lancashire County Library]

Nineteenth-century names

A handful of names still in daily use can be dated precisely to 11 April 1803, when the vestry resolved that William Bibby and Thomas Somner should name all the public streets in the township: their choice of fashionable London names is reflected in Fleet Street, Holborn, Cheapside, Chancery Lane and Pall Mall. The process gathered pace and there was never such a need for new names as in the Victorian era, when the town expanded appreciably with each decade. Some names were bestowed in honour of local people, such as Fazakerley Street, Cobden Street, Lawrence Street. Others reflect the preoccupations of the day. After 1815, for example, patriotic feeling inspired the naming of Waterloo Lodge (at Hartwood), the Waterloo Inn (in Market Street) and a number of streets – Waterloo, Trafalgar, Wellington and Congress. A later war, the Crimean, gave two pubs, in close proximity, the names of Alma and Sebastopol. Royalty were commemmorated, again in pubs such as the Queen's Tavern, British Oak, the George, Princess Alice, and the Queen's Hotel. Streets such as Clarence, Brunswick and Avondale gained added prestige from the royal connotations of their names.

Older names grew less familiar and some – Lidyate Lane, for instance – were totally forgotten as new properties obliterated them and the passing years erased them from memory. The town's green eventually became just St Thomas's Square, while, although 'on't Duke' survived as the Duke Street area, there was no clear picture of its bounds.

CHAPTER TWO

Christ's Croft: Chorley in the Middle Ages

When all England is aloft
Hail are they in Christ's Crofte
And where should Christ's Crofte be
But between Ribble and Mersea.

CHORLEY'S HISTORY in the Middle Ages is but scantily documented. Surviving records deal mostly with land and property, or crime and mischief. Individual people are usually no more than shadowy figures in the legal papers. In the early thirteenth century, for example, one document tells us that a family of serfs from Chorley was given to the abbey of Cockersand by Adam de Charnock.[1] The only fact known about the family is the name of its head serf Ulf. Likewise, Adam's son Richard de Charnock later gave away Gilbert Finch and his family. About the same period the Charnocks granted parcels of land to the Hospital of St John of Jerusalem, including Astley, Bagganley and Charnock.

The *Victoria County History*, quoting final concords, describes how Richard Green of Heapey counterfeited the king's money in Chorley, at the inn of Joan Wastley from 1437 onwards.[2] He passed the 'money' off at Settle and elsewhere, was caught and acquitted. Shortly afterwards he was taken for the same offence, both at his home in Heapey and at Culmariclough (in the area of Lower Burgh).

The purpose of many of the medieval deeds is to record the boundaries of estates, using landmarks which are now often obscured through time. Timberbrook, for example, is the Euxton Brook, but Wetlache and Mykelriding are not so obvious. It was customary to use ditches and cross-marked stones for markers, the so-called 'harestones', one of which was in Hartwood, a second has been changed through time to Horse Stone Farm, off Euxton Lane. The deeds provide clues to the history of the landscape; many 'ridings' occur in place names and assarting is specifically mentioned. In 1377 Nicholas de Haverington granted lands in the Hartwood to William de Chorley, including Driffenacres (later Drenakers), Bordonstrete, and pasture and wood in Hartwood.[3] The latter was already enclosed by ditches, hayes and hedges, but significantly Nicholas kept the right to enter the wood to cut down and cart away any of the oaks.

Woodland occurs in several deeds of the Charnock family, for medieval woodland provided 'pannage' for pigs. One deed from about 1250 pasture for thirty cattle, thirty sheep, ten mares, thirty pigs and twelve goats. Another, from the time of Edward I, quotes a boundary which begins at the burial ground 'near the street above Hestami Field'.

Some local people served their king in time of war—the Standishes for instance—while the patent rolls show that Thomas Hugynson of Chorley, Knight, served with Sir John Stanley in Ireland in 1390. In 1435 a contract for archers was made between Alexander of Clayton and John Clayton of Whittle and James Standish of Duxbury. Alexander was to be ready on the first day of the muster, with an

> able man of arms arrayed as falls for men of arms and six able archers sufficiently arrayed and each archer 32 arrows and some of them duckbill headed and to follow his master James in the king's service for two years . . .[4]

Chorley was intimately linked with the serjeanty of the wapentake of Leylandshire, who was the king's bailiff in the hundred. Gerald de Clayton was the first recorded, in the reign of Richard I, but later the office passed to the Ferrers family; Henry de Ferrers of Groby who died in 1388 held part of Chorley for finding a bailiff and in 1476 Chorley was said to have been given to the Ferrers for this service. In 1526 Myles Bancroft of Chorley was the king's 'bayle arraunte'. In 1476 when the king was on an official progress the duchy council ordered Lord Stanley to seize those parts of the manor held by Sir James Harrington and Sir John Bourgchier for several years' arrears for the bailiwick rents.

The Banastre rebellion

The course of events in Chorley for centuries to come was shaped by the Banastre rebellion of 1315, part of a wider struggle for power between Thomas, Earl of Lancaster and his cousin, King Edward II. Within Lancashire the earl's foremost supporter, Sir Robert Holland, had been raised from obscurity by the earl and was widely seen as an upstart. In October 1315 armed opposition to Holland was begun by Sir Adam Banastre of Charnock Richard and Shevington. His allies included Sir Henry de Lea of Park Hall (a relation by marriage), Sir William Bradshaw of Haigh and many more. At Westhoughton the group met on 8 October and resolved to act. From Charnock they went to Wigan: within a matter of weeks they had eight hundred men under arms, had taken Clitheroe Castle, attacked Liverpool and captured Manchester. Their plunder included weapons, goods, cattle and corn. Success followed success until November, when they went to Preston and a larger force under the sheriff's command crushed them in battle at Deepdale. Banastre and Lea escaped into hiding at Charnock and were betrayed. Both were executed, Banastre beheaded on Leyland Moor by order of the earl. The *Victoria County History* records that goods to the value of £5,000 were taken in reprisal from the rebels in Leyland wapentake alone.[5]

Local families had supported the rebels and consequently paid dearly. Adam Charnock was convicted but pardoned by the king in 1317. Robert Charnock was killed in the fighting at Deepdale. A greater loss of estates was suffered by the Duxburys of Duxbury. Henry de Duxbury forfeited his lands, was impoverished and saw the Duxbury estates handed over to the Standish family, who had been loyal supporters of the Holland faction.[6]

The rule of law was only re-established when the king came into the county in 1323 in order to halt the civil strife. His courts were held at Wigan and dealt with crimes committed by gentry and lesser folk alike. Heavy penalties were laid on the rival bands which had terrorised Lancashire. Markets and fairs had been raided at will, theft and murder committed openly. The court records name scores of individuals tried, among them the Banastres of Bretherton, Adam Taylor of Coppull, William Bradshaw of Charnock and William Brown of Chorley.

Why was the Banastre rebellion important to Chorley's future? The answer lies in one outstanding woman, Margaret Holland, sister of Sir Robert Holland. She had three husbands in all: Sir John Blackburn of Wiswell; Robert de Hepwall, seneschal to the Earl of Lancaster at Clitheroe; and lastly, Sir Adam Banastre himself. By her first marriage Margaret had three daughters: Alice, who married Sir Robert de Shireburne; Agnes, whose first husband, Sir Henry de Lea, was executed after the Banastre uprising, and whose second husband was Robert de Horncliff; and Joan, who married Thomas de Arderne of Rothby. Though Margaret's second marriage was childless, her third produced a fourth daughter, Katherine, who eventually married Sir John de Harrington. These four daughters and the marriages they contracted governed events for centuries to follow.[7]

Crosse Hall, *c.* 1900. The Crosse family lived at the hall from the Middle Ages onwards, but the older name for it was Eaves Hall, the name indicating an area on the edge of woodland. [Lancashire County Library]

Chorley, with Bolton and other manors, had been given by Henry de Lacy, Earl of Lincoln, to Robert de Hepwall, his seneschal, in reward for valuable services: on his death it passed to his wife, Margaret Holland. In a paper written during the 1930s Canon Porteus made an excellent summary of the complex descent of the manor through the marriages of the four daughters of Margaret Holland. Each originally received a quarter-share of the manor lands, while that of Agnes de Lea was included in the Shireburne and Arderne shares at her death.

The Arderne share was forfeited in 1347 when Sir Thomas was caught up in a case of wife-stealing. That share came once more into the hands of the Ferrers of Groby family. More problems arose when Elizabeth Ferrers married Sir Edward Grey. Their descendant, Thomas Grey, Marquis of Dorset, was raised to power by the king, Edward IV, and when, during the Wars of the Roses, the Grey lands were confiscated Richard III was lord of the manor of Chorley directly. He used the manor as one of the many favours at his disposal, granting it to Thomas Stanley, the future Earl of Derby, in 1484. After Bosworth Chorley was once more in the hands of the king but was soon regained by the Stanleys.

In 1596 part of the manor was sold to Edward Rigby of Burgh and this portion remained with the Rigbys, an influential and important family, until the early eighteenth century. In 1713 Sir Alexander Rigby was financially ruined by his trading activities, and in 1715 he was compelled to sell his estates. Burgh Hall was bought by the Chadwick family in 1727, who rebuilt the hall in 1740.

The Scots raid, 1322

In the early fourteenth century, Healey was separate from Chorley township; then, as now, it formed a wooded outcrop of the moors, but in 1266 it was forest land, held by the king. In 1285 the Dacre family paid a rent of four marks for Healey to the Crown. The rent appears once more in 1314, along with a rent for four burgages in Chorley, recorded among the rents due to Thomas, Earl of Lancaster. In the wake of the Banastre rebellion of 1315 the earl's property was seized directly by the Crown.[8]

In June 1322 the Scots crossed the border, raided Cumberland and burned Lancaster in their march south. They took Preston easily; one large group headed up the Ribble while a smaller party crossed the river and got as far as Chorley. The story is still erroneously repeated that Chorley town was sacked and burned. What the Scots did achieve was the ransacking of Healey Park. After breaking down the palings the invaders stole the wild cattle grazing there and drove them off. The herbage alone was valued as 53s. 4d. annually, now lost, while the chronicler reported,

> of the herbage and pannage of the said park and of the herbage of the wood called le Twecheles [Twitchells] he answers nothing this year because the beasts of that country were destroyed by the Scots . . .[9]

Boundaries of the manor

A description of the boundaries of Chorley manor survives in a document from 1726, yet this may confidently be assumed to represent the medieval boundary pattern.

On 5 May 1726 the court leet resolved that

> This jury are appointed to meet at ye top of Hartwood Green by six a clock on Whitsun Monday next and from thence to proceed and walk ye Boundary of this Manor, and afterwards to meet at ye house of James Hodsons in Chorley....

Fifteen jurymen made up the citizens summoned that day, led by James Parker, gentleman, and including Robert Hollinshead, mercer, John Baldwin, joiner and at least four yeomen. James Nicholson, a maltster, was later fined by the jury for not attending the boundary walk.

The description reads,

> Beginning at ye Lane end by Abbot House, & so along Whittle hedge, so up Hunters Slade to Heapey hedge & ditch & so on to Blackbrook gate near Heapey, & so thorow greenhalgh croft to a style in Lawson's ground by Healey, & so along by ye hedge & rivulet to Gibb Close, & so on ye back side of Gibb Close, divideing Healey from Chorley.

> From thence by ye ffleam ditch to ye Paddock gate, & so to Baginley in James Parker's Lane Thoro' a Croft Leading to ye Hardfield – Betwixt Healey & Chorley, & so from Hardfield style neer ye gate at Healey Miln, & so to an oak at ye Carthouse and at Cross Hall So thoro ye Courts into ye Brew house & so thoro ye Brew house and part of ye orchard to ye bottom of ye barley croft. Then to ye Butcher-ridding & so to ye steel in ye Ridge Land & so thoro ye Little Croft then at ye bottom of Worsley Close to a Weare Betwixt Twitchells & Long Shoot & so along ye hedge from ye weare to ye Sneath and then ye brook divides Chorley & Healey to Sr Thomas Standishs' Land in Duxbury To a fforth that formerly went out of James Whittles meadow ffrom a witch Hassle to a Sweet William where ye water went formerly down before it was turn'd & so to Sr Thomas Standishs' Coe & so to a gravel bed in Yarrow & round the stream Ditch to John Holden's Cellar & so up to a Holling Bush where formerly a gate stood wch parted Chorley & Duxbury. But before we come to ye coe There is a Croft belonginge to John Aspden's Tenemt which was taken out of ye Great Bottoms wch is called Paddock that belongs to Duxbury & so thoro The Jewell's Croft to Sr Thomas Standish' Horse-Heys, & so taking Richard Wasley's intack, to ye ffearnely & so to Thomas Wilcocks Tenement & so to a close of ground formerly Edward Waring's called ye acre

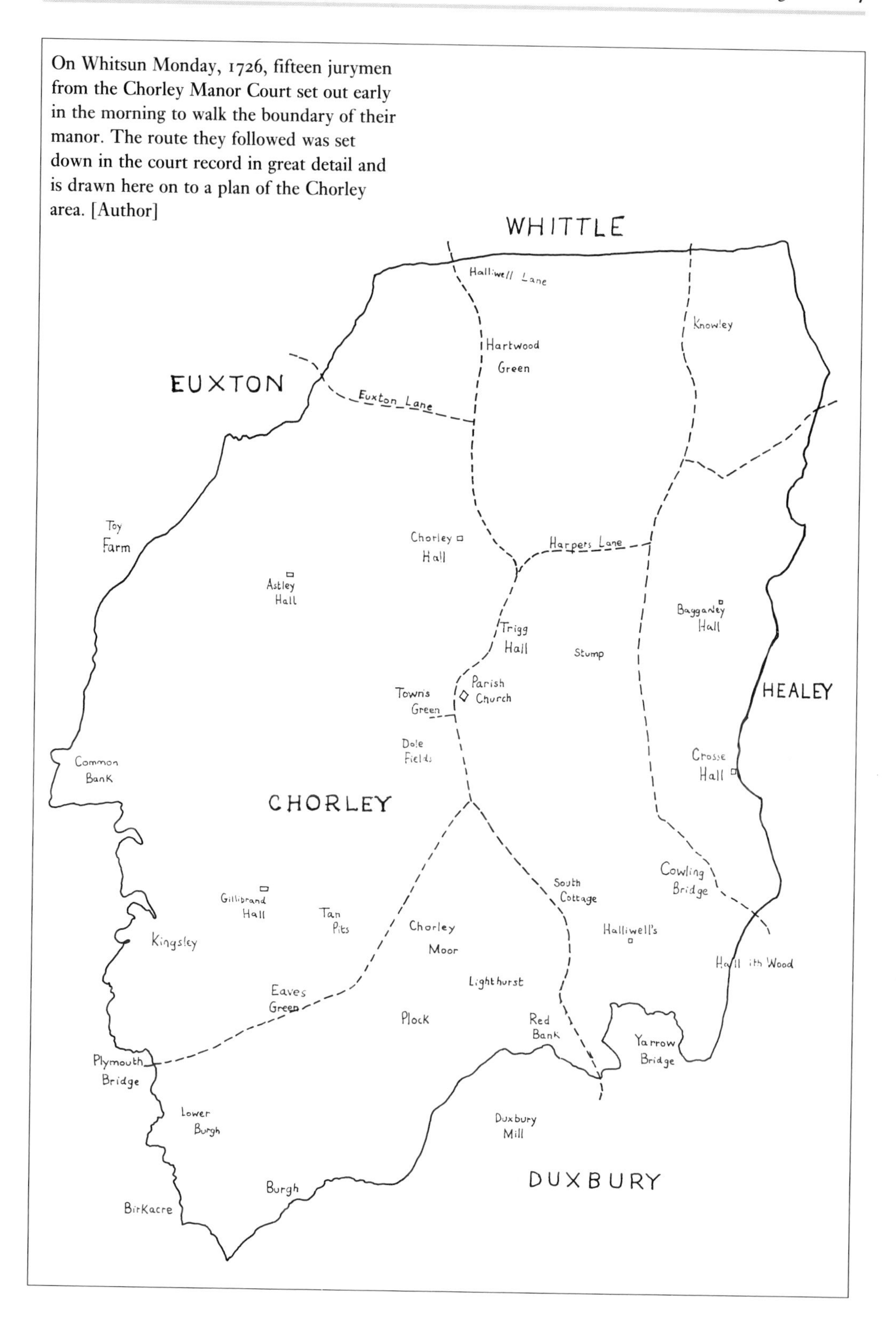

On Whitsun Monday, 1726, fifteen jurymen from the Chorley Manor Court set out early in the morning to walk the boundary of their manor. The route they followed was set down in the court record in great detail and is drawn here on to a plan of the Chorley area. [Author]

> & so to a Close called Comaker being on Rigby's Land & soe to a Rivulett on ye north side of Mr Rigby's Ware-house & there to a Rivulett running thoro Long Hey-wood to a Coe in ye bottom of ye Long Hey-wood takeing in a little houme lying to Jarmand houme and then Yarrow parts Chorley & Coppull to Crosseness Brook anbd then Yarrow parts Chorley & Charnock Ricd to ye Plimmers Bridge (excepting three Crofts, Paddocks, or parcells of Land belongeing to ye Land's of Saml Crook Esqr Decd) and soe to ye Bark-house Bridge (excepting one Hillock) formerly James Charnock's and so down a hedge betwixt Lee Houme & Sis houme abt 2 roods Soe to a corner of Smith's Ramskar's & so down ye sd Ramskar's for ye space of 24 yds over agt Lower Miln Holme belonginge to Kingsley house ground and soe down to ye Bottom of a Little Croft of Tho Waring's & then up a Rivulett to ye bottom of Common Bank, & then up a Rivulett parting Mr Gellibrand's Land & Mr Robinson's Land lyeing in Euxton, and soe takeing in ye acre's Tenemt to Astley Demesne and so after ye Bottom of Judd Lands all along Astley Demesne to Euxton Brook and soe after to Abbot's Tenemt adjoyneinge to Wm Ffoole's Tenemt lyeinge in Whittle and so up to ye Lane End by Abbot's Tenemt divideing Chorley & Whittle.[10]

It is striking how the boundary matches that of the later borough boundary, with the exception of Healey Nab, and how natural features form landmarks. On the western section of the River Yarrow delineates the manor in itself.

Manor house

The manor of Chorley was thus divided among different owners at an early date. There is some evidence to suggest that the running of the manor was undertaken by one bailiff for their joint benefit, and that the manor house in St Thomas's Road was the bailiff's house rather than a residence of the lords of the manor. The bailiff would have been on hand to supervise weekly markets, collect the tolls, control access to the town fields and the doles. He could farm in his own right and take an active role in local affairs. The house is now a Grade III listed building, said to date from the early eighteenth century, though other evidence gives an older date. A carved oak roof beam was removed by its occupier, Mr Collison, early this century – his daughter later recalled that the date 1567 was carved upon it.[11]

When Sumner's flour mill was demolished in 1991 the east gable of the manor house was revealed, still showing signs of the cruck frame timbers. The east gable also had indications of a door and windows being blocked up. The walls, 18 inches thick in places, bore traces of wattle and daub construction, while hand-made bricks, cemented over and whitewashed, make up much of the frontage.

The house of today gives the impression of having been extended, with an added west wing and attics above. Storage cellars, one of which extends under the highway, were perhaps for the bailiff's domestic use.

The house is reported to have been bought from the Rigby family by the Gillibrands in 1700, and the latter's badge of the crossed swords is clearly visible in a stained glass window on the north elevation. There is a later tradition that Titus Salt, the future Yorkshire industrial magnate, lived here for a time, a tradition which may have a grain of truth in it as a John Salt was landlord of the Royal Oak in 1835.

The seigneurial borough

In 1251 William de Ferrers, Earl of Derby, received a grant from the king of free warren in his lands in the counties of Lancaster, Derby and Stafford. Shortly after, in 1253, the earl made the village of Bolton a borough by his own grant of a charter. His family had used this seigneurial power with some success in the Midlands, where three villages alone had 410 burgages. This was a boom period for planting these 'new towns', as Beresford called them, some set up by the king, others by the church and many by great lords.[12] Chorley was made a borough by the Ferrers in 1256–7 and, although the borough charter has disappeared, that of Bolton still survives: it shows that a free burgess had many more liberties and privileges than townspeople elsewhere, but paid his lord a rent of 12d. in four instalments for his land. At Bolton each burgess had one acre of land, his burgage plot, and Chorley's burgesses may well have enjoyed a similar treatment. The burgage consisted of a house and yard, with a narrow frontage on the main street, and extending back in a long strip of land, this being cultivated for his own use and with rights of access to the open fields. All was meant to encourage growth and trade and increased revenue for the Ferrers.

For a time the Ferrers lands were under the control of the king's son and his bailiff, Henry de Lee, gave an account for 1257.

> Of the assized rent of the borough of Chorley for the terms of St Martin, the nativity of our Lord and the Annunciation, 48s 5d.; farm of the vill for the terms of the Nativity and Annunciation, 6s. 8d. . . .[13]

Among the payments recorded were the wages of the forester, 3s. 4d., perhaps a forebear of Robert Woodward, who appears as a petitioner in 1362.

At the death of William de Ferrers in 1288 his borough of Bolton had sixty-nine burgages, each paying 12d. yearly, while Chorley had ninety burgages, paying the same sum in four parts, implying that Chorley was a larger and more important community than Bolton in this period. When an enquiry was made of the Earl of Lancaster's lands in 1323-4 a rent of four burgages in Chorley for 4s. was recorded, while the rent of the farm

The Manor House in St Thomas's Road, 1992. Dating back at least to Elizabethan times, the house was later sold to the Gillibrand family, whose badge of the crossed swords can still be seen in a stained-glass window on the front elevation of the house. [Author]

of the park of Healey was reduced because these had been drastically reduced in value by the Scots raid of 1322.

Where were the burgages in the borough of 1257? If the Norfolk estate map of 1734 is taken as a pointer towards finding them, many of the strips of land running east and west off Market Street would fit the bill, though not to the total of ninety. Porteus argued that some were inside the boundaries of Healey, based on an account of 1509.[14] In 1630 Henry Baldwin collected the rent of four marks for these from William Crosse, William Tootell, Hugh Tootell and William Hawkshead. In Market Street the last apparent burgage site was lost when the presbytery of St Mary's Church was demolished.

The borough died, just as others did in Lancashire—Ulverston, Manchester and Warrington for example—due some have said to the burden and expense of maintaining borough status. Certainly Chorley was no longer reckoned a borough in 1446 when the 'fifteenth' levy was made. Nevertheless, the fact that it had enjoyed borough status had a significant effect upon the topography of the town.

It would be foolish to be too dogmatic about the early townscape of Chorley, given the absence of specific evidence. However, a hypothetical development can be suggested. The first ingredient was the town's green, which was the focus of secular affairs just as St Laurence's formed the spiritual core of the community. The green, roughly triangular in shape, was the site of the market cross, weekly markets (though seasonal fairs were more probably held in the parish churchyard), the parish stocks for punishing wrongdoers, a water pump and pond nearby, presumably a relic of the days when cattle were turned loose on the green. A little to the west of the green stood the manor house. One lane led into and alongside the

When the fledgling parish of St Mary's sought a site for a permanent new church in the 1850s this property was sold to the Church by the Harrison family for that purpose. [Lancashire County Library]

town field to Astley Wood, and another followed a dog-leg to the doles, hence the modern name Dole Lane. Around Back Mount thatched cottages grouped tightly together, shops grew up and at least one inn served the public's need. Skittle Alley, by the Red Lion tap, was the site of a public bowling alley. In the seventeenth century the maypole was sited on the town's green and was dramatically shattered by a bolt of lightning. Spring waters were tapped on the south side of St Thomas's Road, as several Victorian accounts show. Immediately below Terrace Mount the old pinfold was situated where the entrance to Astley Park came to be built, adjacent to another ancient spring.

Early plans show little development to the east of Market Street. Union Street, dating from about 1710, led into the Dingle or Clough, a wooded hollow where a stream ran down from Steeley Lane to join the Chor. Another stream rose behind the modern market place and came down onto Market Street, the area generally being rural in character. A large field, sometimes referred to as Hill Field, extended across the later Chapel Street.

After the Ferrers family had founded the borough in the late 1250s, burgage plots were laid out, running off Market Street. These plots ran back as far as the doles, Peter Wink probably being one of the access lanes to the fields.

The linear plan of the town was the most obvious feature of Chorley's townscape, with the chararacteristic inverted 'Y' shape of the main streets. Chorley's earliest development was thus around the town's green, Market Street and the ancillary streets being a later expansion.

Moated sites

In the Middle Ages it was for a time fashionable to build moats as a defensive measure, and also as a sign of prestige and social standing. Well over 130 moated homesteads are known in Lancashire, and many are located in a belt from Wigan north to Chorley. They are built on clay soils, and usually measure between 120 and 200 feet square. The majority date from the thirteenth and the fourteenth centuries. The Lancashire moated sites usually included a farmhouse and agricultural buildings on an island within a water-filled moat between 15 and 25 feet across. Gillibrand Old Hall is one example which lasted beyond the Middle Ages up to the end of the eighteenth century. Two plans show miniature drawings of the site, the first a plan from 1766 for the enclosure of the commons, the second the estate plan of 1769. Contemporary accounts add to the picture. A directory of 1793 records that

> it had a mote or canal round it, which is well stored with choice fish, a small tower continued all round, with parapets in the inside, secures the passage over a stone bridge in front of the hall; and on the back is a draw-bridge which leads over into delightful gardens and pleasure-grounds.[15]

The plans show the square moat, enclosing a group of ancillary buildings and the hall proper, an H-shaped hall with two wings. Variously called Gillibrand Hall, Chorley Hall or Harrington Hall (Kuerden, 1695) the site may originally be the home of the Harrington family, joint lords of the manor. In 1808 the old hall was abandoned by the Gillibrands in favour of a new Regency-style hall close by on a slope overlooking the sweep of the parkland to the west. Although the field-names of Lawn Meadow and Moat Meadow hark back to the past, the moated site gradually reverted to nature and is now tree-covered, though aerial photography reveals the U-shaped indentation of the moat. Archaeological research would no doubt provide better evidence of its early history. Other local moated sites included Astley Hall, where the moat has long since disappeared, and Lower Burgh Hall.[16]

An impression of Gillibrand Hall as it would have looked in the mid-1700s, when the moat still surrounded the hall. [Author]

The town fields and Lidyate Lane

The farming systems of medieval Chorley must, in general, be deduced from later documentary evidence, principally the Duchess of Norfolk's estate plan of 1734. The compact demesne lands of the Chorley and Gillibrand families, and to some extent the Astley Hall lands, were farmed for the immediate needs of their owners. Chorley Hall's 71 acres, with 37 acres more at Hall i'th' Wood, were detailed in the 1652 Chorley Survey, while other income came from rents of properties in Walton-le-Dale, Liverpool and Chorley town.[17] For smaller farmers and the burgesses the town and dole fields were close at hand. Although it is damaged, the 1734 plan shows the town fields as a triangular section of land covering what is now Harrington Road, part of Southport Road and Queen's Road. The plan shows the familiar inverted Y shape of the main streets but the areas to the west of Market Street are starkly different from later plans. Devonshire Road was not made until about 1900, being no more than a hedge line previously. One trackway running south from Southport Road approximates to Ashfield Road today and the junction of this path with the embryo Southport Road marks an important focal point in the field pattern. To its immediate north west the town fields lie away from the road in five bands of unequal width and length. Alongside the town fields another lane, named Lidyate or Lidgate, runs down to Astley Wood. To the south-east a series of doles, aligned from west to east, terminate in the burgages along Market Street. Field names given on the 1734 plan are useful clues which can often be supplemented from other documents. Along the south edge of the Lords Clough, for example, three fields are known as Great Mill Croft and the two Little Mill Crofts, suggesting either that a mill was nearby on the Chor or that the fields were worked by the mill tenant. A Mill Meadow appears further to the west, next to Astley Wood and in the correct location for the assumed site of Astley Mill. The specific evidence is slim in both cases, but as late as 1846 the OS map shows a building near the mill crofts and at the end of Lidyate Lane, where a bend of the river might have been used for water power.

While the 1734 plan hardly shows a 'town field', these were originally more extensive: a document of 1417 refers to the land abutting on Many Pits 'in the Town Field of Chorley', behind Gillibrand Walks, meaning that the town fields covered areas to the west of Market Street and Gillibrand Walks.[18] Their true extent will never be known – all have been covered by urban growth over seven hundred years. The town field shown on the 1734 plan was entirely part of the Weld/Shireburne estates and this is confirmed by a rental of 1779 in which the five parcels were farmed by Ann Leigh, James Layland, James Mason and Thomas Halliwell. These tenants also farmed large and varied parcels of land elsewhere on the estate. The only evidence for the nature of the land is from an account (1909), saying that sand from the town fields went to form the filter beds of the sewage works (1890s).

When the town fields were built over, a medieval trackway, now known to be Lidyate Lane, also disappeared. The sketch at page 24 shows its situation in relation to the town's green and other features. Lidyate Lane is a common name, originally meaning a lane with a swing-gate to stop

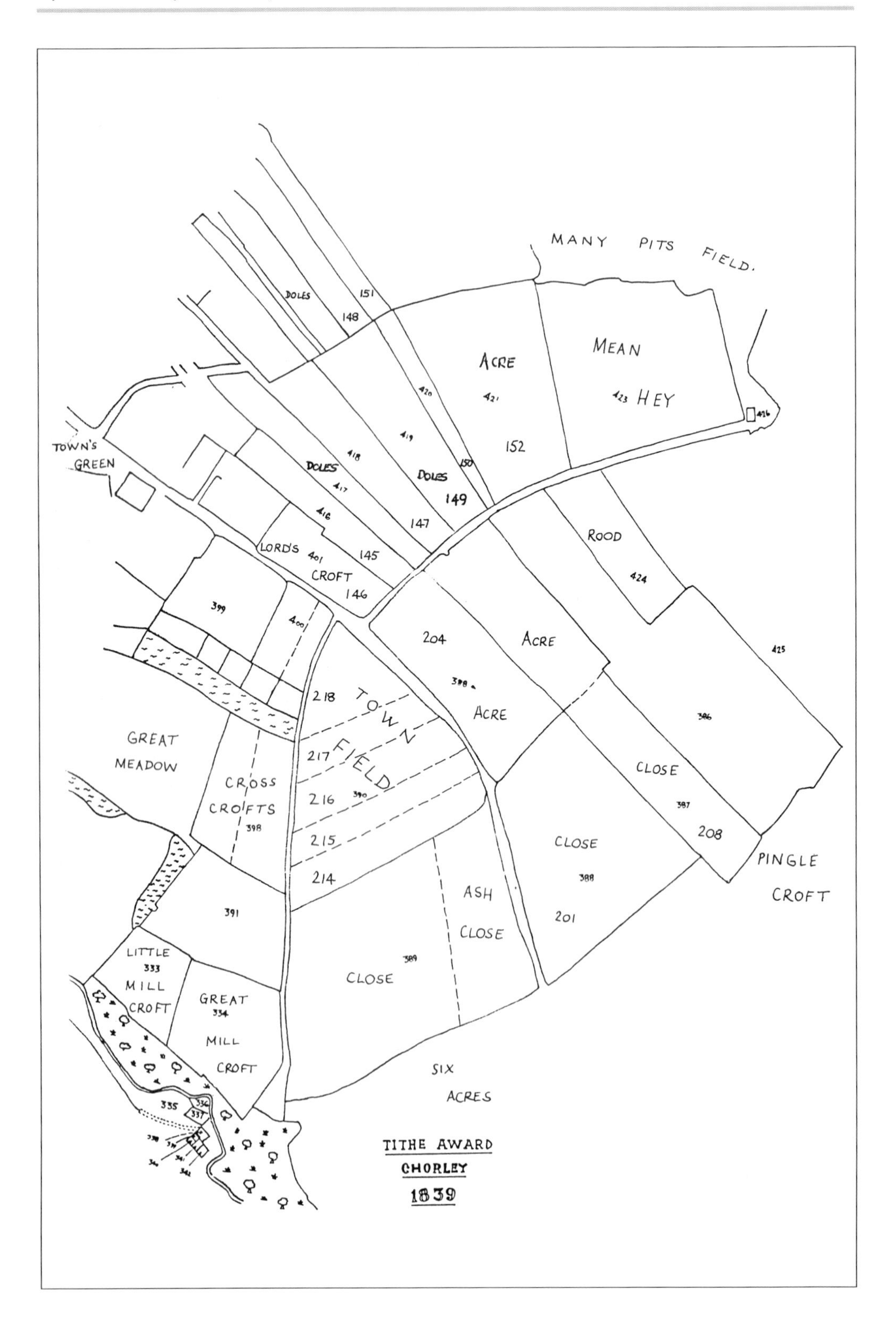
MANY PITS FIELD.
DOLES
151
148
ACRE
421
152
MEAN
423 HEY
TOWN'S GREEN
DOLES
DOLES
149
147
LORD'S 401 CROFT
145
146
ROOD
424
399
204
ACRE
425
386
218
TOWN FIELD
ACRE
GREAT MEADOW
CROSS CROFTS
398
217
216
215
214
CLOSE
387
208
CLOSE
388
201
PINGLE CROFT
391
ASH CLOSE
LITTLE 333 MILL CROFT
GREAT 334 MILL CROFT
CLOSE
389
SIX ACRES
335
TITHE AWARD
CHORLEY
1839

cattle straying, and bounded by ditches or hedges to protect the land on either side. A 1731 reference in the township papers says that

> The Bailiffs do give notice to all persons, complaint being made to this jury that ye hedges on both sides Lidgate Lane down to Astley Wood be cut in all such places as the same in granting by the owners thereof . . .

In 1326 the name was given as Le Lydeyate, in a lease from the Charnocks, while the parish registers show that a house/farm was given the same name, the Parker family living there in the 1600s. The lane seems to have provided access to a mill on the River Chor, for the benefit of farmers on the town fields. When this mill fell into disuse it was possible for the Hoghtons to divert the road through Astley Woods, and for the lane to decay.

The same land grant of 1417 referred to above states that James Bank, fletcher, received two acres of arable land on the east part of Brownsfield, more arable land near Many Pits and three roods in the Faleley (Fellery) between Thomas Trigg's land and that of Robert Brown. Richard Marshall's grant mentions a granary, several houses and tofts. It is noticeable that three hundred years later the same family names occur on Shireburne farm leases. By 1734 the old dole strips, more numerous on the west of Market Street than on the east, were divided between the Gillibrands, Shireburnes, Standishes, Brookes and Cromptons.

As noted earlier, in many parts of Chorley placenames indicate woodland clearances for farming. One of the few documents to confirm assarting (woodland clearance) is dated 1379: in it Thomas Charnock's 7½ acres of reclaimed land is mentioned. There are several 'greens' in the area now, but there were more in past centuries. They are considered by M. A. Atkin to be a major element in the agricultural system of medieval south Lancashire. The oval stock enclosures which she found in the Leyland Hundred were linked by tracks for the movement of livestock. She identifies four enclosures in Chorley, namely Astley, Gillibrand, Healey Park and Kingsley. In this system Chorley would have provided hill grazing. Atkin also records the 'greens' which gave common rights of pasture, again linked to the stock tracks leading eastward from the Croston and Mawdesley area.[19]

The Tithe Award Plan of Chorley from 1839, now in the Lancashire Record Office, shows the town before the intensive development of Victorian housing and clearly illustrates the location of the medieval town fields and doles. [Redrawn by the author]

From the Enclosure Award of 1766 it is possible to compile a list of eight greens in Chorley, which, together with the town's green, can be plotted on the modern street map. Four of them, Plock, Eaves, Booth's and Fool's are grouped around Moor Road and Weld Bank. Others are scattered across the area, though their distribution helps to support the Atkin thesis of a track leading across the north of Chorley to Healey via Hartwood Green.

Corn mills

The mill was vital to the community for many centuries, and had a special role in the local economy. This meant the lord of the manor guarded the mill and its income as his own. Around Chorley several water-mills are known from the 1200s onwards. A Charnock deed from this period speaks of 'Chorlee Mill', though this may not necessarily be Astley Mill on the River Chor. The latter was mentioned in a Charnock will of 1615 and in 1718 when the rent was £6 4s. od. The Chorley Survey of 1652, quoting a medieval land grant to William Chorley from the Hepwalls, says the 'Hall of Chorlegh' goes with the 'Milne, etc.' implying that there was a separate mill on their land. Certainly the name Millfield has survived until today and it is possible that a mill may have stood on the upper length of the streamlet which runs down through Dog Trap Wood, adjacent to the lower field. At Birkacre, on the River Yarrow, John de Coppull granted Robert de Burgh licence to make a mill pool in 1402. In 1423 there was a corn mill and a walk mill (for cloth) here.

The Crosse family deeds mention a water corn mill at Crosse Hall, Healey in 1432: milling on the Black Brook was carried on here well into the last century at two sites. Duxbury Mill, owned by the Standish family, is better documented than most. The River Yarrow provided the power for this mill, which was situated west of Yarrow Bridge and deep in the Duxbury Woods. In 1727 Sir Thomas Standish leased the corn mill, with a malt kiln, to John Brown, miller, of Eccleston for eleven years at £7 yearly. Brown was to run the mill and put the building in good repair, while Sir Thomas agreed to construct a new bridge, maintain the mill race and compensate Brown if ice or drought reduced the flow of water. The mill served two manors, Duxbury and Heath Charnock. By 1742 William Pilkington had the lease of the mill, at a rental of £39 17s. od., and he had to 'Keep up the Banks and scoure the Fleam Ditch between the Coe or Wear above Yarrow Bridge and the said Mill.' An 1867 Duxbury lease refers to nine pairs of stones in the mill, and the property also included sixty-nine acres of grassland.

The use of place-names like Mill Holm at Kingsley's gives clues to possible sites of mills elsewhere, and in some cases they may be linked to processing bark for tanning as in the case of Bark House. Before the turn of the eighteenth century Chorley's only known windmill was built on Chorley Moor; in 1790 it was operated by George Tootell, who ground corn and meal. When the mill was sold in 1808 it was described as a corn mill, with a kiln, fold and garden attached. The best known modern mill is that built by Joseph Sumner in St Thomas's Road. Between 1840 and 1842 Messrs Greenwood and Smalley ran a steam corn mill, while there were several dealers in corn, wheat and oatmeal during the Victorian era.

Chorley Parish Church

St Laurence's Parish Church is probably the oldest building in Chorley; its exact age is impossible to tell. Most experts concur that most of the remaining medieval architectural features date from the fourteenth century, with major additions in Victorian times.

The church has two medieval fonts within its precincts, the oldest of the two dating stylistically to about 1200, while the second would seem to date from the fourteenth century. As Chorley was a dependent chapel of Croston parish until 1793 the fonts may originally have belonged there. The litany bell tower at the east end of the chancel, however, is believed to date from about 1250, suggesting at best that the chapel may have been founded in the thirteenth century.

Fortunately for posterity a local photographer recorded the parish church before the major extensions and alterations were made between 1859 and 1861. [Lancashire County Library]

In 1355 the king granted licence for an acre of land to be set aside in Chorley for a tithebarn for the use of the parson of Croston, and, since no reference to a chapel in Chorley appears in the writ this is taken as proof of its absence. Seven years later, however, a group of Chorley townspeople begged the Bishop of Lichfield to allow a chapel to be dedicated, retaining the status of Croston as the parent church of the parish. Chorley did not, in fact, become a separate parish until 1793. The bishop agreed to the petition of 1362 and William de Huntlowe, rector of Croston, agreed to find a chaplain for the chapel. In that year plague returned, so that a possible reason for the petition was the difficulty of conveying the dead for burial at Croston. With the bishop's agreement came the added comment 'They shall have all sacraments and sacramentals with the consent of the rector and patron, and the licence of the Bishop.'

The petition not only gives a firm date to begin with, but it also provides a list of prominent individuals six hundred years ago. Many of them are familiar: William Chorley, Henry Burgh and John Banastre, Richard Trigg and Henry Asshawe for instance, Robert de Wodeward's name suggests that he was responsible for the upkeep and management of woodland, and William de Wode presumably lived on the fringe of the town. Richard de Kyngeley was probably tenant on the Kingsley estate. In all twenty-five names are recorded.

John Wilson speculated that the chapel was dedicated early in its life to the Virgin Mary – he cited the evidence of the west door, where the letter 'M' carved in a Lombardic style for Mary, as well as the three niches which once held statues of the Virgin with the infant Jesus. Peter de Chorley (of London) made a bequest to the church of St Laurence in 1464, the earliest record of this dedication. The Chorley family were intimately connected with the church very early; a deed of 1380, concerning the family's recovery of Chorley Hall after their attainder refers to 'the whole of the southern half of our chapel, below the step of the High Altar in the church of Chorlegh'. The Chorleys were guaranteed seats and burial ground for ever, a right exercised for burial until 1727. Other families later acquired similar rights.

The old building had a chancel 32 feet by 16 feet 3 inches, a nave 57 feet 6 inches by 27 feet 6 inches, and a west tower 10 feet by 9 feet, much of it medieval. The tower is usually thought to date from the fourteenth century, and is a prominent landmark from the west. From Church Brow passers-by have a clear sight of the arms (three boars' heads) carved on the buttresses of the tower. These were formerly thought to be those of Bishop Booth (through his Barton ancestors) but are now believed to be from the Whyte family who owned land in Shevington. Before the major upheaval of 1859–61 one old quarrel window over the chancel arch in the east wall of the nave displayed the arms of Ferrers of Groby. The account of its removal goes on to say that the shield, some 12 inches long and 9 inches wide, was found on a rubbish heap ready for disposal!

Though the Standishes were landowners mainly outside the township, they always kept an interest in Chorley church. They had a share of the chancel steps, a place of honour, perhaps a survival of a privilege which the Duxbury family enjoyed. Among the many soldiers in the family was Sir Rowland Standish – he fought at Agincourt and was killed at Gerberoy in 1434. During his years abroad he acquired some religious relics, the bones of St Laurence. These relics were given to Chorley church in 1442, recorded in a deed contained in the Harleian Manuscripts.

> Be it known to all men that I, Thomas Tarleton, vicar of the church of Croston, bear witness and certify that Mr James Standish of Duxbury has delivered a relic of St Laurence's head into the church of Chorley, which Sir Rowland of Standish, Knight, brother of the said James, and Dame Jane his wife brought out of Normandy, to the worship of God and St Laurence, for the profit and avail of the said church.[20]

These remains of the saint were placed in a reliquary on the south wall of the sanctuary, and became objects of wonder and veneration to the devout townspeople. The saint was a Christian martyr of the third century, who was tortured on a gridiron, hence the parish church's emblem. However, Croston, writing a century ago, believed the bones were more likely those

St Laurence's Parish Church, *c.*1890. [Author]

of a St Lawrence who held a see in Normandy in about the twelfth century. Around 1790 two antiquarians, Mr Barritt and Dr Ferriar, came to Chorley – they mulled over the heraldry on show, the architecture and the pews, but they announced their disturbing conclusion that the relics were animal bones and not human. Several theories have been propounded to account for this – one is that the true relics were removed by a devout Catholic at the Reformation rather than see them destroyed; another, that a bigoted churchman may have removed the relics from spite. The originals were said to be fragments of skull while the 'relics' examined two hundred years ago were obviously leg bones.

In 1514–30 the churchwardens of Croston were in disagreement with the Chorley townsfolk when the latter refused to pay for the upkeep of Croston, a harbinger of their eventual separation. When the king's commissioners reported in 1552, the church had three vestments, three albs, one silver-gilt chalice, one brass candlestick and one bible. In 1548 there were four priests at the church. One of these, Roger Chorley, lived in the priest chamber, adjoining the house of Roger Allenson off Parson's Brow and across the present Gillibrand Street.

The turmoil of the Reformation and local reaction to it seem little recorded, with the exception of the events of the Pilgrimage of Grace. There were strong feelings in Lancashire against Henry VIII's divorce and the religious upheavals which followed. In 1533 Richard Clerk, Vicar of Leigh, was at Croston to read a proclamation against Katherine of Aragon. A local priest, James Harrison, spoke out boldly and his statement was carried to the Earl of Derby. Harrison said that 'Quene Kathryn was

Quene, and that Nan Boelyn should not be Quene, nor the King to be as King but on his bering'. As the king's men closed the monasteries bitter opposition came in the North; from out of Yorkshire the Pilgrimage of Grace recruited resistance to the closures. The rebellion attracted widespread enthusiasm, though in Chorley's case armed threats were necessary to persuade lukewarm supporters. On 2 November 1536 a minstrel named John Piper and two other men went around the township, wearing armour and carrying weapons, their faces blackened. Percival Sanders was one who said they broke down his door and threatened to wound him unless he swore to support their cause. William Charnock, Laurence Whitell, Robert Bankes and Thurstan Collings all swore under duress, though as they had seen the rebellion fail all across the North, such a claim was a predictable defence.

Thereafter local Catholics kept their faith and learned to tread the delicate line between conforming to the law and the dictates of belief. Lord Burghley's intelligence gatherers provided a map of Lancashire in 1590, showing the homes of gentry likely to be 'recusant' and disaffected. Robert Charnock, of Little Farington Hall, Charnock and Chorley, was said in 1586 to be 'ill-affected towards the new religion but a temporiser', and the map identified him and his neighbours, Farington of Worden, Anderton of Euxton, Hoghton of Hoghton and Anderton of Clayton. The most notable adherents to their old religion were the Charnocks; John Charnock was executed for his role in the Babington conspiracy. Nevertheless, Thomas Shaw of Heath Charnock, from a strongly puritan family, married Alice, daughter of Thomas Charnock.

Roger Wrennall

In November 1987 Pope John Paul II honoured the memory of a man who was born in Chorley, worked as a poor weaver, and died at Lancaster Castle by hanging, drawing and quartering; this man was devoted to his faith and his acceptance of a cruel death displayed a special courage. Roger Wrennall (or Wrenno as he is often called) was born in 1577, second son of Robert Wrennall. He spent his life as a weaver in the town and only came to prominence in 1615, when he was arrested at his home for harbouring a Catholic priest, Father John Thules, another Lancashire man. The prisoners were taken to Lancaster Castle prior to their trial, and although the two escaped they were recaptured within days. When the day arrived for their execution, in March 1615–16, Thules was executed first. Wrennall was next on the scaffold, but the rope broke under his weight and he fell to the ground below. When he came round he went onto his knees in prayer, at which point he was offered the king's clemency if he would take the oath of allegiance as required. Wrennall, it is reported, stood up, saying, 'I am the same man as I was, and in the same mind, use your pleasure with me.' The account of these events goes on to say that he ran to the ladder and quickly made his way to the top.

'How now,' says the sheriff: 'What does the man mean, that he is in such haste?'

—'Oh,' says the good man, 'if you had seen that which I have just seen, you would be as much in haste to die as I am.'

He is now remembered as Blessed Roger Wrennall.

A Protestant church

When Henry Welch took over as minister of Chorley in 1628 the first definite Puritan influence was felt. Welch laboured through the plague years, the Civil War, and the Commonwealth until 1662 when, like many more, he refused to accept the re-enforced Book of Common Prayer and was deprived of the living. At his death in 1671 the register said of him 'Minister there 35 years'.

The church has served several other roles in the past six hundred years. In 1538 it was used as a courthouse; during the Civil War the tower served as a rallying point; and the parish vestry, as its name implies, met here. Chorley's town records were kept in a parish chest within the chancel. In 1734 all the papers in private hands were called in to 'Lodge them in the New Chest standing in the Vestry made for that purpose'. The records describe such matters as the building of the galleries, the erection of the poor house and the appointment of George Sharrock as the first dogwhipper, responsible for keeping the church free of animals. He got a new coat every two years for his efforts.

In the sixteenth century a record was made of the coats of arms displayed at Chorley: those of Chorley, Gillibrand, Standish, Harrington, Ferrers, Brockhole, Worthington, White and Gerard families were noted. The Walton family arms, of the three swans argent, quartered with the Chorleys', may account for the later inn sign of the Swan, in Hollinshead Street. A much later series of funeral hatchments was lost about 1880–1890 – these recalled the Hoghton family, Fazakerley, Brooke and Townley-Parkers.

In 1650 the church was said to be Chorley Chapel, the chapel-of-ease to Croston St Michael and All Angels. It was said that there was 'a Cottage and halfe a roode land of gleabe lands or thereabouts in Chorley aforesaid unto belonginge worth two shillings per annum'. By this time Bannister's charity of £200 was available to pay for a preaching minister. The commissioners recommended then that Chorley should be made a separate parish, but nothing was done to implement this until 1793, when the Revd Robert Master, Rector of Croston, obtained an Act of Parliament to divide his huge parish. Three new parishes and rectories emerged, Croston, Chorley and Rufford, Dr Master kept them all himself until his death in 1798, after which event his three sons, Streynsham, John and Edward, received one living each.

A sidelight on the problem of travelling in these times comes in the preamble to the 1793 Act, saying the people of Chorley 'cannot at any time with conveniency repair to the parish church of Croston by reason of their remote distance from the same, and of the inundations of waters happening in these parts'.[21]

In the last century patriotic Americans were drawn to Chorley Parish Church in search of the roots of Myles Standish, one of the Pilgrim Fathers. The Standish family had many links with the church: their badge is carved on a buttress of the south elevation. [Lancashire County Library]

John Gray

A single line in the 1835 directory sums him up – Gray, John, parish clerk, and town crier, Terrace Mount – but it is a bland statement for a remarkable man. He served as parish clerk for another five years, until his death in 1840 at eighty-one. For fifty-four years, from 1786, he had carried out his duties and a host of stories surround him. One favourite concerns a wedding, in 1810, when two Catholics, Joseph Brimley and Anne Livesey wanted to marry at an Established Church to legalise their union. Armed with a licence they went to Leyland Parish Church but the vicar and curate were both away. They walked to Chorley for the same errand and got there at five minutes to twelve, but marriages after 12 o'clock were not legal at that period. Brimley asked Gray if they could be married that day, and was told to fetch the curate while he, Gray, would stop the clock. Time stood still until the clock was set going just before the service ended.

He and the curate were then near neighbours. Gray was landlord of the White Horse, next to the church, while Mr Cooper lived in the St Laurence's Lodge, now a club. Over the door of the pub was Gray's sign: 'This gate hangs high and hinders none from passing in or going on: John Gray the Parish Clerk lives here and keeps a glass of wholesome beer.' On one occasion he was dismissed from office by Mr Cooper but he walked to Chester, pleaded his case before the bishop, and returned with the approval of the bishop to continue as clerk to St Laurence's.

Graveyard

In 1853 Rawlinson's report on the public health of Chorley spoke of 'serious evils and defects' in the existing practice of burying in churchyards; in his judgement burials had been made at St Laurence's by the thousands in a plot measuring three-quarters of an acre, from at least 1549 when registers were kept. In 1826, he remarked, the graveyard was lowered and thousands of bones removed, clear evidence of a health hazard. He said it was originally a good site, an open soil with adequate drainage and no property to be adversely affected. In 1852 the sexton told him there were 150 burials each year. At Weldbank the problem was exaggerated by a habit of deferring burial until six or seven coffins could be fitted in one plot. His recommendation, which was accepted, was that the graveyard should be closed. As a result the new cemetery was opened in Southport Road.

Parish church pews

From an early date in the church's history the seats and pews were assigned to, and kept strictly for the use of, individuals. It may reflect a long distant apportionment according to the joint building of the church; alternatively the pattern may imitate the social hierarchy of the parish. The best known plan of seating comes from 1655 (itself based on an earlier 1635 layout). Noticeably Catholic families kept both their burial places and seating rights, either from long practice or from privilege linked to property. Charnock of Astley and Chorley of Chorley Hall claimed the most prestigious places at the head of the congregation. Behind them the rows of seats at Sunday service must have been a 'who's who' of Chorley life, sometimes the plan showing a family name, at other times the property permitted to use the seat. Halliwell House was under 'Mr Crosse and his claims', while James Parker had a right from Bagganley and the Stump estate. Way back below the church door were yeoman families such as the Baldwins, Friths of Knowley and Thurston Hodson the shoemaker. Where a home or farm name appeared it is not always clear what the modern equivalent would be, such as 'Rigby ith Towne', though Ackhurst was then associated with the Healds. Apart from the special areas for the well-to-do there were forty-two seats for the remainder.

Because of the numbers of potential worshippers, and the small number of seats, a great many poorer people stood during service. In the eighteenth century galleries were built, one at the west end, for example, was erected in 1713 for 'Mr Riley, Parson . . . And the Profits of it belong to him and his successors forever'. He later built a gallery on the south side and another, for the 'singers', at the west end of the steeple in 1739. The gallery over the chancel was built by Edward Warren and Samuel Crook with a lease from Brooke and Chorley. Riley's gallery was leased from 1714 to John Lawson, tanner, for £4 10s. 0d.; it later passed to a carpenter named Adam Rigby.

The most important seats were, of course, the pews dedicated to the great families. The Charnock pew, now at the rear of the church, is a beautiful canopied oak affair, dating from about 1600. Alexander Standish of Duxbury built a pew for his estate at about the same date, again in oak and decorated with the arms of Standish, Washington, Ashton and many more relations. In 1913 there was a case before the Consistory Court concerning the rector's plan to move the pew, a scheme vigorously opposed by Mr Mayhew of Duxbury Park, although eventually his agreement was obtained. During the 1880s there was an active campaign to make all the seating free, a process stimulated by the mid-century extensions. By 1913 it was said St Laurence's had nine hundred seats, all of them free.

Extending the parish church

The seating capacity of the parish church was a long dispute between the town and the Rector of Croston. Wyke's plan of 1655 suggests a seating capacity of around three hundred; a century later this was patently inadequate for a growing community. Appeals to the rector for enlargement of St Laurence's seem to have been rebutted from the 1770s through to 1793. In 1791 a townsman argued that while the Catholic church of St Gregory's was growing, and two Nonconformist chapels were under way, the Established Church was confined by the whim of its rector, and the problem was one reason for the separation of Chorley from Croston in 1793. In 1804 the vestry resolved to level the church and build anew – happily this plan fell through. As time wore on the situation grew worse: St George's and St Peter's both were built, yet the parish church in some respects was locked in an earlier century. Canon Master took the matter over and set about finding a compromise in the late 1850s – the core of the church would remain, but it would be expanded to the north and south with new aisles. At first under Charles Verelict, a Liverpool architect, and then after his death under T. G. Gilpin, again from Liverpool, the work progressed from July 1859. A contemporary photograph of about 1850 shows how dramatic the changes were, yet with the passage of time the mix of Victorian and medieval is not displeasing. The coarser irregular stone of the older church contrasts with the neat dressed stonework of the 1850s. An array of fierce Victorian gargoyles appeared, now seasonally obscured. The old walls were removed almost entirely, with new arches and columns substituted. Away went the old pews and benches in favour of neat Victorian pews. The three old galleries (from 1714 and 1739) were taken out and a west gallery put in place for the 'orchestra' and the Sunday school. On the south wall the old steps giving access to the gallery disappeared. The cost of the whole of the first phase was £2,650, £300 of which came from Canon Master and a large sum from the Smethurst family. This phase, of 1859–60, was matched by the north aisle paid for by Mr Sylvester of North Hall, the whole being completed by 1861. The seating had been increased by 450 places – it only then remained for the traditional allotted places to be declared free to all after 1882.

CHAPTER THREE

A Wondrous Poore, or Rather, No Market

'A wondrous poore, or rather, no market' Leland wrote of Chorley after his visit in the 1530s. Blome, writing later in the next century, thought better of the town: 'Chorley is seated near the spring-head of a brook or rivulet, called the Chor, not far from the river Yarrow; it is but a small town, yet its market, which is on Tuesday, is well furnished with yarn and provisions.' Nevertheless, Chorley was still essentially an agricultural community. One study, of the period from 1450 to 1558, calculated the relative land use. 'Waste' represented 42 per cent of the total 1687 acres. Of the remainder there was arable of 604 acres (61 per cent of the productive acreage), meadow 155 acres (16 per cent), and pasture 232 acres (23 per cent). In the sixteenth century agriculture always figures large, whether in wills or legal disputes. In Henry VIII's reign Thomas Charnock was plaintiff against Richard Haydock and others over neglect of the ring hedge in Astley Manor. Thomas Charnock of Astley was in a dispute with his neighbour William Chorley over a boundary hedge in 1554.

But there were fledgling industries too, one of them to become dominant three hundred years later. Linen weaving foreshadowed cotton: William Banester of Croston called himself a linen man in his 1595 will. Trading in cloth took him to Coventry and Banbury, and 'linman' is a label given to many in Chorley parish register.

The threat from Spain sent ripples as far as Lancashire. Richard Shireburne joint lord of the manor, was one of the deputy lieutenants who were told to muster the trained bands in 1587, Chorley being one of the centres for foot soldiers. Though the county supplied 700 calivers for its 1,170 men, bows still formed part of the arms available. Perhaps the archers were uniformed as their fathers had been in 1557 when a levy of archers for Ireland wore dark blue cassocks, faced with white, a red cap below their metal cap, a jerkin of stag or bullskin and carried bows of yew.

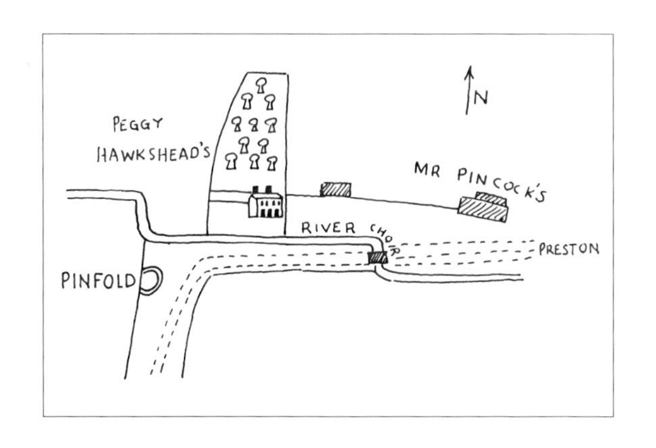

A sketch of Chorley Bottoms as the area appeared in the 1770s, when the highway still followed Water Street. Peggy Hawkshead's house overlooked the spot where a ford crossed the River Chor. [Author]

The Gillibrands: a Tudor success story

The origins of the Gillibrands, who later became the most powerful family in Chorley, are obscure. The name occurs across south Lancashire from the thirteenth century; Henry Gillibrand is the first from the Chorley area to appear in the records when he was fined 20 shillings in the king's court for offences committed as a follower of Robert Holland, in the wake of the Banastre Rebellion of 1315. Humphrey Gillibrand had a lease on land at Eaves Hey from the Hospitallers in 1430: John 'Gelibront' and Elizabeth his mother paid a fine to Richard Crosse for the Eaves Hey lands eleven years later. From this period one line of the family assumes gentleman status, Jenkin Gillibrand being recorded in 1537. Several of his kinsmen in the town appearing in the parish register are clearly husbandmen, however.

John 'Gellybrand' of Chorley, was listed on the Burgess Rolls of Liverpool in 1549 when he paid ten guineas to the subsidy for goods, perhaps implying that he was a Liverpool merchant.[1] By 1565 the same rolls record him as a 'gentleman', and it was about this time he became associated with the Earl of Derby. In 1583 he obtained a lease on Lower Chorley (or Harrington) Hall from the earl for his life and those of Jane, his wife, and Thomas, their son. John's fortunes prospered even more when Edward Rigby bought the Earl of Derby's moiety of the Chorley lands in 1596. One year later Rigby sold him the hall and lands. After 1600 the Chorley Gillibrands increased in wealth and status. Their children were married into the Lancashire gentry, and a pedigree was recorded in 1613. In 1628 Thomas, a considerable landowner, was a convicted recusant who three years later paid a fine of £10 to avoid knighthood. During the Civil War the family, firmly Royalist, suffered and fled, but later returned to rebuild their fortunes anew.

From the 1660s comes the great Gillibrand barn, still standing today and ample testimony to their wealth. The hall, Lower Chorley Hall, became more commonly known as Gillibrand Hall. It was surrounded by a moat, and approached by a drawbridge on one side. The hall, 'a small tower, continued all around with parapets in the inside' (1793), had a group of farm buildings on its moated site. The old hall survived until 1807, when the new hall was built.[2]

After 1717, when Thomas Gillibrand married Margaret, widow of Peter Brooke, one branch of the family lived at Astley Hall. Nicholas Blundell's diary often refers to his visits to Astley at this time. Denied access to many walks of life, as Catholics, the Gillibrands became skilled in other areas. John Gillibrand, lawyer, was steward to the Walmsley family of Dunkenhalgh in 1704 and was paid £100 a year for his services. He was also a trustee for the heir to the estate.[3] The family gave distinguished service to the Catholic Church; two of Thomas's daughters were in the convent at Louvain in 1643, several sons were Jesuit priests, one of them being the sole priest ministering in Liverpool for some time.

Though their fortunes prospered through the eighteenth century, and the estate became richer – farm buildings bearing the cross-swords badge of the Gillibrands survive to this day – the line faced a bleaker future. Thomas Gillibrand, who died in 1733, had five sons and four daughters: Richard and William were priests, and William succeeded on the death of his elder brother, Thomas. His nephew Thomas Hawarden next inherited the estate and adopted the Gillibrand name. His son Thomas took the Gillibrands to the peak of their fortunes, for in 1825 he bought the Shireburne or Weld moiety of the manor, uniting the Chorley manor for the first time in centuries. He demolished the old house in 1807–8 and built the present Gillibrand Hall at a cost of £15,000. From him the line passed to the Fazakerleys who sold their manorial rights in 1874 to the Improvement Commissioners. Miss Fazakerley, one of the last of the line, was an autocratic and determined lady: when jolted in her carriage during one election she laid about her with a horsewhip!

The estates, grand as they were, went the way of most old-established lands – there were sales in 1830, 1845 and 1870. In 1880 the hall itself was offered for sale, with considerable tracts of building land. Out of this came the extensive housing developments of the late nineteenth century, and eventually the development of the present Gillibrand estate by the Langton family.

The mystery of Myles Standish

Myles Standish, one of the outstanding early settlers of America, is thought by some to have been born at Duxbury. The Standishes were an old and important Lancashire family, with lands in several places. Standish itself is their place of origin, but branches of the family later lived at Duxbury, Ormskirk, Warrington and on the Isle of Man. Myles is the best known of the family, but his immediate ancestry is unclear.

His will, made in New England in 1655, is a vital clue, but ambiguous. He claimed to be a Standish of Standish, yet the lands he said were 'surrepticiously detained' from his ancestor were, in fact, part of the estates of the Ormskirk branch of the family. That conflict of evidence creates another mystery, and Canon Porteus set out in the 1920s to seek out clues here and in the Isle of Man. His research, meticulous as ever, was not conclusive, though he deduced that the Ormskirk Standishes were closely linked to those in the Isle of Man.

Were it not for the fame which Myles Standish achieved, his claim to the Standish lands would have been one more obscure attempt to regain lost lands. The nineteenth century saw a revival of interest in the USA, for scholars were keen to retrace the events of the *Mayflower* voyage; several novelists and Longfellow, the poet, recast Standish in a romantic mould, from which he has never since altogether escaped. His descendants, learning that the Standishes' Duxbury estates were without an owner, sent legal representatives to England. The lawyers found the Chorley parish register entries for 1584 (the year of Myles' birth) almost illegible – doubts and suspicions flared, and the page was now assumed to have been rubbed with pumice so that Myles' claims were lost for good! The Rector of St Laurence's was accused of involvement in an elaborate fraud. Dickens wove an imaginative tale around the whole charade. To Englishmen of the time Myles Standish was a founder of the Empire and a genuine hero. The American claim foundered, though one of the claimants, Captain Myles Standish of the American army, looked as though he would have made an admirable incumbent of Duxbury Hall!

The Manx link was investigated by Porteus in 1920 and then undertaken in more depth by G. V. C. Young in the 1980s. The latter's book, *Pilgrim Myles Standish* (1984), has caused ripples of doubt since its appearance. Myles, he claimed, was a Manxman, born at Ellanbane of Standishes linked to the Ormskirk line, a theory pursued by others since. The argument for Ellanbane is a strong one and has convinced many on both sides of the Atlantic, but all the accounts of the early history of New England credit Myles Standish with the founding in 1630 of a separate settlement, near Plymouth Colony, which he called Duxbury. His farm was there and his family buried nearby. None can give a convincing solution to the question – why would Myles Standish, if Manx born, give the name Duxbury (which he knew he could not claim) to a farm and homestead thousands of miles from his birthplace?[4]

The founding of Chorley Grammar School

By the end of the sixteenth century there were schools in many Lancashire towns; those at Preston and Lancaster began during the Middle Ages, though the majority of schools had appeared since the reign of Edward VI. The school at Heskin, for instance, which dates from 1597, was the gift of Sir James Pemberton, who made his fortune as a goldsmith in London, eventually serving as Lord Mayor, but was born in Eccleston. Rivington's grammar school (founded 1566) drew pupils from far and wide; there were several sons of Chorley families among the early scholars, and it is possible that their experience influenced the course of events in Chorley, where the first school dates from 1611. The background was set down in the parish register of St Laurence's by Thomas Ainscough and William Hawkshead. These two churchwardens stated that the town of Chorley had no schoolhouse and that a majority among the parishioners had agreed to remedy the lack of education in the town. The cautious townsfolk planned to prevent their schoolhouse ever being appropriated for other uses, ordering that it

> should be sett part within ye Churchyard and part within ye Tithbarne yard to this End that when the Vicar nor ye Minister of ye said Church or Chappell nor the farmer of ye tythes of ye Chapel should have power to convert it to any other use but that it should Remane Constantly for a Scholehouse . . .

No schoolmaster or his family was permitted to live in the school, and likewise no minister of the chapel could be a teacher. The founders were afraid that children born to the schoolmaster would acquire rights of settlement with the parish charges. Most of the building costs were borne by Robert Charnock of Astley Hall, who gave £6 in money and all the bricks required for the structure. As a certificate of 1634 also shows, however, 'every Inhabitant in Chorley that was liable to a ffifteene gave and paid 20 ffifteens thereunto Accordingly with other charges made only by ye said Inhabitants'. Their co-operative venture succeeded; Charnock's generous gift, coupled with the archaic levy of fifteenths, raised the money needed. In all Charnock paid out £22, not including the bricks supplied from the Astley estate brickfields. The school building survived until 1824.

Regrettably, the curriculum of the first school is now lost. Perhaps it followed the example of similar schools, such as Rivington, where the lessons consisted of 'grammar and other good learning', including the study of Latin, Greek, writing, reading and simple accounts. The first schoolmaster on record is Richard Smith, who appears in 1619 as curate and schoolmaster. Shortly the school was in need of further charitable requests for its upkeep; two in particular are detailed in the Charity Commission's Report of 1898. William Mason, by his will of 1638, made a gift of 20 shillings to be paid annually for the use of a schoolmaster to teach at Chorley. The commissioners knew of four legacies other than Mason's, the interest of which aided the school, but all trace of their origins was lost by 1898. The second, and better known of the gifts, was a result of war. In 1648 the officers and men of Major General Ashton's Lancashire brigade, all veterans of Cromwell's forces, were due to receive arrears of pay following their decisive defeat of the Scots at Preston. Local tradition maintains that the brigade had been quartered in Chorley; consequently in gratitude for hospitality afforded to them they agreed to a request from Richard Standish and Edward Robinson to make over their pay to the parish for the use of the grammar school. The arrears came to £86 3s. 3d, a huge sum of money by modern standards and giving this was a remarkable act of generosity. Nevertheless, the matter was not concluded easily. Giles Marsh of Chorley, draper, received £70 12s. 1d. from Alexander Norris of Bolton, brigade treasurer, while the balance remained in the hands of Humphrey Chetham. Edward Robinson submitted a petition in court to compel Chetham to surrender the money. Another complication came when Robinson himself was sued in the Chancery Court of the Duchy, as he had held onto the capital funds, paying out only the interest to the school on an annual basis. When ordered by the court to pay this money in full to the school in 1667 he paid over £35 18s. 7d. and then only into the hands of two court trustees. According to the later *Notitia Cestriensis* neither the principal nor the interest was made available to the school at this period, though it figured in later income. Despite the shaky start the financial affairs seem to have been augmented from pupils' fees and a handful of boys were admitted to the school annually.

Farms

Lancashire farmers in the seventeenth century took on second occupations to increase their income, as the farms often provided only a bare subsistence. They turned to weaving, to quarrying, mining, or to carting. There were several farmers in the parish of Chorley who had craft skills in addition to farming their land. One such was John Wareing of Eaves Lane. He was a tenant of the Chorley family, but also worked as a tanner, and, judging from the contents of his will, was relatively prosperous. The inventory of his goods made in 1685 amounted in all to £81 9s. od. including sizeable debts owed to him.

John Wareing's eight acre farm in Eaves Lane first appears in the Chorley Survey, described as 'Wareing Woods', at the end of the Middle Ages. Henry Wrennowe got the lease in 1507; by 1586 it had passed to James Tootell, tanner, suggesting that the farm itself had a dual function over a considerable time. When Alexander Wareing, John's father, married Alice Tootell the couple acquired the lease in 1632. Ten years later the Chorleys re-leased the farm for ninety-nine years, to Alexander and his two sons, John and Edward. Edward's name features as a farmer at Plock Farm, yet he was also party to a new lease in 1671 from Catherine Chorley and Robert Holden.

John Wareing died in 1685 and was survived by his wife Mary and daughter Alice. She in her turn married James Ainscough, extending the lease in his name in 1690. Thereafter, it passed to Thomas Mason in 1704, and he was still in possession in 1716 when the Chorley estate was sold. The rent paid for Wareing's from 1642 onwards was 18s. 9d. annually, with boons of two shearings and two hens to the Chorley estate.

Fortunately for us John's will and inventory separately describe him as husbandman and tanner, a fact which is borne out by the contents listed in his will. The inventory of his goods, made on 14 October 1685 by Evan Brindle, Robert Wareing and William Felton, is well laid out and detailed. The debts of more than £20 owed to him included one of £3 due from his brother Edward.

In his storehouse John had leather, tanned and untanned, valued at £1. 19s. od, while his freshly-harvested grain, barley, oats, wheat and hay, were together assessed at £12 3s. 4d. He owned cattle, one bay mare, a colt, geese and pigs. There was a range of farming implements – plough, harrow, seed hoppers and harvesting tools. The most valuable of his possessions in the house were beds and beddings; it is tempting to guess that the 'Standing Bedstead, with Courtains and Vallants' valued at £2 was John's own and the best bed in the house. The inventory had several other beds and bedding, one in the chamber of Oliver, his servant.

The everyday necessities of hearth and kitchen were listed: fire tongs, a cheese press, pewter, trenchers, wooden basins, linen and household furniture, including 'a standing press to put cloaths in'. In his will John

In the early years of the last century the Farthings were bought by the Hoghton family, bringing the boundary of Astley Park ever closer to the town. This entrance to the park was built in the 1820s. [Lancashire County Library]

appoints as his executors his wife Mary and 'my sayde worthy master Richard Chorley'. John Wareing appears as debtor for £6 7s. od. to John Heald in Heald's will of 1671. Henry Baldwin, one of John's contemporaries, had brewing vessels worth 7s. in his inventory, while Roger Breres left goods valued at £34 9s. 4d., £8 of which was accounted for in yarn –perhaps he doubled as a weaver.

Evidence for the range of crops grown is scarce. Nevertheless, clues appear in some documents: the township papers of 1656, for example, give detailed returns of crops for that year on several local farms. Most of the farmers reported crops of wheat, barley, oats and beans with only slight variations. The Chorley estate farm had 1 acre of wheat, 3 acres of barley, 1 acre of beans and ½ acre of oats. Oats were a reliable Lancashire crop, tolerant of local conditions, and figured recurringly in local diets. As late as 1895 a Chorley baker, James Heaton in Brooke Street, advertised himself as the 'Oldest Established Oatcake Bakery in Chorley'. One other crop which seldom occurs in returns but occasionally in field names is peas, which were perhaps less important than cereals in the market.

The extent of farming units in the parish can be gauged from the ley book of 1654. Of eighty-three separate 'farms', 52 per cent (forty-three in all) were of 10 acres or less, 30 per cent (twenty-five) between 11 and 20 acres, 13 per cent (eleven) 21 and 50 acres, while only four consisted of more than 51 acres. Eighteen farms were assessed for woodland as well as arable, usually in small areas of wood of one, two or three acres. Richard Gray appears in the 1654 list as the only occupier of 'barren' land, presumably at Heapey in 10 acres with 20 acres of arable land.

The durability of farm buildings from the seventeenth century is testified by the number of farm houses, barns and outbuildings where the basic structures have survived almost into the twenty-first century. Gillibrand Hall Barn, a Grade II listed building, dates from 1669 and is an impressive building by any standards. It was restored in the 1970s and used as an arts centre. Its function as a key element in the management of a large estate is reflected in its quality. Halliwell's Farm, in Yarrow Road, dates from the same period as Gillibrand Hall Barn, showing the type of farmhouse from the reign of Charles II. At Heath Charnock the barn at Ivy Cottage in Long Lane also dates from the 1660s and uses local stone in its fabric.

Roads and transport

In the early years of the seventeenth century Lancashire's local officials were not as rigorous in rooting out illegal Catholic worship, nor in pursuing Catholic priests as government officers would have wished. The king's officers regarded the physical landscape of the county as a hindrance to their efforts: 'To penetrate into the country was like penetrating into the heart of a forest. The roads were rough and ill suited to much travelling; the people were uncouth and suspicious of travellers.'[5]

Lady Anne Clifford, when a redoubtable old lady, recalled over sixty years a stay in a Chorley ale-house in 1616. Her diary for 1676 relates,

> March – the second day. I remembered how this day was 60 years since I went out of the Inne at Manchester in Lancashire into the poor cottage at Chorley where I lay in a poor ale-house there that one night . . . I went out of the poor cottage at Chorley (though it was Sunday, by reason the lodgings were so bad) into the inne at Preston . . .

One up for Preston!

A few years later the townspeople of Chorley showed their attitude to travellers, as well as their own frugality, when they petitioned the justices of the peace in July 1628 for permission to block the highway with chains as and when they wished.

> We the inhabitants . . . of Chorley, having a great charge of sundry highways lying upon us, which with much cost for many years past we have repaired and amended, and do continue the same, to the great ease of our country and others who have occasion to travel in and by the said ways which said ways . . . are by several persons of other towns and places, being strangers and far remote off, foully of late spoiled, decayed, made foul and many of our causeways broken, by carrying and carting of coals, and such like affairs in unseasonable weather and at inconvenient times, to our great grievances and damages and to the utter spoiling of the said ways, and for that the Lords and owners of the Manor of Chorley who chiefly ought to see a redress therein, do not now inhabit in this our Country, but dwell afar off.

The townsfolk claimed the precedents of other towns where stoops (posts) were chained to regulate carriages and carts in bad weather and were presumably successful in their request, for in later years a house, whose location cannot be fixed, was known as the Stoophouse. There were good reasons for the frugality of the townspeople on the upkeep of roads, for the cost of repair and maintenance came out of their pockets. The quarter sessions papers for 1650 include a return from Roger Haydock, in which he says that 'the highways in Chorley betwixt the market towns of Bolton and Preston are very foul and in great decay.' He submitted a list of all the property owners who were in default of providing six days' labour on the roads, a list headed by Charnock, Gillibrand, Chorley and Crosse, followed by dozens of others; local people often felt unwilling to maintain highways for the benefit of persons travelling long distances.

Apart from the burden incurred by the upkeep of the king's highway, other local roads caused problems from time to time. In 1647, for instance, the manor court ordered John Heald of 'Ackers' (Ackhurst) to 'mend and make a fair passable footway fit for passage both for Church and market the way lying in his own field'. Failure to obey the order would cost Heald 6s. 8d. in fines.

Travel by coach enjoyed a revival in the years of peace after the Civil War. The *Mercurius Politicus* for April 1658 announced that stage coaches would set out from the George Inn in London, travelling north via Wigan, Chorley, Preston, Garstang, Lancaster and Kendal.

When Dr Kuerden recorded his Lancashire itinerary in 1695 he gave one clue to the validity of Chorley's complaint in 1628. Referring to his route, he says that: 'having pass'd Blainsco Brook you shortly after meet with a Road on the right hand leading to Chorley; passing over the ford into Duxbury there are 2 Halls called Burgh one belonging to Mr Alexr Rigby, the other to Justice Crooke and passing over Chorley Moor you leave on the left a fair built Hall formerly the seat of Harington but now of Gillibrand of Chorley. Here are great quantities of Coal.'

The Protestation Return of 1642

In 1642 the House of Commons ordered that all adult males over eighteen years of age should make a vow, before approved witnesses, to maintain 'the true Reformed Protestant Religion expressed in the doctrine of the Church of England'. The Chorley list, dated 18 February 1642, contains the names of 209 men of the town, together with the occupations of most of them. Clearly, those townsmen who were firm Catholics refused to take the vow. One, Mr Thomas Charnock of Astley, was excused attendance at the Chorley witnessing of the vow as he had already done so at Manchester. Overseeing the formalities at Chorley were John Wasley, Alexander Wilcock, John Heald, Thomas Hawkshead, Roger Allenson and Evane Brindle.

The equivalent list for Euxton, testified by James Langley, Vicar of Leyland, lists seventy-three men who made the protestation, and twenty-seven who refused, headed by Hugh Anderton of Euxton Hall. The Recusant Roll of 1628 and other contemporary documents tend to suggest that Chorley's firm Catholics numbered one in four of the population. The return indicates a township population of about seven hundred. The Protestation Return for Chorley also gives valuable clues as to occupations. Forty-six men are listed as 'husbandmen', eleven as yeomen farmers; however, a number of individuals whose occupation is not given are known, from other sources, to have been involved in farming. If these are added, agriculture emerges as the principal occupation of more than half the adult males.

Twenty-four men are shown as 'Websters' or weavers, one intriguingly as a 'silck weaver'. The list of occupations also includes joiners, coopers, shopkeepers, feltmakers, alehouse keepers, wheelwrights, tanners, eight tailors, one vintner (Richard Burton), and an essential member of the community in Thomas Crook, who is described as a bonesetter. The surnames reflect the old-established families in the town: Anglezarke, Anderton, Baldwin, Bailey, Breres, Brown, Dickinson, Hawkshead, Heald, Lowe, Melling, Taylor, Tootell, Waring, Wastley and Whittle.

The plague takes its toll

'Here beginneth the Visitation of almighty God, the Plague'

A quick search through Chorley's parish register might contradict the impression that our ancestors lived short lives. Given the right circumstances of a healthy life and good fortune some people lived to a ripe old age. In 1698, for instance, the body of Bridget Garstang, 'alias Husks', was laid to rest in St Laurence's Churchyard, having lived 104 years and 6 months. If this statement is true she was born in 1593 when Elizabeth I was a mere sixty years old; Bridget's lifetime spanned the reigns of six monarchs, the Civil War and Commonwealth had come and gone, she had survived the perils of daily life.

A citizen of the 1600s faced a catalogue of hazards, from starvation, through periodic warfare and the recurrent nightmare of an unseen, deadly enemy – the plague. In the seventeenth century the plague was common in Lancashire, whose JPs levied taxes on the hundreds to pay for the relief of victims. In 1605 one Anglezarke man assaulted the tax collector rather than pay his due. Chorley and surrounding areas were badly hit by an epidemic disease in 1623-4, but this was mild compared with the outbreak of plague in 1631. In the autumn of 1630 Preston was a centre of infection and within a year 1,069 people died; more than one third of the population. Neighbouring towns and villages with contacts through trade were sure to be affected. The clerk of St Laurence's duly records in the register the first deaths with the phrase 'buringes of the Plake the year of our Lord 1631' Humphrey Layland is the first, buried on 1 June 1631. Perhaps the plague had come with the May fair, conveyed by traders or fair showmen.

The Layland family suffered indeed; Elizabeth, Humphrey's wife, was buried on 18 June, Janet, born 18 June, buried two days later. Altogether the plague accounted for 120 deaths in seven months, which might represent one-sixth of Chorley's population. The absence of names from the gentry families suggests that Chorley followed the national trend, inasmuch as the poor were more prone to infection.

It is significant that the register shows that burials from 13 June were made, not in the churchyard, but 'At Halliwo Barne', which was identified by Canon Porteus as Halliwell's Farm in Yarrow Road.[6] John Wilson, meanwhile, suggested that this was more likely Hall-ith-Wood Farm at Cowling. The first is more likely, as 'Halliwell' means 'Holy Well'. Coupled with the evidence that medicinal springs at Yarrow Bridge were known in the past, it is easy to see how a popular belief in these would suggest that this spot, well away from the town proper, might be the best location for plague victims.

The authorities hurried to halt the spread of the plague. The Ormskirk quarter sessions ordered the constables to keep watch and ward, and to detain suspected persons and wanderers. At the Wigan Sessions, too, the case of Chorley was cited: 'the contagion of the sickness within Chorley is verey ferefull and is dispersed into many parts of the said Townshipp'. Corn could not be ground, the essentials of living could not be bought and an extra levy was raised to be given to Ralph Lever, Alexander Liptrot and John Parker to aid the poor and needy. In early March 1632 the plague ended, its last recorded victim being Richard, son of John Bancroft.

The repercussions of the plague were felt for months, and the outbreak of 1631-2 was not the last. A serious problem arose again in the 1640s, just as the Civil War was wreaking a different scourge. In 1644, Preston, Rochdale and Ormskirk were hard hit, and six hundred died in Manchester in 1645. From 1646 to 1648 travel restrictions were put on ordinary travellers to limit the infection. In 1649 James Hyet, Pastor of Croston, signed the appeal for aid, describing the hard-pressed county.

> The hand of God is evidently seen stretched out upon the county, chastening it with a three-corded scourge of sword, pestilence and famine . . . In this county hath the plague of pestilence been raging these three years and upwards, occasioned chiefly by these wars.[7]

Astley Hall

No building in Chorley has such a well documented history as Astley Hall. Its secret lies, perhaps, in that it has something for everyone: the park and woodland for a pleasant stroll; the hall and associated buildings for the historically minded, and for students of architecture and period furniture. Like all old houses Astley has its legends and tales of ghosts. Whatever the season of the year, its fascination never dims.

The first settlers have only come to light in the last thirty years. In

Astley Hall, built around a Tudor core, was extensively added to in the seventeenth century when the magnificent glass façade appeared. It was refashioned in the 1750s under the Brookes and again in the 1820s. [Lancashire County Library]

1963 Mr Peter Clitheroe unearthed the remains of a pottery jar from the roots of a felled tree. This was a burial urn of the Middle Bronze Age, dating from perhaps as early as 1400 BC, and inside were the bones of a woman who had suffered from arthritis. Later excavations were carried out in the 1970s during the Astley Park Village development. The site of this discovery is marked by an inscribed slab.

Although the Charnock family were principally resident at Charnock Old Hall, in Charnock Richard, documents associating Astley with the Charnocks appear from the Middle Ages onwards. From Charnock the family's estates extended almost into Chorley itself, where the east-ley in time became Astley, home to younger branches of the Charnock family.

They had a chequered history. In 1194-5 Adam de Chernoch was a rebel in arms against Richard I and paid a fine of four shillings for the peace and favour of the King. Richard Charnock gave lands in Charnock Richard to the Hospital of St John of Jerusalem in 1199, followed later by a grant of land in 'Chorlee called Astelee'. The Charnocks paid rent for the estate to the order throughout the Middle Ages, though the Earl of Derby gained the order's land after the Dissolution. In 1650 Robert Charnock paid rent of 2s. 6d. for the capital messuage of Astley and for Moorfields, the latter equivalent to Halliwell's Farm and Bolton Road. The fuller extent of the Charnock estates can be deduced from the grant of Bagganley to the Hospital of St John by Richard Charnock and by his settling his estate of Birkacre on his sister Ellen.

The Banastre rebellion of 1315 implicated some of the Charnocks: Robert was killed fighting at Preston; Adam, son of Jordan, although caught up in the revolt, was given a pardon by the king. The head of the family, Adam, was summoned to the Great Council of Westminster in

1324, implying that he was no longer thought a rebel. Early in the fifteenth century Henry Charnock's rental for Chorley included separate headings for Brown's Hey, Wymundsley and the Lighthurst.[8] His descendant, Robert Charnock, made a grant of land in 1498, in which he refers to the 'Judland' and 8 acres of meadow in Rugh-Astley and Chorley.

The Charnocks increased in importance and, as they become more successful, they married into the leading families of Lancashire, the Norrises of Speke and the Molyneuxs, for example. A tradition says that a fire at Charnock Old Hall in Elizabeth's reign induced the family to transfer to Astley as their chief home though as early as 1554 Thomas Charnock 'of Astley' made an agreement with William Chorley of Chorley Hall concerning a boundary hedge. Thomas recorded a pedigree at the visitation of 1567, and died in 1571. The family played active roles in local and national affairs. John Charnock was executed after the Babington Plot, Edward Charnock was Page of the Wardrobe to Ann Boleyn, while Thomas Charnock in 1557 was in the army which was sent to meet the invading Scots. Robert Charnock was largely responsible for the rebuilding of Standish Church and for the setting up of Chorley Grammar School in 1611.

From the Tatton Papers at the Lancashire Record Office comes a graphic account of the disputed rights of way on the Astley estate, a valuable short cut before the construction of Southport Road in 1865.

> Edward Dicconson, of Coppull, aged 57 . . . says that, about 30 or 40 years ago he was well acquainted with Robert Charnock of Astley, Esquire, deceased, and very much in his company at Astley Hall, walking with Mr Charnock on the Green between the back gates and a . . . Tree on the side of the said Green. 'We saw people go over the Green from Euxton to Chorley and from a place called the Ackers to Chorley'. He heard Mr Charnock find fault with those people for coming that way and told them that their way . . . was not there but at the back of the wood. Dicconson says that he believes this to be correct, as he was once coming from Euxton with Hugh Rigby, Esq., deceased, his master, they had stopped at a gate near Astley Mill where Mr Rigby rode behind the mill at the back of the wood.[9]

The phases of Astley's development

It has often been observed that Astley shows building styles from different eras; the most detailed and expert account of these changes is given in Herbert Cescinsky's 1922 Report to the Council, while the work of George Birtill and Canon Porteus complete the story.

To date no definite evidence has been found for a medieval hall on the site, though the frequent references to the Charnocks of Astley from the thirteenth century imply its existence. The *Victoria County History* states that Astley was a moated homestead site, but this, too, is doubtful. Porteus argued that such a hall would have been of the 'H' pattern of a Lancashire vernacular design. Only with the reign of Elizabeth I does Astley's story become clearer. Robert Charnock is credited with building a new hall and the datestone showing his initials and those of his wife, with the date 1577, is assumed to relate to his work. Later rebuildings have meant that only part of the house of the 1580s has survived: the gables on the west wall are believed to be the oldest remaining parts of the half-timbered house. More work occurred in 1600, as witnessed by the corbel beam in the courtyard. The courtyard, a typical Tudor feature, even now gives a special attraction to Astley. It is a small yard, and the entrance from the north is perhaps the original entrance to the house. When the walls of the courtyard were restored in 1952 the wattle and daub of the original building was uncovered above the stone base of the wall. Cescinsky described a two-storeyed timber building, with the great hall at its heart, and containing around thirty rooms. It may also have had a much larger kitchen than today, and there were galleries inside the Great Hall, one for minstrels. This was the hall which Cromwell might have seen after the Battle of Preston.

The most important changes came after Margaret Charnock married Richard Brooke of Mere in 1665. The impressive stone and glass façade of the south front was built by the Brookes, who also redesigned the great hall with a contemporary moulded and decorated ceiling. The morning room was partitioned off, and the carved panelling and painted panels showing historical figures seem to have been added around this period. The ceiling, decorated with elaborate skill by continental craftsmen, incorporated the badges of the Charnocks (the lapwing) and the Brookes (the badger). The Brooke mansion transformed the Tudor shell after 1666, and thereafter there was a steady increase in Astley's comfort and elegance. Cescinsky suggested that there had been a long gallery above Robert Charnock's hall, but the later adaptation of this room was not a success. It did, however, allow the display, in its 72-foot length, of a shovel-board table (23½ feet long) made in the seventeenth century, and now one of Astley's special features.

An eighteenth-century painting of Astley, though topographically incorrect, still conveys the layout of formal gardens, surrounding walls and corner tower alongside the dam. Blundell's diary, recording visits there in the 1710s, tells us that Astley had orchards with fruit trees of various kinds. More alterations were made in the 1750s, as instanced by the spoutheads on the south frontage displaying the initials of Peter and Susanna Brooke and the date 1752.

Further work was carried out in 1787-8 – the stables were built, and a new staircase provided from the great hall. In 1825 the east wing was completely rebuilt, with a new dining-room, the inlaid room and the half-timbered extension on the lakeside. John Bannister's compilations of the 1880s included one recollection that, in about 1810, some of the portions of the hall which were taken down appeared to pre-date the 1600 rebuilding work.

When Peter Brooke died without issue in 1787 Astley Hall was inherited by his sister Susanna. She was born in 1762, became a noted beauty of her day and married Thomas Townley-Parker of Cuerden in 1787. Thomas, High Sheriff of the county in 1793, died in 1794. Their eldest son, Robert Townley-Parker, was High Sheriff himself in 1817, MP for Preston twice and Guild Mayor in 1862. Cuerden Hall was the chief family home of the Townley-Parkers. Susanna remarried, in 1797, to Sir Henry Philip Hoghton and bore him an heir, also named Henry. According to Tootell the father came to live at Astley Hall in 1814, and many changes to the estate followed. The east wing of the hall dates mainly from 1825, the new stone boundary wall which is seen on old photographs was made facing the new Park Road, the Farthings were brought into the estate and the lodge situated just inside the entrance was built, as well as a second on Euxton Lane.

Lady Hoghton was an autocratic lady, who lived into her nineties, dying in 1852. At her instigation the almshouses at Whittle-le-Woods were built in 1841, and the land given for St Peter's in Chorley. She also diverted the old route through the park to guard her privacy and is said in her old age to have had a servant to push her wheelchair from Astley to St Laurence's. At the Lancashire Record Office a series of tradesmen's bills records building and rebuilding work at Ackhurst Lodge in 1842. This work was apparently commissioned by her ladyship, as a summary is

Thomas Townley Parker's stable block, built at Astley in the 1780s and now a Grade II listed building in its own right. The Townley Parkers were avid sportsmen, maintaining a stud of hunters here in the 1790s. [Courtesy of Ann Tout]

headed 'For Mothers Whim or Folly', implying family misgivings about 'Wood Cottage'.

By the end of the Victorian era Astley Hall had assumed most of the features it has today, showing elements of design of three earlier centuries. Building features apart, the hall has kept some remarkable plasterwork and period furniture, notably 'Cromwell's Bed', in fact a carved Jacobean bed of a date earlier than 1648.

At the end of the First World War, Chorley sought a way to provide a memorial to its war dead. Eventually, in 1919, Reginald Arthur Tatton, the owner of Astley Hall, decided to offer the house to the corporation as a memorial. Though the land would have to be bought from the estate the offer was a remarkable and generous move. A War Memorial Committee eagerly approved the idea and set about raising money to buy the park. Peace Day was celebrated inside the park in August 1919, complete with the replica of the market cross which would be placed inside the entrance to the park. From the Gillibrand estate the committee purchased the impressive archway which now marks Astley's entrance.

When the details of the park purchase had been settled, the formal handover of the hall and park came on 24 February 1922, followed by an official opening ceremony on 31 May 1924. The park had been used occasionally in the past for special events, but it now became completely free to the public of Chorley, a year-round delight situated only minutes away from the busy heart of the town.

The Astley estates

The Hawkshead papers give interesting sidelights on life at Astley in the mid-eighteenth century, when Peter Brooke was still a minor under the guardianship of Richard Wharton Brooke. From the late 1740s until the 1760s routine matters are recorded – income from rents, roofing repairs, wages paid – but a good deal of restoration seems to have been under way. In 1754 William Woodcock was paid £7 11s. 9¾d. for reflooring the parlour in deal. There were repairs to Astley mill, and the existence of brickmaking, hinted at in the Tudor period, is confirmed by references to Ben Latus carting clay for 100,000 bricks at Astley in 1755, and being paid £15 12s. 4d. for making bricks for sale in 1756. As Brick Kiln Field appears on estate maps to the north-east of the hall, we may surmise that one of the estate kilns was there.

Building work at the stables also figures among the tasks under way, and the hall and its vicinity must have been busy with masons, carpenters and joiners, glaziers, slaters and flaggers. Confirmation of the presence of a deer park is given: '1752 To Rob. Butterworth for mowing two crofts at Astley for the Deer.' Young Mr Brooke went up to Oxford University in 1751, and a sum of £2,120 was debited.

A survey of the Brooke estates was made by R. and J. Lang in 1760. It details property in Chorley, Whittle-le-Woods, Euxton, Charnock

Astley Park, Chorley's playground, is an important expanse of parkland, surrounded by a residential area. This section of the park, as far as the start of the woodland, was once known as the Farthings. [Author]

Richard, Coppull, Leyland, Goosnargh, Whittingham, and Bradford (Manchester), where a coal mine had been worked for the Charnocks for over a century. So far as Chorley is concerned a substantial number of farms were on the estate: Halliwell Farm, mentioned in medieval deeds; its near neighbour, Kingsley's Tenement (now South Cottage); Lion's Tenement, from which Lyons Lane is named, was near the top of the lane, on the south side. Harper's Tenement was at the foot of Lyons Lane, straddling the new Morrison's store site.

Canon Porteus' transcript of the 1760 Survey, with additional notes from his antiquarian knowledge, explains that the Astley mill was south of Mill Croft and south-west of Far Old Orchard; with its site on the River Chor and a dam, separate from the Great Dam near the hall, this water mill must have been in the same location for many centuries. The Survey of 1760, reinforced by later evidence, such as the estate plan of 1822, reminds us that Astley was a working agricultural and industrial estate, its role as the stately home at the heart of decorative park and woodland being primarily a product of the nineteenth and twentieth centuries.

Farming the land

Astley Hall Farm was not accessible to the public until the 1970s. The hall and parkland opened to the public after the First World War, but the farm complex remained private until the construction of Astley Village by the Central Lancashire Development Corporation enabled a car park to

Wills from the seventeenth century frequently include an inventory of the person's goods and belongings. This example is attached to the will of Henry Baldwin, a yeoman farmer who died in 1680. [Lancashire Record Office, ref. WCW]

be made behind the hall. The fact that the farmhouse is now visible from the adjacent footpath reinforces the point that Astley Hall was dependent upon, and the centre of, an agricultural estate. The main building had the appearance of an extended farmhouse or long barn with additional wings at the north-east corner.

In 1571 an inventory was made by George Browne and Roger Allanson of Chorley, together with Hugh Boulyng and Henry Fyssher of Charnock Richard, detailing the property of Thomas Charnock of Astley. The livestock included thirty-seven sheep, eleven hogs and six young pigs, one old gelding and three mares, and six pairs of oxen, which would have been used for ploughing. The oxen were valuable enough to be named, Pike and Palmer, Gibb and Gye; Thomas' cattle are likewise given homely names such as Maryon, Swallow, and Cromphorne. The record of his crops included oats, wheat and barley in store with 3 acres of wheat sown in the ground. The farm equipment is shown in detail, with three turf wains, one old and one new dung cart, scythes and pitchforks and the rest. The estate supplied its own milk, cheese and butter, and there was flour from Astley's mill. The lake would no doubt have supplied fresh fish and it is likely that Astley (like Chorley Hall) had dovecotes for alternative fresh meat.

The water-driven corn mill was always a source of income as well as of estate supplies. When Robert Charnock died in 1615 a note concerning the mill was made.

> In the Mill
> 1 pare of bed stockes and clothes for the same £0 18s. 0d. One croe of Iron and one picke and chissill £0 6s. 0d. A great stone senteron at mill £0 16s. 0d.

The miller was clearly meant to stay on the premises for some time! Reference to the mill site appears elsewhere in this text and it has been argued that the lake next to the hall was originally dammed to provide water power for the mill. George Birtill has argued that the discovery of stones with the Charnock crest is one clue to the location of the mill on the River Chor. Ultimately, archaeological excavation may solve this mystery and give us a clearer picture of Chorley in the Middle Ages. The gardeners of Astley were busy in the eighteenth century with its ornamental gardens, orchard and later the deer park. One account from the last century refers to large areas of woodland disappearing from the park in the early 1800s. When the farm was let for tender in 1844 it consisted of just over 55 acres with pasture and meadow, then tenanted by James Clieveley. The land agent, Thomas Gaskell, had offices in Bolton Street.

CHAPTER FOUR

The Civil War and its Aftermath

The Civil Wars

SHORTLY AFTER Christmas in the year 1655, Edward Robinson, of Buckshaw Hall in Euxton, lately major in the Parliamentary forces of Lancashire, wrote the preface to his history of the Civil Wars in Lancashire. As he worked, Robinson reflected on all he had seen over the past thirteen years – his thoughts echoed those of countless veterans of war as he expressed a heartfelt weariness of war, despair at the privation and hardship which followed for soldier and civilian alike, and regret for the chaos and bloodshed spilled over nine hard years from 1642 to 1651. He concluded with these words,

> Reader, judge of me as having no particular envy against any man . . . I freely forgive all and to speak Truth I verily think that there was not any man of my rank in all the county where I live and of the side I took was plundered deeplier, but God forgive us all. Amen.[1]

If Robinson, one of the victors, felt like this, what must the many local people on the losing side have felt? When the war started in 1642 people from all levels of society were quickly caught up in events. Most of the gentry lined up for the King, while ordinary people often followed the lead of their masters and landlords. Regardless of conscience, they could be called on to fight at someone else's whim. At the end of the first Civil War many of the gentry had been impoverished and their estates lost through sequestration by Parliament. Survivors of war struggled to stay alive. John Hilton of Wheelton, for example, fought for the King under Sir Thomas Tyldesley. When he appealed to the authorities for aid in 1673, he said that in 1644 he was wounded eighteen times at Marston Moor, 'sixe in the head, in his armes and hands nine wounds, one wound in his side, another in his thigh and another in the leg.' Medical bills had depleted his funds, taking a full year for him to recover.[2]

Chorley had mixed fortunes during the wars. It had little strategic importance, though its position astride the north–south highway meant that bodies of armed men were a common sight. Most local people,

Buckshaw Hall, now within the confines of the site of the ROF, was the home of Major Edward Robinson, a prominent local supporter of Parliament during the Civil War. [Lancashire County Library]

however, seem to have opted for cautious neutrality, but some were more committed, and others were involved in the local militia. As individuals, however, some townsfolk were firmly for King or Parliament. A muster roll of the Leyland Hundred 'trained band' survives from 1635 when Robert Charnock was captain and Alexander Rigby was an officer. Six men from Chorley appear on the roll, James Lucas, John Heald, Richard Tootill, Thomas Rigby, Robert Whittle and Edward Aynscough. Training took place at Chorley for two days in July.[3]

There was a rehearsal for war in 1638–9, when the King called out the northern gentry to fight the Scots. William Farrington of Worden wrote to a group of them – Ralph and Thomas Standish, Robert Charnock of Astley, William Anderton and William Hoghton – telling them to assemble at Chorley as part of a force of mounted horse. The gentry were also expected to attend, and so were the trained band. Lord Strange's list for the muster included Alexander Rigby of Burgh and Richard Ashton of Croston, Royalists in the Civil War to come. Charles's army avoided conflict and battle was averted by the Treaty of Berwick.

The breaking point in the quarrel between King and Parliament was in September 1642, but it had been preceded by a period of growing tension. There was a rowdy meeting at Preston in June, after which the town's magazine of arms and powder was seized for the King. In turn Manchester was seized for Parliament.

In September 1642 Lord Strange succeeded to the title of Earl of Derby. He launched an unsuccessful Royalist attack on Manchester with 2,500 men. There was one notable Royalist casualty:

> Captain Standish, a Captain of the Trained Band of Leyland Hundreds, eldest son to Mr Standish of Duxbury, . . . quartered in a house upon the north side of Salford, well up towards the Chapel, washing his hands in the morning at the door, was by a bullet shot from the top of Manchester Steeple slain . . .[4]

So reported Edward Robinson. Another account, by Halley, says that the Duxbury tenants, who had accompanied young Standish, slipped away after his death and returned home to Duxbury. Thomas Standish was buried at Chorley four days later. The Standishes faced a dilemma of divided loyalties: Thomas, the eldest son, fought for the King, but his father, Thomas senior, was a firm Parliamentarian, as were the younger sons. Shortly before the siege of Manchester Lord Derby wrote to William Farrington, instructing him to seize the magazine at Chorley, with its arms, armour and equipment, to keep them in the hands of Captains Robert Charnock and Thomas Standish.

In Lancashire efforts continued to prevent fighting. Letters passed between the two sides, calling for a local truce to be arranged. William Farrington, Alexander Rigby of Burgh and John Fleetwood of Penwortham wrote from Chorley to Sir Thomas Burton, concerning the truce, but Parliament blocked the meeting when it learned of its purpose. The county was committed to war.

In the wake of Edgehill the Earl of Derby resolved to take Lancashire for the King, and local gentry played a prominent part in the subsequent fighting. At Wigan, Captains Charnock, and Chisnall of Chisnall Hall, and Captain Barrow were in command of three hundred foot soldiers. In 1643 a desperate assault by 1,500 men on the town of Bolton failed, and a son of Alexander Rigby of Burgh and many of his men died during the attack.

Robert Charnock of Astley was early in the field, as was Thomas Gillibrand, of Lower Chorley Hall, sixty years old in 1642, who declared his support for the King and was joined by his son and heir, John. When the war turned against the King the two escaped to the mountains of Wales, while their families were sheltered among friends. A letter from Thomas Gillibrand from 1643 sheds light on the often lukewarm support for the war: 'I have maintained all this year above the ordinary arms. I am charged withal one Dragooner on horseback and like to be still, God knows how long.'[5]

In 1643 Edward Robinson, a captain at this stage, was captured in a lightning raid on Chorley. Lord Molyneux's troopers, in a night attack from Rufford, seized Robinson's company with their arms and equipment and took them to Lathom House. Among the captains during the later siege of Lathom were Farrington of Worden, Robert Charnock of Astley and Edward Chisnall of Chisnall. Legend says that Charnock was wounded during the siege and afterwards was known by the nickname 'One-Eyed' Charnock.

When Prince Rupert besieged Liverpool in 1644, Captain Chorley of Chorley was among the attackers, perhaps anxious for the estates he owned at Walton. By June 1644 Prince Rupert's army was fifteen thousand strong; now he planned to relieve the siege of York. He took a leisurely route, passing through Chorley en route to Preston. The only earlier occasion in the war when a large force had been in Chorley was in 1643, when Lord Molyneux's army assembled at the church tower before setting off to join the King at Oxford.

For Robert Charnock of Astley the surrender of Lathom House on 5 December 1645 meant more than the ignominy of defeat. Thereafter he was treated as a 'delinquent', a rebel against Parliament. Many of his assets were seized and sequestrated, and for his support of Charles I Charnock was fined £260. Robert's brother Roger, as well as his kinsman Thomas Charnock of Leyland, also suffered financial penalties. Parliament later intensified the sequestrations, and some 'rebels' were outlawed – the Gillibrands are a local example. In 1648, when war broke out again, Cromwell prepared to meet the Scots and their English allies in battle somewhere in Lancashire. As they moved towards Preston the Scots army outnumbered Lambert's five thousand Parliamentary force, until Cromwell advanced from Skipton. He stayed the night of 16 August at Stonyhurst Hall, home of the Royalist Shireburnes. This gave rise to one of the inevitable Cromwell legends, saying that he slept on the kitchen table! The Scots, overly confident, were strung out along the highway, their foot soldiers north of Preston while their horse were on the outskirts of Wigan.

On Thursday 17 August Cromwell moved onto Ribbleton Moor, splitting the Scots army in two. The battle lasted for three days, although victory was settled when the Scots were pushed over the bridge at Walton-le-Dale. The Lancashire brigade under Assheton fought hard throughout the battle. The evening of 17 August saw some Scots retreating north, their commander Hamilton remaining at Walton before his army moved south under darkness.

At this stage it is appropriate to examine another Cromwell legend – where did he sleep after the Battle of Preston? Astley Hall, the Unicorn Inn at Walton and Preston town are all contenders. Astley Hall maintains a tradition that Oliver Cromwell spent some time at the home of Robert Charnock, commemorated in the Cromwell Bed (in the east wing), the Cromwell Room (at the rear of the hall), together with a pair of the great man's boots left behind in his haste to chase the enemy. Some authors maintain that Cromwell's visit to Astley Hall fits 18 August or the night following. His much-quoted remark about travelling twelve miles of the worst roads he had ever met describes his journey, but a letter from him says he slept in the field that night – a detail which may still accommodate a stay at Astley Hall. The next phase of the battle came with the morning of 18 August. Those Scots trapped south of the Ribble retreated through Chorley with Cromwell in pursuit. General Middleton's Scottish horse, recalled from Wigan, were in Chorley when Cromwell's cavalry caught up with them at Red Bank on Chorley Moor, so tradition says, where the open common lands provided room to manoevre. Cromwell lost a valued cavalry leader in the action.

> I ordered Colonel Thornhaugh to command two or three regiments of horse to follow the enemy, if it were possible to make him stand till we could bring up the army.
>
> The enemy marched away 7,000 or 8,000 foot, and almost 4,000 horse; we followed . . . with about 3,000 foot and 2,500 horse and in prosecuting that worthy gentleman, Colonel Thornhaugh pressing too boldly was slain, being run through the body and thigh and head by the enemy's lancers . . .

The conclusion to the battle came on 19 August when the Parliamentary army caught up with the Scots at Winwick; one thousand Scots were killed before a surrender was negotiated at Warrington. Wardale, writing in 1932, argued that Cromwell's actual visit to Astley took place on the night of 21 August when the general retraced his steps before travelling to York. There is no hard evidence to verify the traditions and Cromwell gave rise to new legends wherever he went; the oral tradition at Astley, however, seems current from the seventeenth century onwards.

There is a certificate in the Lancashire Record Office collections showing that at least one of Cromwell's troopers was still billeted locally long after the battle, as he accidentally shot a young woman when unloading his pistol at the window of his billet, the home of Roger Haydock, in October 1648. Along with the cessation of hostilities, arrears of pay came to Assheton's Brigade and at the instigation of Richard Standish and Edward Robinson the officers agreed to give their pay to Chorley town for the benefit of the grammar school.

There is very little evidence to show how Chorley's townspeople fared during the wars. The parish register for 1644 includes the burial of William Doson, 'Killed at York', meaning that he was a casualty of Marston Moor. In 1645 Richard Heald was killed at Duxbury though no engagement is known there. Similarly, Peter Bannister was killed at Haigh in October 1645 and John Dans, soldier, was buried at St Laurence's in January 1646.

The last phase of the wars came in 1650, when the future Charles II landed in Scotland only to see his army beaten by Cromwell at Dunbar. The Scots invaded England again, and were in Lancashire in August 1651. On the 14 August Charles stayed at Euxton Hall with the Andertons.

> This day Charles Stuart lodged at Euxton Burgh, six miles on this syde of Preston being Sir Hugh Anderton's house, who was prisoner at Lancaster, but sett at liberty by the Scotts. This Anderton is a bloody papist, and one that when Prince Rupert was at Bolton, boasted much of being in blood to the elbows in that cruel massacre.

Support in Lancashire was disappointing. Charles moved on to Cheshire while Derby drummed up recruits where possible for the Crown. While he was at Warrington on 20 August the Royalist army assembled at Chorley on the 21st. Lilburne, in command of Parliament's horse regiments, took his troops to Brindle where they fought off an attack on 23 August. Two days later battle was met at Wigan Lane, where the Royalists were roundly defeated. Colonel Tyldesley was killed in the battle, a loss so profound that in better times Alexander Rigby of Burgh, his cornet of horse, erected a memorial to his old commander, which is still there to this day.

Major Robinson bought the sequestered estate of Chorley Hall in March 1653 though only for the lifetime of Richard Chorley. When Chorley died in 1662 the estates reverted to his son and Robinson's family fell heavily into debt. Eventually Richard Brooke of Astley bought the debt and Buckshaw Hall passed into the hands of a Royalist.

The Restoration

Under the Commonwealth an uneasy peace prevailed, but uncertainty dragged on until the republican sentiments died in the ineffectual rule of Richard Cromwell. In 1660 Charles II was restored to his throne; the erstwhile ruling powers now endured a period of bitter defeat, various factions challenging for influence. The restored Royalist faction set about reforming the county militias, recognizing the fact that the new legally constituted authority might need the weight of armed forces in local communities to establish firm rule. The authorities still focused their fears on the disbanded and returned Cromwellian soldiers scattered all over the country. Sir Roger Bradshaigh of Haigh, on behalf of the king, had agents gathering information from far and wide of rumours of disaffection.

One of these was apparently Robert Baldwin of Chorley, a Royalist sympathiser, who wrote to Sir Roger in January 1660 with an account of an armed uprising supposedly being planned for Chorley. He reported a conversation with William Melling of Hartwood Green, whose servant, John Smith, had overheard a secret night-time meeting of plotters. The two alleged plotters talked about the recent militia reforms, one of them asserting, 'They can raise none, but theire will bee a Hundred Souldiers raised in this towne with Armes upon Dayes Warninge, and those which will not rise wee will hang them att their own Doores'. No rising took place: perhaps Sir Roger took steps to prevent it.

Two years later, in 1662, Sir Roger Bradshaigh was on the trail of Presbyterians around Aspull, who, although they were Royalists, would fight to protect their religious freedom. In June Sir Roger's agents reported that Quakers would join the Presbyterians in an uprising, and that various Presbyterian ministers (including Welch of Chorley) would go to Scotland rather than conform. Plots and rumours continued. In 1665, after the Conventicle Act of 1664 and the Five Mile Act, Nonconformists still were suspected of treasonable activities. The militia were called to readiness in August and arms and ammunition were seized from dealers. The homes of suspects were searched for weapons, among them four families in Euxton, three in Eccleston and a number of people in Chorley. They included Alexander Brears (Breres), Eaves Lane; Thomas Wareing, Yarrow Bridge; James Roscoe; Thomas Moody of Heapey; and John Lowe of Duxbury.

Chorley's best known Nonconformist of the time was, of course, Henry Welch, curate of the parish church of St Laurence. Although he was a minister in the Established Church Welch's outlook was fundamentally Puritan. He was appointed to St Laurence's in 1628 as curate, and Welch's superior as Vicar of Croston was James Hyett, BD., an even stronger supporter of Presbyterianism than Welch himself. When the call came for ship-money to be paid by the clergy of Lancashire in 1635 several local clergymen of Presbyterian leanings paid up – Dr Parr of Eccleston, Mr Leigh of Standish, Hyett of Croston and Bispham of Brindle – yet Welch (whose name appears as Walsh) and Mr Bradshay of Penwortham paid nothing. Hyett's generosity to those who suffered hardship during the Civil War enhanced his reputation, though he was deprived of his benefice in 1662 for refusing to submit to the Act of Uniformity. He died a year later, Welch preaching the funeral sermon at Croston.

During the Civil War the Presbyterians predominated, and Hyett and Welch became members of the local classis. When the Lancashire Church Survey appeared in 1650 it reported, 'Mr Henry Welch doth Supply the cure there, & is a godly painfull preachinge Minister.' Welch's modest income derived, they said, from the various charities attached to St Laurence's, Mr Hyett's regular payment of 53s. 4d., and the profit of the glebe lands (a cottage and half a rood of land worth two shillings per annum). Welch's best income, however, had come from the county committee via Mr Hyett in the sum of £18 annually. Welch's Puritan stance seems to have been tempered by an ability to get on with others of different religious views; he was well regarded even by those who would be supposed to be his enemy. Nevertheless, in common with two thousand other clergymen, he declined to agree to the terms of the Act of Uniformity of 1662. Consequently he was expelled from his curacy of St Laurence's. There is a local tradition that Welch then opened a new preaching house in the town for his Nonconformist parishioners, on the site of what is now Park Street Unitarian Chapel. Prior to his death in January 1671 Welch acted as tutor to Sir Richard Standish of Duxbury. Edmund Calamy, writing in 1775, wrote of Welch that he was

> a very humble, mortified man. Tho' he did not excel in gifts, it was made up in grace . . . he was of so blameless a conversation that most gentlemen had a good word for him; and was esteemed so faithful, that Mr Standish of Duxbury (a person of a great estate) left the tuition of his children to him, after his own and his wife's death. And he discharged his civil as well as his ministerial trust so faithfully that the most critical adversary had nothing to say to his charge.[6]

According to the Revd Oliver Heywood, a Puritan minister, Chorley people rejoiced in the restoration of the monarchy under Charles II in 1660. The prohibitions on dancing and old customs were thrust aside and in celebration Chorley saw a fine maypole erected on the town's green. It bore a crown, coat of arms and a cross. For six years it was decorated with garlands for special events, and a piper was hired to play. In July 1666, however, during a severe thunderstorm it was hit by a bolt of lightning. Heywood witnessed the devastating effect on the maypole, which was shattered to pieces though set six feet into the earth.

Trade and economy

During the seventeenth century there were cottage textile industries in Chorley, producing both linen and woollen cloth. In addition there was a felt-making trade, which processed by-products of the woollen industry. The felt was used particularly for hats. On 18 January 1631 John Rede of Shevington and Gilbert Barnes of Wigan, feltmakers, gave evidence to the JPs that Ann Tootell, widow, of Chorley was guilty of 'unlawful feltmaking', employing two of her sons and Robert Lee, 'contrary to the Statute'. The matter came to light when widow Tootell sacked Lee, who took a bow and four blocks to Barnes looking for work. A Robert Lee died of the plague in Chorley in August 1631, though this may be a coincidence of name. Local people still carried on the work however, as John Parker and Robert Heald, both feltmakers, appear in the parish registers for 1661-2 and 1666-7 respectively.

A shortage of copper coinage during the period of the Restoration disrupted commercial trading and led to the issue of tradesmen's tokens in many towns, among them several examples from Chorley. [Courtesy of J. G. Shaw]

The civil wars between 1642 and 1651 wrought havoc with the nation's trade. One result of this was observed in the coinage, hitherto a royal prerogative. After 1649 hundreds of individuals began to make and circulate their own copper coinage, properly known as tradesmen's tokens, as an informal currency; they were made in forty-five towns in Lancashire. Where people gathered to trade and buy in markets and fairs these tokens were especially useful, generally being made in small denominations. Five tradesmen in Chorley are known to have produced these tokens: Robert Dicconson, mercer; Thomas Wasley, Thomas Allanson; James Wolstenhome and Hugh Cooper. The earliest coin issued is that of Thomas Allanson, a farthing of 1653 showing a roll of tobacco and two pipes. Wasley was a shoemaker: his halfpenny dated 1666 shows the arms of the Cordwainers' Guild. Hugh Cooper was another mercer but apparently a man of considerable importance. His family, originally from Ormskirk, was extensive, with members in Charnock Richard and

Chorley, two of them at least in business dealing in textiles. Hugh's halfpenny, issued in 1667, pledges his allegiance to Charles II with the motto 'God save the King'. He served as High Sheriff in 1657, and on his death in 1682 was buried in St Laurence's church. Cooper was the benefactor who founded the almshouses in Pall Mall. Another Hugh Cooper, possibly his nephew, appears in the Kenyon Manuscript as a witness to a reported criminal activity of clipping the king's coins in Chorley in 1684.

> Lawrence Lowson of Chorley in Lancashire hath been seen to clip money by James Roscow who will evidence the same. Peter Breyares hath filed money in his house in Chorley town, near the Cross and seen to do it by Richard Blackburn and Hugh Cooper.[7]

The Calfe-Coat Club

Today 'clubs' are generally no more than associations of like-minded people for recreation or sporting activities. In the reign of Charles II there were fears that republicanism would rise again to overthrow the Crown. Accordingly, in 1675, clubs were banned by royal proclamation, in the hope that preventing secret assembly would ensure public order. Nevertheless, a record of one club was kept among the private papers of the Talbot and Parker families of Bagganley Hall Rejoicing in the name of the 'Calfe-Coat Club' it was, in the opinion of Canon T. C. Porteus, an illicit drinking club. A calf-coat is a shelter for calves, without windows and having loopholes without glass. The deed for this club, dated about 1670, was written in the manner of a royal proclamation, 'in the Thirty-Twelfth yeare of Rowley, the tw'ot chiefe water weaver in Moonland'. The members were instructed to bring no furniture, 'only pottles, bottles, flagons, jugs, mugs, pots, cans, stands and noggins, English or Scotch pipes, tobacco, some victuals to kneag on and Old Axe'. The tone of the text, again echoing royal edict, was signed Robin Rex, at Cob-Castle in Lubberland. Canon Porteus speculated that other similar clubs may have existed like this one, well away from the town and careful to avoid drawing attention to themselves. The Walton-le-Dale Mock Corporation of the next century was akin to this in some respects.

Witchcraft

For many seventeenth-century Lancastrians primitive superstition was as much a part of their lives as the familiarity of formal religion. From the use of charms to ward off evil, and of spells and potions, to the celebrated trial of the so-called witches from the Pendle area in 1612, the concept was ingrained in the life of the county. Sudden illness, or unexpected and unaccountable happenings seemed to some people to be the certain result of witchcraft.

In Chorley there was a case in the 1660s. When Elizabeth Hodgson, a widow of Chorley Moor, fell seriously ill for almost a whole year, the cause of her illness was laid at the door of Alice Dewhurst, a thirty-two-year-old spinster of Duxbury. Three witnesses testified to the fact that Alice had bewitched the woman on Christmas Day 1667-8. Alice was in Lancaster Gaol in March of the following year accused of the capital crime of witchcraft, but fortunately for her, she was found not guilty. The parish register of St Laurence's shows the burial of Eles Deuresh, who may have been the same woman, on 31 August 1672. Elizabeth Hodson, however, lived on for many years, and was buried in Chorley on 15 November 1690.[8]

CHAPTER FIVE

'Alas for Richard and for Charles!'

IN THE Public Record Office in London is a survey made in February 1716 by John Wicker, a Crown official. In its businesslike way the survey measures, numbers and names the fields, farms and cottages comprising the estates of Richard Chorley of Chorley, a condemned traitor, whose story is the most tragic in the town's history.[1]

How did he become a 'traitor'?

By the end of the seventeenth century the Chorleys were, like other Lancastrian gentry, clandestine Jacobite supporters. Groups in the county worked in secret to promote the cause. At Walton-le-Dale the Mock Corporation was founded in 1701, meeting at the Unicorn Inn ostensibly as social gatherings but in fact acting as a meeting ground for like-minded Jacobite sympathizers. The Earl of Derwentwater, John Winckley of Preston and Charles Chorley of Chorley, all members, were later actively involved in the 1715 Rebellion.

Richard Tootell, Chorley's postman in 1735, reputedly walked to Preston and back each day with his pack of letters. [Lancashire County Library]

In 1715 an army of lowland Scots crossed the border aiming to strike at once for the Stuart cause. Hoping to attract Lancashire support in strength the Scots moved south into the county: Lancashire Catholics were held to be the backbone of the Jacobite cause. June 1715 saw noisy support in Manchester and Warrington for James Edward Stuart. The Scots were at Lancaster on 7 November and their mounted troops reached Preston on 10 November. Here the Scots relaxed, waiting for their extended forces to come into the town and as word spread into the hinterland sympathizers travelled to Preston to join the army. Richard Chorley and his son Charles went to the town on 10 November, bearing the red and white cockade of English Jacobites. Neighbours and acquaintances were there too – Ralph Standish of Standish, Sir Francis Anderton of Lostock, Richard Townley of Townley and many more, of high and low rank.

The immediate aims of the army were to seize the fords at Warrington and capture Manchester. However, General Wills' government forces advanced quickly from Wigan, secured the Ribble crossing at Walton, and pushed the Scots into the heart of Preston.

Here the Scots, four thousand strong, barricaded the main streets: they gambled on defeating the government troops. The fighting began in the early afternoon of Saturday, 12 November. An attack by two hundred dragoons against the Churchgate barricade resulted in one hundred and twenty casualties, and tradition says that the two Chorleys were among the defenders there. Reinforced on the Sunday, Wills' forces secured the surrender of the combined Scots and English on Monday 14 November.

Defeat turned the erstwhile revolutionaries into traitors in arms against the Crown, their lives and property forfeit. The gentry were kept under guard in Mr Winckley's house in Fishergate, pending a decision on their fate. The government acted swiftly and decisively. Judges were sent into Lancashire to try the prisoners in local courts. The intention was to deal out a lesson which would last for a generation, quashing any further dreams for a Jacobite succession. Richard and Charles Chorley both perished in the aftermath of Preston. Their fate is particularly poignant compared with the fortunes of the rebellion's leaders; the great lords went south to London for trial, where a majority decision in the House of Lords overturned their death sentences.

Lesser Jacobites, though, were despatched for public execution in Preston, Wigan, Garstang and Manchester. The two Chorleys, Henry Walmesley and James Drummond were tried at Liverpool on 21 January 1716. Walmesley was acquitted, but the rest were sentenced to die. Richard Chorley was taken back to Preston and executed there on 9 February 1716, alongside the Scot, James Drummond. Execution then meant the barbaric sequence of hanging by the neck, drawing and quartering, all in front of a curious crowd of Preston townfolk. The final touch of indignity came when Richard's head was hacked off and displayed on a pole in front of the town hall. The witnesses, it was said, wept at the sight of 'Old Mr Chorley', his white hair blowing in the wind. He was fifty-six years old.

And what of Charles Chorley? Following the trial he was kept in the Old Tower Gaol at Liverpool, consisting of seven cells 10 feet or more below ground level. Measuring no more than 6 feet in any direction the cells were crowded with inmates: Charles Chorley contracted 'gaol fever' there and died before he could face execution. It used to be said that Richard Chorley and Drummond were buried on Gallows Hill, Preston, but the Chorley parish register proves this false. They were buried in Chorley on 9 February 1716 and Charles' body came home for burial in March.

So much for the factual account of the passing of the Chorleys. A crop of legends surrounded their deaths. It is recounted, for example, that one of the maids at Chorley Hall, putting out sheets to dry, found the sheets spattered with blood on the day of the execution of her master. Another tells of Mrs Chorley's death from grief at her double loss, and of her ghost haunting the area at the bottom of Harpers Lane, once on the edge of the Chorley Hall estate. Mythology apart, the aftermath of their deaths had its own grim tragedy. The government exacted one more penalty on the family – their estates were forfeit to the Crown – hence the survey made in 1716. The estates were put up for sale and bought for £5,550 in 1718 by Abraham Crompton, banker, of Derby.

The aim of the government was realised; sympathy for the Jacobites was extinguished or went underground. Thirty years later, when a new Scots army, led by Bonnie Prince Charlie, marched south on the same journey, the streets of Chorley, so it is said, were lined with silent, curious townspeople. The lesson taught at Gallows Hill was deeply fixed in memory; would-be monarchs apart, the Chorley family were crushed for their blind loyalty to a doomed cause – with their passing a vital link with Chorley's past was broken for ever.

The Cromptons at Chorley Hall

The new owner of Richard Chorley's lands and estates could not have been less like his predecessor. The Chorleys were Jacobite, Catholic, old-established gentry: the Cromptons were strict Presbyterians, nonjurors and firmly rooted in the world of commerce. Abraham Crompton was, according to his descendant Beatrix Potter, a man with a special abhorrence of Catholics, the divine right of kings and all that Richard Chorley lived for. Crompton came from Derby, where his father, another Abraham, had built up Derby's first bank. Despite their stern, puritanical image no evidence survives of the Cromptons penalising Chorley's Catholic tenants.

The town's small Nonconformist community found ready champions in the Cromptons. John petitioned the quarter sessions in 1719 to licence Chorley Hall as a meeting place for Dissenters and two of the Crompton infants were baptised at home. When old 'Abram' died in 1724, he left £10,000 to his son Samuel and two bequests to the Dissenters. £150 was left with trustees to build a permanent chapel on his own land.

> One good and convenient building, the same when built to be made use for and on a Chapel or Meeting House for a Congregation or Assembly of Dissenting Protestants of the Persuasion commonly called Presbyterians.

The second bequest, of £850, was meant for the maintenance of a minister. The chapel was built in a field called Drenacres, overlooking Chorley Bottoms and clearly visible from the grounds of St Laurence's church. From Water Street a footpath led to the chapel, named Chapel

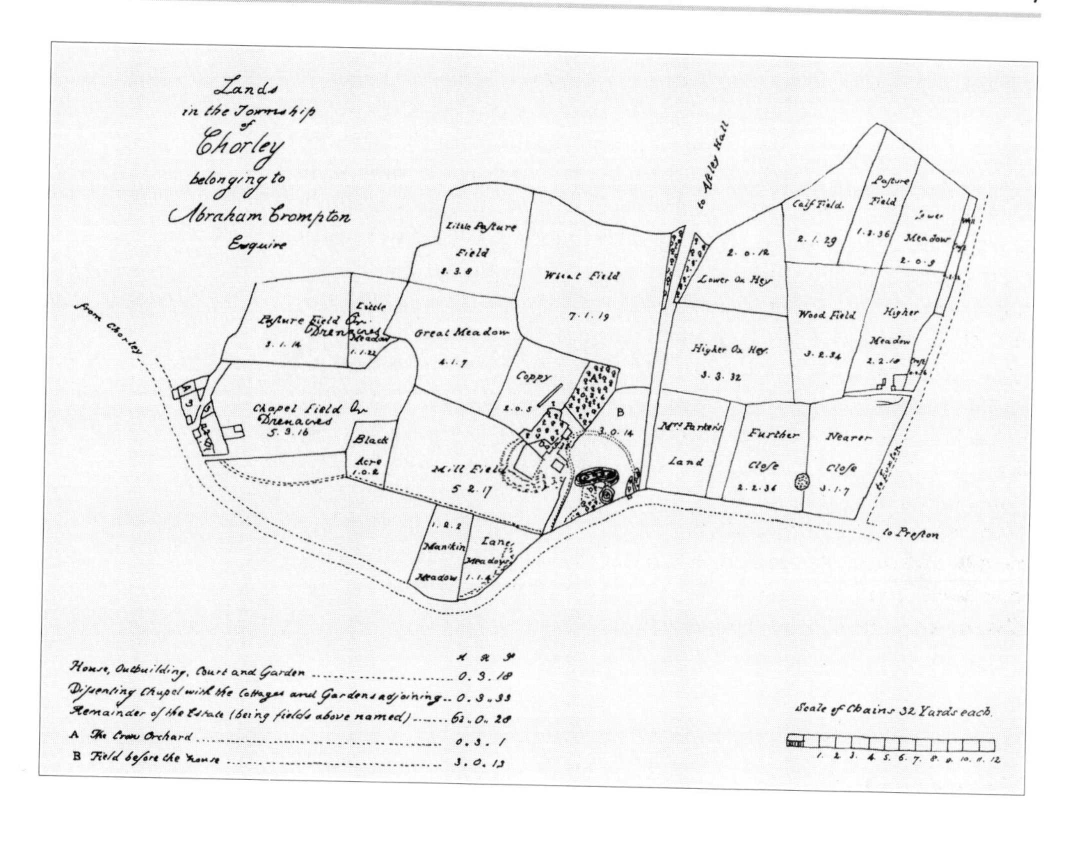

The Chorley Hall estate passed to the Crompton family in 1718. This plan dates from the 1730s and shows how extensive the old demesne lands were. Park Road had yet to appear but the old road to Astley Hall through the estate is marked from the highway. [Lancashire Record Office, ref. DDH 438]

Steps in later times. According to tradition, the chapel was nicknamed Jeroboam Hill.

The chapel was completed in 1726 and acquired a minister, Revd Samuel Bourn, in 1727, followed by Revd John Bent in 1732. The Sunday School was built in 1860. One source says that thirty-six Highlanders were quartered on Revd Bent in 1745, probably in the chapel, during the Jacobite Rebellion. Revd Bent was paid £5 extra in 1747 'on account of his sufferings from the rebels', who ate 41lbs. of his best cheese before dinner. A legend in the Crompton family told how Bonnie Prince Charlie himself dined at Chorley Hall.

One of the few allusions to commercial investment is the case of Samuel Oldknow who built a mill at Anderton in the 1770s, financed by £3,000 from Arkwright and £1,000 by loan from Abraham Crompton. It was a shrewd investment – Oldknow's muslins were popular in London. As landowners the Cromptons figure in contemporary events such as the enclosure of the commons in the 1760s, when they were allotted portions of the old commons out of the Chorley estate claims. One further link with the family was the old presbytery attached to St Mary's Roman Catholic Church in Market Street. The presbytery, demolished in the 1980s, appears to have been one of the old farms in the town centre. One phase of its building was shown by a rain spout marked A. C. 1745, for Abraham, younger brother of John Crompton. This Abraham left a fund in his will to encourage learning by paying for basic skills to be taught to poor children. The first surviving accounts of this charity date from 1768 and they continue until 1829. Dame schools were the principal recipients of the payments, though Revd William Tate, father of the famous Sir Henry Tate, was one teacher paid by the fund. The first child named is Ann Blackledge, eight years old, daughter of John Blackledge of Harpers Lane. The bill requests Elizabeth Layland to 'teach the English tongue' to her. Typical fees were 3s. 9d. for a half year and it is pleasant to note that a high proportion of the pupils were girls. Tate came as minister to Park Street Chapel in 1799, staying until 1836. During the 1770s meetings for Independent Presbyterians began to be held in a house in St Thomas' Square. These were the origins of the congregation which became Hollinshead Street Chapel. The Park Street Chapel may have converted to Unitarianism in the early 1790s.

After 1800 the Cromptons seem to have cooled in their affections for Chorley Hall. In 1817 Abraham, great-grandson of the purchaser, sold the estate to the Townley Parkers of Astley Hall, who promptly had the hall demolished piece by piece, much of the material going to build a new hall at Cuerden. The last reminders of the Chorleys were the old barn and the fishpond which lasted into this century.

The Duchess of Norfolk's estates

One of the most intriguing items in Chorley Library's Local Studies Collection is a copy of a plan of private estates in Chorley, surveyed by Joseph Dickinson in 1734 for 'Her Grace the Duchess Dowager of Norfolk.' Crude as it is by modern standards, this is the earliest known plan of the town. Dickinson's main purpose was to show exactly what his client owned but in the process he showed the extent of Chorley at that period.

He used the conventions of his time, and buildings are drawn with childlike elevations. This at least identified the parish church; next, a cluster of houses and cottages around Back Mount and the town's green. A narrow strip of properties, houses, farms and a few shops line the present day Market Street, shown by the surveyor as 'Chorley Town'. There are no side streets, though narrow strips of land lead east or west from cottages behind the highway. Bolton Street is shown, though Pall Mall is little more than a general indication. Chorley in 1734 was a country town, and the plan names thirty-five tenant farmers, but there would have been many more on the Gillibrand, Standish, Crompton, Brooke and Lee estates. Despite the evidence of the market and commercial growth the community of 1734 made its living from working the land.

Why did the Duchess of Norfolk own land in Chorley? The answer goes back to the fourteenth century when the division of the manor gave one share to the Shireburne family of Stonyhurst. Sir Richard Shireburne's rental in 1563 amounted to one quarter of the manor. His

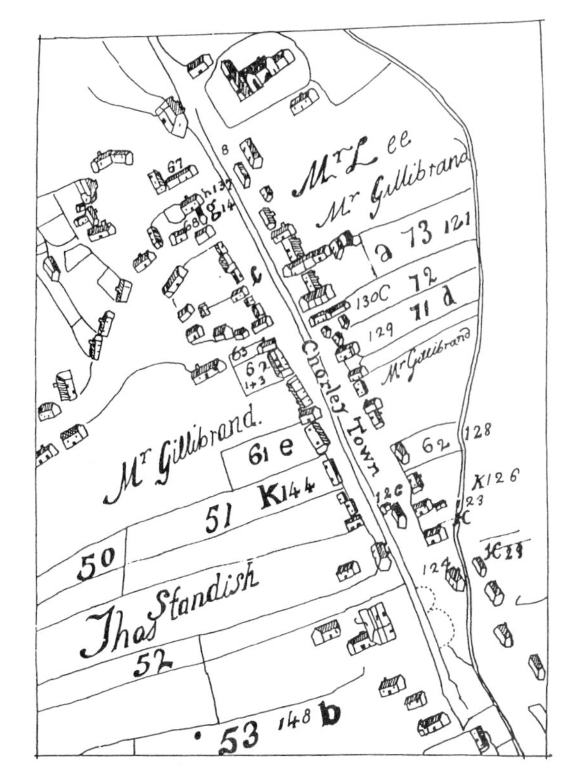

The oldest map of Chorley, of which this is only a fraction, was drawn in 1734 for Mary, Duchess of Norfolk, who had inherited the old Shireburne portion of the manor. [Lancashire County Library]

descendant, Mary Shireburne, born in 1692, married Thomas, Duke of Norfolk, in 1709, and at the time of their marriage Mary was sole heiress to the Shireburne estates with an annual income of £3,000. When Thomas died in 1732, his widow remarried later that year. She lived on until 1754. The Stonyhurst estates passed by the terms of her will to a cousin, one of the Weld family of Lulworth in Dorset. This connection gave the name Weld Bank to the town. The Shireburnes, being a Catholic family, were made to register their estates in 1717.[2]

Where were these estates in Chorley? The largest block stretched from the doles, immediately behind Market Street, as far west as Common Bank, sandwiched between Astley on one side and the Gillibrand land on the other. The whole of the modern Astley Park east of the Lords Clough was Shireburne land, including the Farthings. One scattering of fields along Eaves Lane and at Crosse Hall was overshadowed by a larger chunk of land adjacent to the manor boundary on the north, including Hartwood Green and below Knowley.

By virtue of the date of the map, and because of Shireburne interests in the land, the town's field is shown intact. Lidyate Lane, leading to Astley Wood, is clearly marked, a survival from the Middle Ages. One property from the Shireburne estate has a special interest, the Mount Pleasant site where St Mary's Roman Catholic Church was built in 1854. The old presbytery, fronting Market Street, seems to have been an ancient tenancy, possibly a survival of a medieval burgage plot. With its farm buildings nearest the highway the land stretched back almost to Ashfield Road. When the house was demolished in the 1980s its interior walls revealed that the last frontage had been one of several added to the core farm building over centuries. According to legend the Harrison family acquired the property for services rendered to the Shireburnes during the Jacobite Rebellion.[3] John Harrison was certainly a tenant of the family at Bailey during this period. A rain spout dated 1796 evidently exists from the rebuilding and extension work by the Harrisons, and James Harrison, cotton spinner, was living here in 1841.

By the late eighteenth century the Welds not only owned large areas of land but also several of Chorley's pubs, such as the Royal Oak, Anchor, and White Bull. At this period Messrs E. and W. Leigh bought some of the Weld estates, including Brindles Tenement off Knowley and the Leigh farm itself in Market Street, together with land at Eaves Green.

The piecemeal disposal of the estate continued until 1811, when talks began for the Gillibrands to buy the Welds out altogether, a process completed in 1825.

Enclosing the common lands

One of the complaints of Revd Oliver Cooper in 1776 was that St Laurence's and its incumbent had not benefited from the enclosure of the commons, while the lords of the manor, being Catholics, had set land aside for the benefit of their own clergy.[4] The poorer people of the town relied on the commons for grazing rights and ancient rights of collecting moss, but over the years their rights had been eroded. In 1737 John Parker recorded a number of questions for the court leet, including one revealing statement,

> the Lords of the aforesaid manor have got, by the neglect of the charterers, into their possession of the aforesaid encroachments, which by the pound rate amounts near to a hundred pound a year.[5]

Enclosure was under discussion thirty years before the award of 1768. The arguments for and against enclosure were familiar and well-worn, apportionment frequently being to the great landowners. The Enclosure Act for Chorley (1767) said that common and waste land then produced little profit, but could expect to do better afterwards.[6] A survey of 1620 by Thomas Borne recorded 333 acres of common land in Chorley (excluding a few parcels of land), while the award of 1768 showed 318 acres. The largest areas of land were on Knowley Mosses and Banks (149 acres), Chorley Moor (77 acres) and Eaves Green (38 acres). At Hartwood Green there were 30 acres: this was one of several 'greens' associated with commons.

Healey township had a close interest in the matter. It was distinct from Chorley, but the lords of Chorley manor did not object to Healey freeholders lifting clay for burning bricks and rights of pasture were condoned. The Healey folk were concerned that all their rights might be lost if the enclosure went through. Although Healey Nab did not figure in the enclosure act (most of Healey was owned by the Standishes) the two townships drew closer together through custom and use to the extent that in decades later there seemed no distinction between the two.[7]

The major landholders petitioned parliament and the commissioners duly met from 1 June 1767 at the King's Head in Bolton Street. These men were Robert Lang and John Nixon of Leyland, with Henry Porter of Rufford. They deliberated for weeks, mulling over the issues; a survey plan was displayed in St Laurence's church and appeals were heard. Mr Brooke of Astley argued an exclusive right to Knowley Mosses, producing Elizabethan documents in support.

Of course, the award was made in favour of the petitioners. The Brooke, Weld, Crompton and Standish estates were enlarged, and smaller landowners such as Wasley, Tootell and Hollinshead also benefited. After

Right. Chorley in 1769. The striking feature is the proximity of farmland to the heart of the town and the relatively under-developed pattern of urban form. [Lancashire County Library]

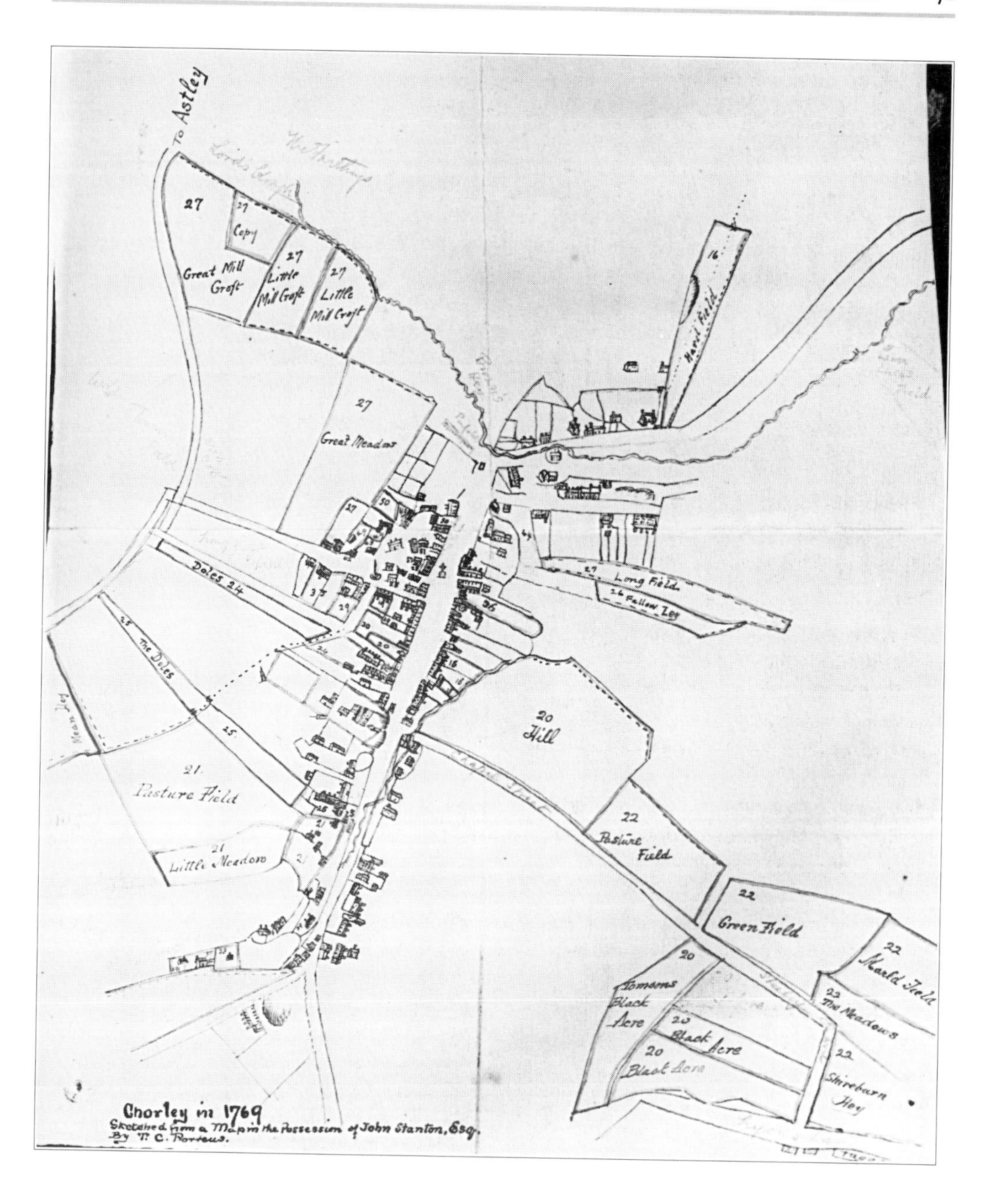

the enclosure of Chorley Moor took place – bounded by Pall Mall, most of Weld Bank Lane, Pilling Lane and Bolton Street – distinctive field boundaries with straight-line divisions typical of parliamentary enclosures appeared, a pattern which set the street plan for the nineteenth century. If the loss of common grazing rights produced hardship there is no evidence left; the benefits that accrued fell into the hands of those already well provided for.

Hollinshead Street and Chorcliffe House

From 1750 onwards a new mood of prosperity was abroad in Chorley's middle class. John Hollinshead, a mercer in the town, was a major landowner in the area east of Chorley Bottoms; he began to sell or lease plots of land for building purposes in what became known alternatively as New Street or Hollinshead Street. Fashionable new town houses appeared, built in a contemporary style and designed for comfort as the homes of the gentry were. Within fifty years Hollinshead Street became the home of many leading citizens. As early as 1757 the *Manchester Mercury* advertised 'a very good dwelling house, outbuilding & garden suitable for either a Gentleman or Tradesman' in the street.[8]

In April of that year a contract was signed between Richard Ward, a Chorley joiner, and Thomas Norris, chapman. The joiner was to build a house on the south side of Hollinshead Street, following detailed instructions from Norris, with plans attached to the contract. The front walls, of brick, would be of Flemish bond, the windows of best Leeds glass, Wheelton flags for the kitchen, Whittle Hills stone for the chimney and Roddlesworth flags for the lobby. Best oak was required for the roof timbers, deal for flooring, and best slate from Upholland for the roofing. Outbuildings such as the brewhouse and 'the Little House' were to be to a fixed standard. The rent was set at £7 15s. 0d. *per annum* or Norris could purchase outright at £155.

John Hollinshead was born in 1717 in Chorley, son of another mercer, Robert Hollinshead. The father's name occurs several times in local affairs. When John died in 1802 his estate was valued between £40,000 and £50,000; he was lord of the manor of Tockholes, and owner of Hollinshead Hall as well as being an influential tradesman. He gave the town money to build the first town hall on the east side of Market Street in 1802.

In 1792 the Independent chapel was built in Hollinshead Street. At the corner of Fellery and Hollinshead Streets a mill for muslin manufacture was operated by William Hodgson until 1835. In 1814 Benjamin Hodgson was one of five muslin manufacturers in the street. From its highly fashionable beginning the street gradually changed after 1800, with more

Number 24, Hollinshead Street, an eighteenth-century town house. George Testo Sante, circus strongman and owner of the Grand Theatre, lived here in the 1890s. [Lancashire County Library; courtesy of Mr E. K. Chapman]

cottage properties being built – the aspiring gentry moved away to newer, more fashionable locations such as Park Road, developed after 1823.

The most enduring property in Hollinshead Street is certainly Chorcliffe House. Built about 1790, supposedly for the Silvester family, this has been extensively restored at the time of writing and it is a Grade II listed property. Handmade brick, probably from nearby sources, made up most of the construction. It was built in three storeys with stone plinths and eaves cornice as a gentleman's residence of a high standard, and has survived perhaps because it remained for so long in the family's hands. Nestling under St Laurence's Parish Church, Chorcliffe's status was increased when the Silvesters developed the grounds. In the early part of the last century it was laid out with formal walks planted with choice trees and featured a stream which had come down across the Fellery and through the Clough. The Silvesters kept a large retinue of house servants and were noted as sporting people with a stud of hunters. They were originally a Manchester family; John's marriage in 1788 to Joanna, daughter of John Threlfall, a Chorley brewer and banker, led to their inheriting the estate on which Chorcliffe was built. One drawback of the site of the house was its tendency to flood when the Chor was in spate and backing up from the Astley estate. This happened in 1886 when the house was flooded to a depth of four feet.

From the door of Chorcliffe Colonel Silvester set out to read the Riot Act to the millbreakers at Hilton's Mill in 1826, fulfilling his magisterial duty, much as he had done in 1819 at Peterloo. On both occasions, of course, his efforts were wasted. He died in 1827. By 1886 Chorcliffe was in the hands of Alderman A. G. Leigh and it was to see considerable change over the years. During this century it was once converted to flats and this seems likely to be its future once more.

The Birkacre Riots of 1779

For a short time in 1779 national attention was focused on the Chorley area. At Birkacre and several other locations the new cotton factories were the scenes of sporadic and bitter attacks by angry crowds of working people. They guessed, rightly as it turned out, that a building filled with the ingenious spinning jennies and water frames, would take up the work latterly done by cottage industries. When they could gain entry to a mill they smashed the hated machines and sometimes tried to fire the buildings too. Central government, as well as local JPs, grew alarmed, anticipating a people's revolt over a wide area. Troops were sent in, and inevitably reprisals followed. The events at Birkacre in October were for a time the pivot of the whole unrest.

The Chadwick family, active, and ambitious businessmen, had ventured into mill building at Birkacre. John Chadwick entered into an agreement with Richard Arkwright, leasing to him a newly-built spinning

Birkacre, a bustling industrial complex of calico printing, coal mining and textiles in the early 1900s, was the setting for one of the bitter riots of 1779 directed against factories which used powered spinning machines. [Lancashire County Library]

mill on the Yarrow at Birkacre. The lease sets out Arkwright's use of the mill, forges, slitting mill and parcels of land.

> 29 November 1777 – It is agreed between John Chadwick of Burgh, gentleman, Richard Arkwright of Cromford, in the county of Derby, merchant that the said John Chadwick will lease . . . the new erected Spinning Mill, the Higher Forge, the Lower Forge . . . to hold for 84 years . . . The yearly rent is to be £150 . . .[9]

Arkwright was in partnership with Samuel Need and Jedediah Strutt (his business partners elsewhere), John Cross, and Thomas Walshman, a Preston merchant who may have been the group's on-site member. Accounts differ regarding the number of workers at Birkacre; some say that the mill was built to employ four hundred to five hundred, but another account refers to no more than fifty employees. All versions agree that the workers were largely young people and women. It is known that the mill had been running for several months before the October troubles began.

Early in 1779 the stocking workers of Nottingham petitioned parliament for a bill to regulate framework knitting. The manufacturers mounted a concerted opposition – when the petition was rejected in June riots began, one of them directed against Arkwright's principal mill at Cromford. By the autumn three more factors combined to fuel the disturbances. The American sea captain John Paul Jones' raids on the British coastline threatened trade and the nation's confidence. Secondly, a French fleet seized the British islands of St Vincent and Grenada, the major sources of raw cotton. When a drastic fall in demand for cotton goods came in the autumn, the third element was in place. The cotton industry slumped and the workers were badly hit. In the face of falling wages and with little hope of rescue, some of the cotton workers blamed the factories and their new machines, resolving to take matters into their own hands.

On Monday 27 September a cotton mill at Aspull was attacked by 'a violent and unruly mob', and fourteen carding engines and two spinning wheels were destroyed. On 1 October the Wigan JPs appealed to the Secretary for War, pleading for a military force to guard the town and nearby mills from the mobs. Fearing the worst the people of Wigan barricaded the streets. More trouble followed on Saturday morning, 2 October; a crowd of five hundred people smashed machines in the area between Bolton and Chowbent. That afternoon the first riot at Birkacre began. The mob reportedly came from Blackrod, gathering support as it neared Chorley, until it numbered two thousand people, with an estimated three hundred to four hundred curious onlookers from Chorley itself. When the rioters descended Burgh Lane to the mill it is said Chadwick pleaded with them in vain to turn back. The first attack was beaten off, leaving one man killed, others wounded.[10]

Arkwright's representatives at the mill had already been warned of the impending trouble. A first-hand account of what followed was given in a letter to Thomas Bently by Josiah Wedgwood, the potter.

> I wrote to my dear friend last from Bolton and I mentioned the mob which had assembled in that neighbourhood, but they had not then done much mischief, they only destroyed a small engine or two near Chowbent. We met them on Saturday morning, but I apprehend what we saw were not the main body for on the same day in the afternoon a capital engine, or mill, in the manner of Arcrite's [sic] and in which he was a partner, near Chorley, was attacked but from its peculiar situation [they could approach it by one passage only and this circumstance enabled the owner, with the assistance of a few neighbours, to repulse the enemy and preserve the mill for that time]. Two of the mob were shot dead upon the spot, one drowned and several wounded. The mob had no fire arms and did not expect so warm a reception. They were greatly exasperated and warned revenge. Accordingly they spent all Sunday and Monday morning in collecting fire arms and ammunition and melting their pewter dishes into bullets.
>
> They were now joined by the Duke of Bridgewater, Colliers and others to the number we are told of eight thousand and marched by beat of drum and with colours flying to the mill where they found Mr R. Clayton guarding the place with 50 invalids armed, but the handful was by no means a match for enraged thousands they (the invalids) therefore contented themselves with looking on, whilst the mob completely destroyed a set of mills valued at £10,000 this was Mondays employment. On Tuesday morning we heard their drums about two miles distant from . . . purposed design was to . . . Bolton, Manchester and Stockport on their way to Grimford, and to destroy

> all the engines not only in these places but throughout England. How far they will be able to put their threats into execution time alone can disclose.
>
> Etruria 9 October 1779.[11]

Wedgwood's letter is the best-known first-hand record of the trouble at Birkacre, important in one sense because he voices the anxiety of all men in his position – would the anarchy swamp us all? Wedgwood refers above to 'invalids', not in the modern sense of the word, but in his day army pensioners who were valued for their training and skills. The Wigan justices, writing to the Secretary for War on 5 October, reported that the forty soldiers had been brought from Preston to Birkacre. They said that the rioters were armed at the outset, and in a mood of panic claimed that the rioters 'threaten to ravage the whole county and particularly destruction of the property of persons not only of their Sufferers but also of the Justices.'[12]

At Liverpool, Sir George Saville, commanding the 1st Regiment West Riding Militia, had contradictory claims on his military command. His role was to guard French prisoners of war in the town, yet when he received an appeal from Wigan he sent two hundred men there on the night of 3 October and one hundred men to Prescot, gambling that he could react to trouble in either Wigan or Liverpool. The government's response to the Wigan JPs was lukewarm, agreeing to send Sir George's militia but turning down a request for dragoons. Their reply reinforced the principle that the JPs should 'not call upon the military for their assistance until every effort of the civil powers had been exerted and proved ineffectual'.

A consensus maintains that Sir Richard Clayton of Adlington brought forty army pensioners to the mill from Preston on Sunday 4 October. Each man was given six rounds of ball and powder, a bag of swan shot and six pounds of battle powder held in reserve in the mill. On Monday, Sir Richard and two other magistrates met the mob of three thousand to four thousand people, now armed with sixty-five guns, axes, hatchets and other arms, their drums beating and colours flying. The magistrates concluded that the rioters would not be persuaded to disperse peacefully, nor could forty men hold them off.[13]

> the mob might go into the works and destroy them, but save the buildings. They then went in about 2 o'clock and before 4 destroy'd all the machinery, the Great Wheel, and set fire to the broken frames in the yard, rear'd some of them agt the wall which communicated to ye building and ended it . . .[14]

This was the report sent to Arkwright on 5 October by Cross and Walshman. One detail of the riot appears in a collection of historical notes published in the *Chorley Standard* for 1865.[15]

> One man, a workman in the premises, endeavouring to pacify the

> rioters, was shot by some one of them. It was never clearly made known who fired the shot but one of the Chorley rioters to his dying day was blamed for it and used to be asked over his cups if he knew who shot —.

Several people were eventually indicted for the Birkacre riots, two men from Aspull, one from Haigh, a man named William Ainscow of Whittle-le-Woods and a young woman called Mary Lister (alias Knight) from Chorley. The indictment of Mary Lister shows that she was one of a body of twenty or more who went into the mill; she was seen to have carried out a hamper of cotton twist to be thrown onto a bonfire, and was sent to the House of Correction at Preston.

And what of Sir George Saville's militia at Wigan? Having marched from Wigan the troops were exhausted when they got to Birkacre, only to find the machinery wrecked, Arkwright's mill in flames and the rioters dispersed. The military authorities were perplexed as to where they should turn next. Unrest was brewing in Preston, Bolton and Blackburn and no dragoons were available for rapid response. Within weeks a total of ten mills were wrecked, but Birkacre was reportedly the most valuable: there machinery worth £4,400 was destroyed. According to the Quarter Sessions papers Arkwright and his partners lost twenty spinning frames, twenty spinning engines, twenty carding engines, twenty roving engines, twisting wheels, cotton wheels and cotton reels.[16]

Once the rioters had left Birkacre the Chorley area was quieter than the rest of the industrial districts. Blackburn's Wensley Fold Mill was badly damaged on 11 October. One week after Birkacre more troops were sent to restore a semblance of order across the county. In fact the army was fighting against guerrilla forces, assembling, moving and dispersing at will.

In the aftermath of Birkacre Arkwright and his partners severed their links with the mill. A deed dated 20 September 1780 describes their initial venture, the riots of the previous year and the payment of a sum of £200 to Edward Chadwick, surrendering the lease. In June 1780 the partners petitioned parliament for recompense of the losses they had suffered. In a suitably dramatic manner the petition describes

> a most riotous and outrageous Mob assembled in the Neighbourhood, armed in a warlike manner, and after breaking down the Doors of the Buildings, they entered the Rooms, destroyed most of the Machinery, and afterwards set fire to and consumed the whole Buildings . . .[17]

The petition was ultimately unsuccessful. It contrasts sharply with one submitted by a body of cotton spinners in April 1780; in the latter stress was laid on the loss of work to the 'thousands of individual poor' occasioned by a 'Domestic Evil of very great Magnitude,' by which they meant the cotton machines used in works such as Birkacre. Their plea, too, fell on deaf ears.

The Lancashire magistrates came up with a conclusion which managed to face both ways. They acknowledged 'that it is the Unanimous Opinion of this court, that the sole Cause of the Riots, Tumults and Insurrections that have lately happened . . . is owing to the Erection of certain Mills and Engines . . . for the Manufacturing of Cotton, which in the Idea of the Persons Assembled tend to depreciate the price of Labour.' On the other hand they recognised that the cotton machinery, whether carding, roving, spinning or finishing, was of great benefit to the industry, and gave work to the poor 'who have not had any pretence for Committing the late Riots from the want of work'.

To be LETT,

For any Term of Years, and Entered on Immediately,

ALL thoſe Works at *Birkacre*, lately occupied as a Cotton Mill, ſituate on the *Yarrow*, in the Townſhip of *Chorley*, together with a good Farm Houſe, ſeveral Cottages, and any Quantity of Land not exceeding twenty Acres.

The above Premiſes are ſuitable for any Branch, where a large Head of Water is neceſſary, either in the Cotton, Linen, or Printing Buſineſs. All the Lands are well watered with fine clear Springs, which may be conducted all over them with a ſmall Expence.

Alſo all that Work called *Burgh Forge*, lately occupied as a Plating Forge, at preſent in very good Repair, and very ſuitable for any Branch in the Plating or Whiteſmith Buſineſs.

For Particulars apply to Mr *Edward Chadwick*, or *Thomas Moore*, of *Burgh*, near *Chorley*.

Following the Birkacre Riot the mill was put back into use relatively soon. This newspaper advertisement of 1780 offers the works with a source of water power to intending buyers.

With the advantage of hindsight it is clear that riots such as those of October 1779 were no more than one skirmish in a long campaign which lasted into the next century; in the process industrial unrest, increasingly ugly, occurred in the growing towns. Often long-established skilled crafts were pitched into conflict with the inevitability of progressive change. In such conflicts the latter invariably won. Within one generation craftspeople saw their skills devalued; in 1764 a woman spinner could daily earn ten to fifteen pence. By 1780 the same worker earned between three and five pence. Men's wages in the same period dropped from seventeen to ten pence a day.[18]

The events at Birkacre in 1779 were a hiccup in the tide of progress. Arkwright pulled out for richer pastures while others, of sterner stuff, set up mills and printing works around Chorley. In 1788 a petition was presented to the Board of Trade by the local MP, Mr Blackburn, on behalf of 'the Spinners of Cotton Yarn and Manufacturers of Callicoes and Muslins in the Township of Chorley and its environs'.

Twenty-eight signatures follow the petition, perhaps half of them attributable to Chorley, including Edmund and William Leigh, Peter Heatley of Gorse Hall, Richard Sanderson, Robert Lightoller of Trigg Hall, Richard Salisbury and John Parkinson. They jointly sought a trade protection measure against the East India Company, whose recent imports of calico and muslin from the Far East had undercut the prices of local producers. Having claimed that they had invested large sums in works and machinery they begged the government to give them preferential treatment.

CHAPTER SIX

Turn from the land

LOOKING BACK over seventy-six years, a newspaper article of 1865 asserted that Chorley's first cotton mill was built by Samuel Burton.[1] Although this claim was not, in fact, accurate, the mill built by Burton was of considerable interest and did date from the earliest phase of the industry. It was built in 1789, on a site at the top of Hollinshead Street, facing the old Independent chapel (now the United Reformed Church). The machinery was operated by a horse and whim of the type more commonly found in the small coal pits. John Ryding, a cooper, and Thomas Hindle, surgeon and apothecary, were the joint owners – an unlikely pair perhaps to speculate in textile machinery.

This was not a mill in the classic mould, for on the sale of the property in 1827 it was converted to three cottages on the lower level, with a schoolroom or warehouse on the upper level. In 1789 the land, owned by John Hollinshead, was leased to the proprietors at £3 a year. Ryding soon pulled out, while Hindle kept an interest until the 1820s. Lessees ran the factory, which produced a yarn for the town's handloom weavers. In 1806 Thomas and Ann Hindle were divorced, the mill being part of the settlement, and in 1817 Hindle borrowed £60 from the Hornbys of Kirkham, using the factory as security. In 1827 Joanne Sylvester bought the building, in what became Bengal Square.

The 'old' town hall was built in 1802 thanks to the generosity of John Hollinshead. It served the town as a market, committee rooms and lockup. [Lancashire County Library]

Handloom weaving

Weaving was one of Chorley's core domestic industries, for cloth must always have been produced from local resources to serve local needs. The Protestation Return in the mid-seventeenth century lists many 'weavers' and in the following one hundred years cottages built specifically for handloom weaving appear in the region. The weavers moved from wool in the Middle Ages, to linen, and then ultimately to cotton. They became a skilled and successful workforce. In 1690 James Roscowe of Chorley was agent for Nathaniel Mollineux who sold fustians in London,[2] and in 1726 one Manchester fustian maker sent warps and bobbins to Chorley. The Tootell family, fifty years later, were running one of Chorley's loom shops.

Handloom weaving and the factory system overlapped for a considerable time. The former was on a modest scale, with single men or families working as a unit, selling cloth to middlemen – the putting-out system; these next sold the cloth to merchants in regional centres such as Bolton or Manchester, the final market for the best cloth being London.

Thomas Taylor (1803-1872) began his working life as a weaver, and started to 'put out' looms and fibre about 1840. His business in Hollinshead Street and Halliwell Street was prosperous. Though he bought Smith's powerloom shed in 1868 he also kept thirty handloom weavers busy weaving jaconet and fine mull cloth at the same time. These high quality cloths were the last mainstay of handloom weavers, as late as the 1870s. John Marsden of Wheelton was a large-scale 'putter-out'.[3] Each week he made up one thousand pieces of cloth, which he sent by canal packet to Manchester each Sunday to reach the market. Like many such 'cotton men' he now lies in the churchyard at Brindle.

Several villages around Chorley sent cloth to the traders based there. The Brindle weavers used a wallet for transporting their wares, a bolster five feet long with a slit in the middle. With the middle section resting on his shoulder, the weaver would fill the 'panniers' either side with finished cloth (up to sixty pounds in weight), coming home with warps and wefts. The White Horse in Chorley was their destination – there the doors were left unlocked for them to arrive early in the morning. Mr Dewhurst's large room was used for sampling cloth; here, too, the weavers' favourite tipple of coffee at a penny per basin could be bought. He would also leave a sovereign at the local pub in a village for the weavers' treat.

In 1835 there were twenty-eight muslin manufacturers in the town, among them John Cairns, a Scots Presbyterian whose warehouse in Queens Road still carries his initials and the date '1833'. Gorse Hall on Blackburn Road was earlier used by the Heatley family who traded with Richard Arkwright and Samuel Oldknow at Roscoe Lowe in Anderton. From Water Street in the 1850s William Gillibrand hired out looms and supplied warps and weft to weavers from as far afield as Mawdesley, and also to Chorley weavers in Bolton Street, Chapel Street and elsewhere.

The middlemen had a paternalistic relationship with the handloom weavers. Unlike the mills, the handloom weavers could respond to demands for short runs of quality cloth, and this was more likely to reflect the skills of individual men and women. Marsden of Wheelton was reported as saying to weavers coming to him after an absence, 'Wod did tha leeov mi fur? Wen oi want tha o'll send for tha'.

The industry had a strength in that it was a lifelong employer, whether a man made it his sole income or combined it with farming, for instance. William Tootell learned to weave, under his father's tuition, at the age of ten. At the other extreme in 1881 William Crook was still weaving in a cellar in Water Street, aged seventy, while John Barnes, who died in a dreadful accident by burning in 1895, was said to be still weaving at eighty-three. Ralph Brindle of Bolton Road still had two men on his books in 1899.

From the 1820s the pendulum began to swing heavily towards power-loom weaving, although this caught on relatively late in Chorley, always a spinning town. Nevertheless, a wage of £2 a week could be made in 1847 for a handloom weaver. Within Chorley they were geographically concentrated. The area 'on't Duke' was a principal location, as the 1816 poverty survey showed: it noted 190 looms in the Bolton Street, Fox's Square and Red Bank area. Princess Street was said to have more weavers than any other street. Eaves Lane, Cheapside, Botany, Anderton Street, Chapel Street and Parker Street all housed these weavers. Often weavers lived in 'up-steps' houses, while others had a cellar below ground. The common factor of these cottages was intended to be a lower level with an earth floor – on this surface looms could work in a warm, moist atmosphere, so helping threads remain intact. Some cellars in Bolton Street could house six looms. Individual weavers made the transition to the factory system, occasionally with great success: George Brown of Euxton ended his days owning a group of mills – a factory master in the classic style.

The canal boom

Canals and the industrial development of the eighteenth and early nineteenth centuries are inextricably linked. As early as 1712 plans were drawn up for making the Douglas navigable below Wigan, and this scheme had considerable success. Forty years later the first suggestions for a trans-Pennine canal from Leeds to Liverpool were made. This was intended to link two thriving industrial centres, and to allow the exploitation of rich reserves of coal, stone and slate along the route. Work began at each end in 1770. The earliest plans would have avoided Chorley altogether, though one version cut directly through the town, another ran from Hall oth Hill, through Limbrick and Healey, but later changes meant that the town was eventually served by the canal. The eventual route was determined by the line of the Lancaster Canal. John Rennie planned his canal from Lancaster to Westhoughton in 1792. The Lancaster Canal Company was thus responsible for much of Chorley's canal; 1795 saw one length finished from Aspull to Adlington. Two years later the navvies had pushed on to Knowley, making an 8½-mile route to move coal for onward transport to Blackburn and Preston. John Hollinshead of Chorley, a member of the canal committee, sought potential profits from the canal in several ways – in 1787, for example, he was planning to move stone from Parbold

Quarry along the cut. At Blackrod the family's pits were ideally sited to supply coal. Hollinshead also had a licence to run packet boats between Liverpool and Wigan.

The navvies building the canal had a fearsome reputation for their tough, hard-living ways. At Chorley in 1795 Vickers and Lewis, the contractors, were taken to task for their workmen's riotous behaviour in the town: 'Some of your men have been behaving in very riotous and very illegal manner at Chorley . . . such conduct will bring disgrace upon the works.'[4] Other relations with the locals were happier, as several entries in the parish register show marriages between local girls and 'canalmen', or 'canal contractor', between 1795 and 1799.

It is possible that the riot of 1795 has some connection with Knowley Wharf being renamed Botany Bay. Before 1795 the name was always Knowley; thereafter Botany became synonymous with the basin, where goods were unloaded and barges moored. Why was this innocuous wharf given a name which conjured up a picture of a lawless penal colony at the far ends of the earth? The most likely answer is that the navvies gave the name Botany Bay in a grim sense of humour, as they usually gave names to each wayside camp. Alternatively, the Chorley townsfolk may have given the nickname to a new community, remote and isolated from the town proper. Several other contemporary examples survive, one at Worsley (on the moss), another at Ashton-under-Lyne.

On 20 October 1816 the proprietors and their guests reached the locks at Johnson's Hillock as part of their celebratory journey along the 127-mile-long length. Many useful developments came with the arrival of the canal; coal, cotton and timber supplied mills throughout the length of the canal. Mills such as Cowling, Hall ith Wood and Bagganley's Talbot Mills (from 1906) were obvious beneficiaries. The Whittle Springs Brewery (built in the 1850s) was a major landmark, while the millstones for which Whittle-le-Woods was famous were also easily transported. The passenger use of the canal was advertised in directories of the time; boats left Knowley for Blackburn at 6 a.m. daily, while others went to Wigan and Liverpool. Excursions became commonplace and until the advent of the railways and motor vehicles the canals were a quick, cheap and efficient transport system.

The Royal Oak and other inns

The earliest Chorley inn we know of is Joan Wastley's, where Richard Green of Heapey counterfeited the king's coinage from 1437 onwards. Much later in the records appears the Royal Oak, which two centuries ago was distinguished by a magnificent oak tree in front of the inn, its thatched roof in keeping with the rural character of Chorley. Some sixty years ago it was said that an oak chest belonging to the inn carried the date 1704, and the Royal Oak does crop up in records frequently thereafter. John Markland was tenant in 1770, when the inn's value was £25; the rent in

1827 had risen to £140 a year, but an important transformation occurred in the years between. Coaching services had come through the town at least since the 1670s, but the mail coaches started to run though Chorley from 1785, at first stopping at the Black Bull's Head, now the site of the Royal Bank of Scotland. Prestige was attached to the task of servicing the mail coaches – some years later the Black Bull (renamed the Gillibrand Arms after 1815) acquired the honour for itself.

The regular stagecoach services had a choice of inns, any of the three above or the Red Lion, opposite the parish church. At one point the Gillibrand Arms had stabling for seventy horses, and the Royal Oak a similar number. The coach services using the improving turnpike roads, put Chorley in daily contact with all of its larger neighbours.

The Royal Oak was sold in 1797 by the Weld estate to Edmund and William Leigh. At this date a farm and lands came with the tenancy. Now the inn assumed a more vital role in the town's life – the vestry met here, trade and business were carried on under its roof and gradually it became the town's social gathering point. The temporary peace of 1814 was celebrated with a grand dinner at the Royal Oak, balls were held for raising charities' funds, theatre companies performed in the great room and meetings were conducted between masters and men during cotton disputes. It was sold in 1886, but the saddest day came when the old inn was demolished in 1937 in order to widen Market Street. New premises rose, but further back from the old line, and without the rich history of the original.

In 1860 Chorley had fifty-one inns and taverns and as many beerhouses, little more than front parlours decked out to serve a local trade. One on Eaves Lane had the wonderful name 'Thumbs Up', while another was named 'Luck's All'. At one period many hotels and inns were known for their special allegiances. The Fazakerley Arms and Gillibrands Arms, for example, belonged to the lord of the manor. The Brookes Arms (alias the White House) displayed a connection with Astley Hall. The Standish family owned the Black Bull, and the Silvesters the Swan, a matter of yards away from Chorcliffe House. Another group had 'royal' links – Red Lion, Rose and Crown, George and Dragon, Duke of York (1782) and Britannia in Water Street – a patriotic pub crawl! The White Horse, not obvious now, would have attracted any Hanoverian sympathiser two hundred years ago. The Anchor (or Rope and Anchor) in Market Street was a farmers' pub on market days, likewise the Wheatsheaf in St Thomas's Road (now the George and unofficially called the 'Vatican').

In early times inn signs had to be visually explicit, the White Bull, Black Bull, Anchor, Fox and Goose, Millstone (1819), Joiners' Arms or Black-a-Moor's Head (1793). Pubs like the Seven Stars in Eaves Lane may be very old, for this was a popular inn sign in the Middle Ages, signifying the early Christian churches in Asia Minor. The King's Arms, long gone now, may have been the former King's Head in Bolton Street. In 1718 this was run by Mr Cowling and well patronised by the gentry, according to Blundell's diary.[5] Like the Standish Arms at Duxbury (better known to us as the Yarrow Bridge), the King's Head had the bonus of a bowling green, as did the Robin Hood in Clifford Street (demolished for the new town centre bypass).

The Siege of Duxbury Hall

Sir Frank Standish died at his London home in Lower Grosvenor Square in May 1812. His body was brought back to Lancashire, and was buried in Chorley Parish Church on 2 June. The Duxbury estate was left without an heir, as Frank was unmarried. In the wings the claimants prepared for action; one, Frank Hall of County Durham, born in 1799, was a great-grandson of Sir Thomas Standish [who had died in 1758], by virtue of his grandmother, Margaret Standish. Though he was a minor in 1812 Frank Hall's guardians installed a bailiff at Duxbury Hall to safeguard his claim.

A counter-claim was mounted by a Standish male 'heir', Tom Standish, a handloom weaver who lived in Coal Street, Horwich. Perhaps there was a belief in Tom's family that he and his kin were descendants of the Duxbury line, but it is more likely that a shrewd guess was exploited by other people to further the idea in Tom's mind. He grasped the nettle and in 1813 made a determined bid to seize the hall and its estates, giving rise to the infamous Siege of Duxbury Hall. This developed into a compound of tragedy and farce, which gave the newspapers a wonderful story.

Duxbury Hall, seat of the Standish family from the fourteenth century. After a period of mixed fortunes the house was damaged by a fire in 1952 and razed to the ground, although the coachhouse and walled garden, together with the Duxbury cruck barn, survived to testify to Duxbury's more prosperous days. [Lancashire County Library]

William Tootell, that keen observer of local events, recorded the attack on the hall on 4 June 1813:

> Thos Standish of Blackrod Weaver Entered Duxbury Hall at 5 o'clock in the Evening attended by the Colliers &c from Blackrod and turned all the family out and made great Depredations that Night and the Day following.

The *Preston Guardian* of 12 June confirms the substance of the account. Tom had about one hundred followers, miners from the Blackrod area. The occupants of the hall, seeing the numbers outside, gave in without a struggle, allowing Tom and his friends to move in. Tom Standish's supporters immediately claimed for him the title of 'Sir Tom', and he, decked out in the finery he found there, played the part. He was fifty years old at this time and 'a great bony fellow'. As there were now so many people inside the hall, provisions were a serious problem, and Bill Harrison recalled sixty years later that his father had supplied meat to the new lord and his retinue.[6] One account from the 1870s, by Mary Roberts, tells us that the hall was barricaded from within, all windows barred and only one door kept usable for access.[7] Genteel eyes were alarmed at the sight of the colliers and their families, some from as far away as Wigan, turning the park into a recreation ground. The sports and fairground atmosphere gave rise to the infamous Duxbury Races and Yarrow Bridge Fair.

Tom's tenure was short-lived; on the Saturday, at 5 p.m., a troop of the Queen's Bays arrived at Duxbury to evict the 'rioters', but not before Mr Houghton, governor of the House of Correction at Preston, had been driven off with his constables on two separate occasions by the miners, once as far as Yarrow Bridge.

William Tootell reports that Tom and five others were taken to Lancaster Castle by a party of the Queen's Bays on 6 June to stand trial at the assizes. On the next day a larger group of seventy or more were taken to the JPs at Bolton, bound to appear at the next quarter sessions at Ormskirk. The accounts are vague as to the situation at Duxbury thereafter; Tootell says that more dragoons of the Queen's Bays came to Chorley at the end of June to keep Duxbury under guard, while Mary Roberts implies that the 'funfair' continued for weeks after the eviction. A popular song of the time ran.

> From Wigan the constables brave did repair,
> To Duxbury Races and Yarrow Bridge Fair,
> To keep our true landlord our efforts did fail,
> They carried Sir Thomas to Lancaster Jail.
> But we'll fetch him back,
> He nothing shall lack,
> And in spite of the lawyers and Mister Frank Hall,
> He shall ride in his carriage to Duxbury Hall.

If brave words could have swayed the issue, Tom Standish would indeed have won. In fact, he did not, for Frank Hall succeeded to the estate, though not to the title of baronet; he adopted the name Standish and promptly removed himself to Seville, indulging his interests in art, travel and literature.

Tom served his sentence in Lancaster Gaol, being released in September 1814. Tootell tells us that the Orange Society came out from Wigan to welcome him home. The issue did not end there, however, for Tom went to law and was back inside the prison again in 1820 with debts of over £2,500! His assets, he claimed, were the title to the Duxbury estates, worth £15,000 a year. Frank Hall Standish was still expecting a recurrence of the siege from Tom as late as 1832; Tom, however died in 1836 and was buried at Bolton on 13 July. The story of Tom Standish's claim lingered on for years, engendering a good deal of genealogical research; this showed that Sir Frank Standish and Tom Standish did indeed share the same ancestor in Alexander Standish, who was born in 1567 and died 1622.[8] Tom's descent was from Ralph, younger brother of the heir, Thomas Standish, who was buried in Chorley Parish Church in 1642.Tom's son and heir, James Standish, pursued the claims for many years afterwards, with no more success than his father had achieved. A gaggle of other claimants appeared in the 1830s, Peter, James and John Standish all bidding for the estates when Frank Hall Standish died at Cadiz in 1840. But Frank Hall Standish's will nominated William Standish Carr of Cocken Hall, Durham, to succeed him, and this he duly did in 1841.

Bill Harrison recalled one legend, which said that Tom Standish's claim was hampered by the relevant pages of the Chorley parish register being removed from the record surreptitiously (shades of Myles Standish again!). This was echoed in Canon Porteus' account of the curse flung at Revd Oliver Cooper by a woman in Hollinshead Street: 'You'll die with your shoes on for what you did to Tom Standish.' Mr Cooper, it is said, did indeed die with his shoes on at a dinner party, supporting thereby the alleged prophecy made for him.[9]

The diary of William Tootell, 1796–1817

William Tootell, remembered now solely for the diary which he kept between 1796 and 1817, was a descendant of one of Chorley's oldest yeoman families; he was born in 1789 and spent all of his long life in his birthplace, dying at the age of ninety in 1879. Those ninety years encompassed a period of unparalled changes, the world he was born into being almost wholly wiped away in the course of one lifetime. There emerged a society more familiar to this century, and an industrial landscape so alien to the sleepy market town in which he grew up. The 'Chronology', as he called it, was written in a plain notebook with marbled paper covers – in its pages he jotted down those events, such as the births, marriages and deaths of family and friends, as well the price of foodstuffs and everyday shopping. He collected sensational local news and odds and ends of scandal, so that his diary is a unique picture of Chorley in the years spanning the Napoleonic Wars.

Since Chorley's first local newspaper did not appear until 1864, the diary gives the only first-hand account of many key events. In 1815, for instance, Tootell records that the chapel at Weld Bank was opened on 12 March, high mass being performed on that occasion. In the same year he tells us that the Black Bull's Head Inn was pulled down on 17 May; the new inn was begun on the same site on 10 June and in August the inn must have been completed, as it was then renamed the Gillibrands Arms Inn.

It is not surprising that one of the preoccupations of the diary is the price of food. William, according to other sources, was one of the town's officers for regulating weights and measures on the market, which would have given him a regular opportunity to follow the market prices. The commodity featured most often is oatmeal, underlining the key role which it played in the everyday diet of the common people. In 1800 a pound of oatmeal could be bought for 6d. (2½p), the same quantity cost 5d. in 1812 (which he commented on as 'dear' for the time), with a steady rise in cost from 3s. 6d. (17½p) a peck in 1814 to 8s. (40p) a peck in March 1817. Other foodstuffs quoted by Tootell include sugar, fresh butter, bacon, pork, beef, potatoes, cheese and molasses. Candles, bought by the pound weight are also quoted: they were of course essential to handloom weavers when working beyond twilight. The average weekly earnings of handloom weavers in 1817, an especially harsh time for the weavers, amounted to no more than 4s. 6d. (22½p).

William Tootell's background was handloom weaving; his father Thomas apparently ran his own weaving shop, employing members of his family and two or more apprentices. One of the first entries in the diary records that his sister Nancy learned to weave in 1798, while William himself was taught the family trade in 1799 (at the age of ten). At the end of his life his obituary commented that he later became a weaving master in his own right, presumably having taken over the family business.

Two incidents, which are coincidentally the first and last entries in the *Chronology*, are particularly striking to modern eyes. The first refers to a thwarted raid by body-snatchers in the burial ground of the parish church: '1796 March – Wm Winstanley Died Aged 87 the morning after he was Interred his corps was attempted to be took up for Dissection.'

This entry, like several others, must have been made long after it happened, for William was a mere seven years old in 1796 and, as the Winstanleys were Tootell's maternal family line, it is likely that this was a family relation. The story is confirmed in the *Blackburn Mail* newspaper of 1796: it adds that Winstanley had been parish clerk shortly before his death. The body-snatchers had tried to open up several graves in their search for suitable corpses but were disturbed at work and scared away. The second entry, made on 19 August 1817, tells us that 'Ann, wife of Thos Morris Publicly sold at the Obelisk at St Thomases Squair by auction for £0 11s. 1d'. It was, perhaps, a meagre price for a wife, yet the practice was not too rare. Many nineteenth-century accounts verify this drastic form of divorce, which Thomas Hardy illustrates in the *Mayor of Casterbridge*. The last sale in this county occurred in the 1920s.

The 'obelisk' in St Thomas's Square was one of the casualties of nineteenth-century change. It was evidently used for public events, proclamations and punishments. In 1801 Tootell wrote that John Allenson was publicly flogged at the obelisk, having been sentenced for rioting.

War and threats of invasion governed the lives of Britons throughout this era; at the age of twenty William and his elder brother Richard enlisted in the Leyland and Ormskirk Local Militia, based at Ormskirk. William's diary records a number of training periods and musters, but it was not all drilling and marching, for the two found time to attend the races at Ormskirk in July 1809. Their only excursion under arms, however, came in May 1812 when the militia were mustered to police the Luddite riots prevalent that month. Nevertheless, on returning home, William took a keen interest in the movements of other units through Chorley – the Lancaster militia, plus cavalry and several Scots militia units. His father's employees left to enlist into the Artillery or the Royal Marines. William provides a solitary clue to the existence of a Chorley 'militia', when he notes an incident in 1804, in which the Duke of Gloucester was escorted to Bolton by the Chorley Corps of Cavalry.

Everyday tragedies crop up among the entries: accidental deaths such as falling into the canal and drowning, death from fooling with a loaded musket, suicide, or the case of John Astin who died in the winter of 1815.

> Dec 17 and 18. Heavy fall of snow average depth from 11 to 12 inches. 20 Dec. John Astin died being lost in the snow and darkness betwixt St Thomas's Square and the Hacust [Ackhurst]. Coroners Inquest Perishd through the Inclemency of the Weather aged 43.

According to the 1801 census the population of Chorley township was about 4,500, but Tootell's diary conveys an impression of a close community, where every event was everybody's business. New streets were being laid out – for example Halliwell Street, and the new road through Astley Park across the Farthings, and these were newsworthy items, as was the building of gentlemen's residences in Chapel Street in 1799 for Richard Smethurst and William Gent.

Three changes caught William's eye in May 1813, the first being the building of St Gregory's, Weld Bank; the second was the construction of the Lodge at the entrance to Astley Park; the last was the removal of the town's pinfold from near the Astley entrance. With the loss of this relic from earlier times Chorley severed one more link with its rural, agricultural past, for the pinfold had been used to pen strayed livestock, until it could be claimed by its owners. A pinfold of some sort, however, must have survived until 1864, as an advertisement in the *Chorley Standard* informs its readers of a strayed donkey being kept there.

The year 1813 also saw the start of the market coach services from

Chorley to several towns, operated by William Ashworth; these usually set out at eight in the morning.

Day	Depart	*Destination*	*Fare (inside)*	*Fare (outside)*
Monday	8 a.m.	Bolton	3s. 6d.	2s. 6d.
Tuesday	6 a.m.	Manchester	7s. od.	5s. od.
Friday	8 a.m.	Wigan	3s. od.	2s. od.
Saturday	8 a.m.	Preston	3s. od.	2s. od.

The *Chronology* comes to an end in 1817 with the wife sale described above. It is not clear why Tootell stopped at this point, as there are ample blank spaces in the notebook. Tootell's name occurs in a number of contemporary documents – he acted as secretary to the Chorley Adult School, for instance, and was a dedicated and active member of the Auxiliary Bible Society, engaged in the distribution of Bibles and religious works. His obituary emphasised his interest in religious matters and chronicled his progress through the various churches and chapels. He first worshipped at St Laurence's Parish Church, where the gravestones still testify to the involvement of the Tootells. From the late 1810s he changed his allegiance to the Hollinshead Street Independent Chapel until the 1860s when he moved to the Primitive Methodists. For the last twenty years of his life he worshipped among the Free Methodists at the Railway Street Chapel. He married at some date after 1817, though he was widowed for many years, but there were no children of the marriage.

Although he came from a relatively modest background William was a multi-faceted man for his time. He had a personal library of two thousand books, which would have been remarkable in itself, but was especially so for a tradesman in a provincial town. He was deeply religious, and a promoter of adult education, yet in spite of all that his fame rests on a slim volume, recording everyday events over twenty years.

> 1813 23 Decr. Rejoicings Grand Dinner &c. at the Oak Illuminations at the Oak Thos Browns Warehouse and the Work House occasioned by the Late Victories in France.

James Talbot at Bagganley Hall

The diary of William Tootell has long been recognised as a unique document detailing the social life of Chorley during the Napoleonic Wars. One of William's contemporaries left a record of a different kind, which shows us the life of a gentleman yeoman farmer. James Talbot (1772-1853), of Bagganley Hall, kept a meticulous and detailed account book between 1815 and 1836 in an admirably legible copperplate.[10] The Talbot family were in Wheelton two hundred years earlier, and then moved to

Hindley and Ince as tradesmen. James' grandfather, William, went up in the world when he married the daughter of Mr Parker of Bagganley; from this marriage the Bagganley estate came to the Talbots. In 1812 James married Cicely Hawkshead of Heskin, descended from a Chorley yeoman family which in 1737 quit the Hartwood Green estate for Heskin. James' son, William Hawkshead Talbot, thus had an impeccable pedigree from Chorley's oldest families. His day book, never meant to serve as a document of social history, survives in faded leather covers.

The household consumed impressive quantities of liquor and spirits; in November 1815, for example, Henry Dawson was paid for four gallons of port wine at twenty shillings per gallon, four gallons of 'Shirrey wine', four gallons of gin and three quarter-barrels of ale, the first of numerous such purchases. In August 1818 James bought a pig at Chorley market from an Irish trader for three guineas – fattened up and slaughtered, the pig yielded twenty-one score and eleven pounds of meat, and seventy-five pounds of hams. James bought a washing machine from Joshua Richardson for £1 14s. 0d. in December 1815 and then on several occasions paid for repairs to this essential household utility.

A series of accounts shows that James and his wife were restoring the fabric of Bagganley Hall at some expense and were also building a new farmhouse, re-thatching the barn, clearing the weir on the brook and stocking the orchard. James bought, for example, Lord Nelson and Liveseys Imperial apple trees at sevenpence each, 'Portugal Laurels', Scotch firs and spruce and a drum of figs from his cousin at Liverpool. We learn of the birth of his daughter, later of his daughter's dancing lessons, and his son's education at Standish and elsewhere: 'August 1819. My son William began to go to scool to Mr Brierley to lern to reed at Chorley this day.'

Talbot paid out sums for domestic comforts, buying a coffee pot at Wigan Fair, a waterproof hat for himself, a slip bath for his wife at £2, a canary bird, and clothes for the family when they journeyed by coach to spend a holiday at Blackpool, for the waters.

His income included rents from cottages and farms, and the balance of his wife's marriage settlement, totalling £1,039 11s. 8d. At Chorley market he sold potatoes, cherries and apples from his orchard. The day book includes what seem to be acts of generosity, such as in 1821, when he gave £1 to the widow of a man named Halliwell in order to pay for his burial, and paid money to Peter Eastwood after his mill at Plymouth Bridge burned down.

As a gentleman, he was able to indulge his taste for sport: he coursed for hares on the Hartwood estate, and shot partridges. He paid tenants for the upkeep of his hunting dogs: 'To cash paid . . . for a Cock dog answers to the name of Bob for which I paid 5 shillings he is a light red spotted dog with very long ears.'

Talbot paid his subscriptions to the News Room at the Red Lion, gave evidence to the Charity Commission in 1825 at the Yarrow Bridge Inn and settled family affairs, whether his brother's income or the welfare of his servants. In a sober, plain entry he notes the deaths of his wife and his son, as well as the costs of the services and coffins. From the churchwardens in 1823 he received £150 for the land to build a new tithe barn. He sent a guinea in 1835 to free Joseph Anderton, the town's constable, from the gaol at Lancaster where he had been imprisoned 'for an error in his office.' Berry and Nightingale, cloggers, each bought alderwood from Talbot for clogging in 1832. There is an old saying that 'boys will be boys', and one entry shows that James Talbot endorsed this: 'Expenses for some lads setting fire to a fence at Bagganley . . . I forgave them and paid the expence myself £0 14s. 0d.'

Vestry Survey, 1816

William Tootell's diary is a valuable record of contemporary events in Chorley, yet certain issues are hardly touched in its pages. He omits, for instance, the distress of 1816, even though he was himself a weaver. The end of the Napoleonic Wars resulted in severe economic hardship. Weaving was suddenly poorly paid, and thousands were impoverished. The distress was on a regional scale and Frederick, Duke of York, promoted a scheme to alleviate the hardship in manufacturing districts. John Silvester brought the duke's letter before the Chorley vestry in August 1816; although the eventual benefits of the exercise were doubtful – £300 was granted for poor relief in Chorley – the local response resulted in Chorley's first social survey.[11]

On 26 August 1816 the vestry resolved to find out how individual families fared, the 'amount of their earnings, their occupation, the number of the family under 5 years of age'. They divided the town into eight districts, each to be 'surveyed' by three gentlemen. The volumes which recorded the survey are not available but the summary remains: 673 families were visited, including 1,300 male and 1,002 female children. Of the families surveyed, 125 were labelled 'well off', 246 'in middling circumstances', 302 'very poor and wanting assistance', although the precise definition of what was understood by the labels is not clear. There were 720 looms for 673 families, handloom weaving clearly being a major source of income. When a scheme emerged it involved the employment of men on road-mending and other labouring work. The survey showed a relatively small number of individuals unemployed, but the distress must have involved men who were working as normal but earning well below their previous wages. One revealing statement was made in the submission to be sent up to London: it referred to 'the major part of the Inhabitants belong to other Parishes who have taken up their residence here for the sake of employment'. An appeal was launched locally to solicit donations but this had a poor response and by November 1816 the vestry was compelled to fall back on the familiar provisions of poor relief.

Poverty Survey, 1816: districts.

1. Back Mount, Back Square, Chapel Street, Dole Lane, Mealhouse Lane, Market Street, Peter Street, St. Thomas' Square, Union Street.
2. Bengal Street, Bengal Square, Hollinshead Street.
3. First part of Bolton Street, Back Street, Leigh Row, Leigh Street, Standish Street.
4. Second part of Bolton Street, Fox's Square, Red Bank.
5. Bagganley, Cowling Bridge, Eaves Lane, Lyons Lane, Stump Lane.
6. Cheapside, Chorley Moor, Elbow Street, Eaves Green, Fleet Street, Gillibrand Walks, Moor Street, Pall Mall, Tootell Street.
7. Botany Bay and Knowley
8. Hartwood Green, Preston Street, Water Street.

The vestry survey of 1816 revealed the appalling extent of unemployment in the town, especially among the handloom weavers, caused by a postwar slump in trade. [Lancashire County Library]

District No.	*No. of Families*	*No. of Heads of Families*	*Those Well Off*	*Those Middling*	*Those Very Poor*	*No. of Males*	*No. of Females*	*No. of Looms*	*No. out of Employ*
1	103	201	17	42	46	144	134	33	16
2	87	171	28	24	35	113	112	82	4
3	110	213	–	57	53	185	195	117	28
4	100	195	19	26	55	163	177	190	53
5	36	68	4	12	20	66	67	67	5
6	88	162	14	41	31	140	104	89	107
7	67	126	30	22	15	89	102	89	20
8	82	164	13	22	47	102	114	53	4
Total	673	1300	125	246	302	1002	1005	720	140

William Hall and the Chorley spinners

During the long history of the cotton industry in Chorley there were many bitter disputes between masters and men. Some were of a local nature, others part of wider conflicts. One local dispute developed when Samuel Hilton and Co. stopped running their Water Street Mill at the end of 1823. Messrs Harrison and Lightoller took over in January 1824, at an annual rent of £2,000, for which they got 26,000 spindles, 400 workers and 80 power looms. In a short time trouble flared between the new masters and the skilled spinners. Each side in the dispute published its version of events. Harrison and Lightoller's *Statement of Facts* came out in 1824, while William Hall's *Vindication of the Chorley Spinners* responded in 1826, in a thirty-two page pamphlet. The two versions agree on certain facts, but differ widely on the interpretation of events and the motives behind them. Bitter accusation marked the dispute, there was sporadic violence, and Hall argued that the newspapers sided with the employers.

The chief protagonists were William Harrison who, Hall said, was little more than a petty builder and carpenter before 1824. Thomas Lightoller, meanwhile, he claimed was bookkeeper at his brother Timothy's mills and an undischarged bankrupt. Hall intimated that they did not have the experience to run a mill. The third, Hall himself, we will come to shortly.

As far as the spinners were concerned, the changeover was carried out secretly, leaving them in a dubious position with new employers. The thirty-six spinners went to Lightoller to seek reassurance that their rights would be safe. Hilton had run the truck system, while the spinners protested that they would prefer payment in cash to enable them to shop where they chose rather than to buy only from the mill shop. They asked, too, for the rates paid at Timothy Lightoller's Standish Street Mills to apply at Water Street – Thomas gave them a brusque but apparently favourable reception. In keeping with custom, the spinners accepted his offer of £13 to spend on celebrating their agreement. All seemed well until the first pay day in February – the wages were late, their reckoning dubious and the truck shop remained in use as before. A turnout, or strike, looked likely.

On the spinners' side Hall seemed well versed in the industry. He was born in about 1800 in Preston. From the age of seven he began work at Ryley, Paley & Co.'s mill. The days were long and tedious for all employees, and punishment was frequent and brutal. From there he moved to Bolton but earned little pay. A half wage of 3s. 6d. left only 9d. for food – that paid for porridge twice on working days and a treat of fried cabbage. From the age of nineteen he worked at Hoghton Bottoms Mill but found it a cruel and vicious regime. He next went on a fruitless tramp north to Glasgow looking for work and on returning home worked at Cuerden and Hindley. Pennington, his last boss, was thought generous in employing his hands for only seventy-two hours per week. Many Wigan mills worked between eighty-four and ninety hours.

When Hall came to Chorley in about July 1823 he had a varied, practical experience of the spinning mills; moreover, judging from the *Vindication* he had acquired some learning, had read the parliamentary reports and, most importantly, had a keen sense of injustice. Conditions in the mill where Hall now worked were not out of the ordinary. For young and old alike, each day began at 6 a.m. and ended at 9 p.m. A breakfast break lasted for thirty minutes and forty minutes was allowed for lunch.

Discontent simmered. Lightoller spotted one group of men in a field near the mill, obviously holding a meeting though all would know that it was illegal under the Combination Laws for such a gathering to be held for trade union purposes. In the days which followed claim and counter-claim blurred the course of events. Hall said he was assaulted at one point by Harrison – one night he was shot at under cover of darkness but escaped unhurt. The employers enforced a lockout at the mill, causing the spinners to grow more determined than ever. A dozen men were apprehended by the magistrates, and four held under a warrant. Some were discharged from their employment, and this encouraged Harrison to bring a new group of spinners from Manchester. They walked to Chorley but spent no more than a morning in the mill before they were persuaded to leave by the old spinners.

Harrison, not to be outdone, brought in a second group of Manchester spinners. This time they were escorted to the mill by the town's constable. By night their lodgings were stoned, fights broke out and in the absence of Mr Silvester, the magistrate, special constables were enlisted by Harrison and Lightoller for their protection. The dispute continued for some months. Claims were brought by Hall before the magistrates at Rufford and at Walton-le-Dale, asserting that the masters were in breach of the Factory Acts, employing children under age – they were duly fined. Hall was labelled an informer and vilified, his labours having no tangible success. In the end the masters learned to combine for their interests, just as the men would do in years to come.

The Riot of 1826

Not long after the dispute of 1824, Samuel Hilton's Mill was the scene of a more serious riot. The year 1826 saw widespread poverty and distress in Lancashire. The handloom weavers, working from home and a sturdily independent and proud workforce, were starving in thousands. They compared their lot with better times in 1792, when a yard of cloth earned a man three shillings. In 1826 the same work brought a mere 3½d. Meanwhile, the price of foodstuffs had climbed inexorably. The weavers laid the blame for their plight chiefly at the door of mill owners who used the hated powerlooms, of which thirty thousand had been installed by 1826. The weaving industry predominated in east Lancashire, so that when trouble flared up in that area towards the end of April its effects rippled outwards in a few days. A meeting of distressed weavers near Accrington led to an armed mob wrecking the powerlooms in a local mill. Reinforced with pikemen the rioters moved west to Blackburn, where more mills were attacked in the same fashion, in spite of military forces being sent to protect them. Working to careful plans the rioters sought out the mills which used the detested looms and it was thus inevitable that they should find vulnerable sites in Chorley, the next town which they visited.

The Chorley weavers were suffering from the same acute distress. A meeting held in the town hall on 9 March sought to organise a relief effort for the town's needy. A subscription scheme was begun, and conspicuous acts of generosity were made. The calico printers at Cowling Bridge, for instance, gave £27 from their wages to swell the coffers. Relief was doled

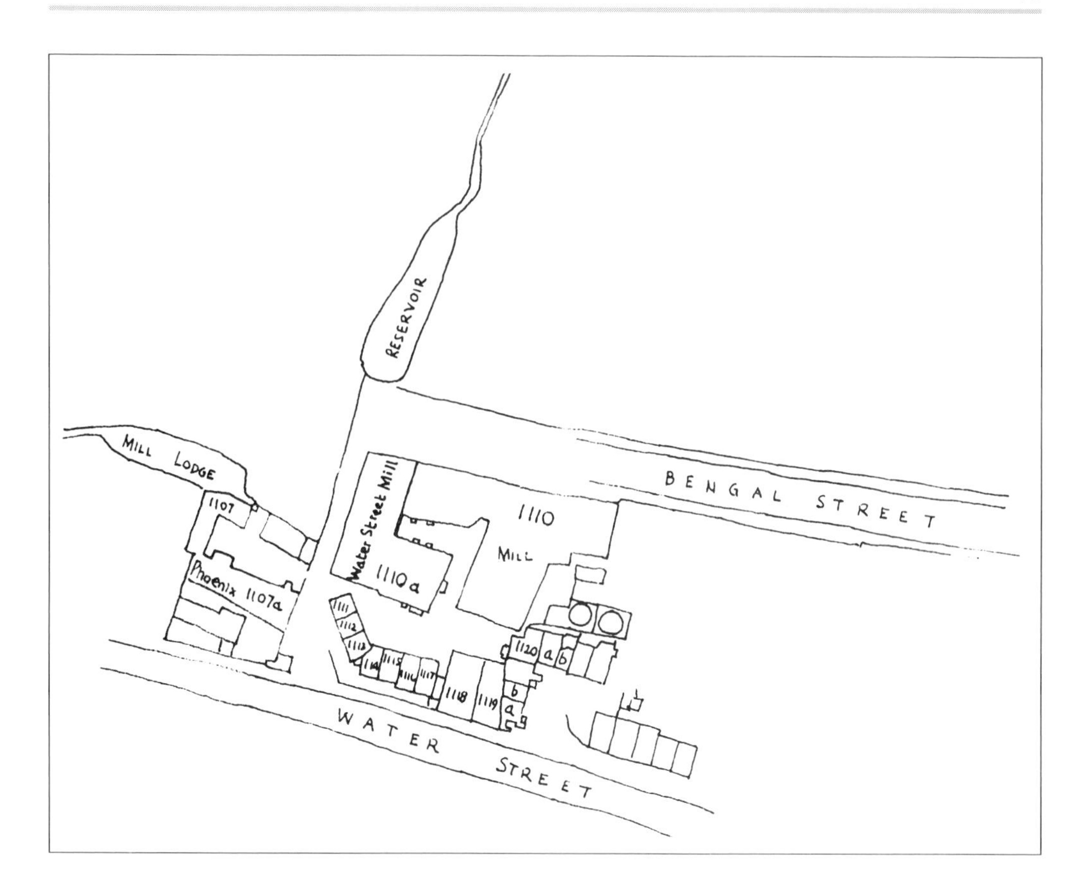

No illustrations survive of Hilton's Water Street mill. This sketch, based on the 1839 Tithe Map, shows the site of the mill, which witnessed one of the loom-breaking riots in 1826. [Author]

out, in the form of oatmeal, potatoes, bacon and meat, to three hundred families in a single week. One week later six hundred families were recipients of food aid. The *Blackburn Mail* reported on 26 April that Chorley's relief fund totalled £170 9s. 6d., though the town was unique in selling food-stuffs back to the poor for £122 11s. 6½d. – a grudging relief effort!

On the next day a body of men came from Blackburn to Chorley, their target being Hilton's Mill in Water Street (operated by Harrison and Lightoller). In this one mill ninety-five looms were powered from a steam engine; Henry Sudell of Blackburn was the owner of the looms. Despite the fact that most of the rioters were east Lancashire men a few were locals, one from Tockholes, another from Brinscall. It was their local knowledge which guided the men to their goal. Estimates of their numbers range between 40 and 150. They avoided the highways, came over the moor tops and crossed the Blackburn road near Gorse Hall. They crossed the canal at Cabbage Hall and followed the line of the River Chor through to Water Street.

The men arrived at 1.30 p.m., but the authorities had had a little time to prepare. The manager of the mill, Mr Farmer, locked the gates and tried to dissuade the men from their purpose. He claimed that the looms had been stopped for some time and the owners would dismantle them voluntarily if the rioters withdrew. The obvious reply came back from the crowd: 'If you don't intend to use them to work any more with them, they can be of no use, so here goes.' The gates were forced open and in they went.[12]

Colonel Silvester, in his role as magistrate, was called in. He raised special constables and marched into the mill. It was a scene reminiscent of Peterloo; as on that fateful day in 1819 he attempted to read the Riot Act. Then he had been under pressure from the huge crowd, now he spoke under a hail of stones from the men. His duty done and the law heard – if not obeyed – he watched as the men smashed the looms one by one within twenty minutes. The constables settled for taking names of the culprits but all they got were aliases. One man called himself 'Hammering Jack', small in stature but destructive with his hammer.[13] The alarm was raised and word was sent to Blackburn, whence sixty cavalrymen departed at 3.30 p.m. Swords in hand, they followed the highway, intending to catch the rioters in Chorley or returning home. The mob, however, left by the route they had taken earlier and evaded the military at Botany.

Time was on the side of the authorities: dozens of men were taken up and sent for trial. Many were given the death penalty imposed on convicted rioters, but mercifully this was commuted to transportation for many of them, including James Chambers, who had led the raid on Hilton's Mill. Sudell sued the constables of Leyland Hundred for the loss of his looms, and was awarded £468. From May of 1826 a body of dragoons was stationed in Chorley to ensure peace but the locals by now were more concerned with food for empty bellies than with any mischief.

A survey was made in that month of 5,030 people: only 803 were fully employed, 509 were on half work, and 1,551 wholly unemployed.[14] A total of 1,844 children were also unable to work at all. Ten months later the county's calico weavers were no better off. Around one hundred thousand were in abject poverty through the winter months. At best hard-working men and women could earn no more than a pittance for survival. The balance between hand and powerloom weaving was not yet tilted in the latter's favour – the change began to occur when the handloom weavers exchanged their independence for the discipline of the mill.

The culture of cotton

The textile industry infused every aspect of life in Chorley for over a century, but within a generation all of the outward signs slipped away. When Sidney Campion came to Chorley in 1913 he suffered what a later age calls 'culture shock', and in a letter home gave his first reactions.

> I came here last week but I shall not stay a minute longer than I can manage. The people are very rough in their ways and speech. I don't like the clatter of the clogs before six in the morning. All the men wear caps and all the women wear shawls . . . Nearly everybody is employed in the cotton mills or in the coal mines.[15]

This commercial property on the south side of Queen's Road was built in 1833 for John Cairns, cotton manufacturer, as a warehouse for the handloom weaving trade. It was later used as a chapel, barracks and meeting hall. [Author]

Working conditions improved over the century because of a long campaign for the ending of abuses. Children regularly worked long hours until the 1840s, when legislation was passed to curb this. Some employers, however, still ignored the law. In 1844 children were found to be cleaning machines during a lunch break at Wallwork's Mill. The management of the same mill were similarly at fault when one girl, Ann Peel, was injured in a lunch period in 1848. Twenty years later, the inspector found that at Lower Healey children had been sent out of the mill to hide in a hedge when he made his visit.[16]

Groups of workers met secretly, and later in open association, to press for more pay, better safety at work and improved working conditions. In 1888 the issue at stake was steaming in weaving sheds, a system ideal for machine running but injurious to health. In 1902 the Chorley Weavers' Association opened the Weavers' Institute at the corner of Chapel Street and Clifford Street. The weavers had 4,041 members, and there were also associations for spinners and bleachers.

Some employers, such as the Smethursts, could be as conscientious as the best anywhere. Occasional treats for workpeople were granted to mark the opening of new weaving sheds, or other events. It was common for mill managers to rise from the ranks of ordinary spinners or weavers, so that they were thoroughly in touch with their way of life. A story is told that the managers of Lightoller's two Standish Street mills agreed to go to a circus one Saturday afternoon. The first, after a hasty wash, went along in his work clothes and qualified for the workers' fee of 6d. admission. His colleague, washed, and dressed in Sunday best, was a gentlemen to all appearances and so was made to pay the gentleman's fee of one shilling.

Richard Cobden at Crosse Hall

Calico printing in Lancashire began in 1764 at Clayton's Bamber Bridge works. Block printing was started at Robert Peel's works in 1785. In that year James Duxbury opened the Crosse Hall Print Works which, after a period under the management of Birch, Rees and Evans, was vacant for two years until 1839. In that year the printworks reopened, under the management of a most remarkable man, Richard Cobden. He had worked in calico printing since the 1820s, when he had been involved in a works at Sabden. A man with a keen social awareness, he was politically active from the 1830s onwards, and after 1838 was one of the pillars of the Anti-Corn Law League.

The mill in Chorley was on the east side of the Black Brook, bordering on the canal. The sheds ran along Cowling Road; there was a dyehouse to one side with the machine shop situated along the Black Brook. A warehouse was behind the print shops and an office at the rear of the complex. Cobden's reputation as an employer was exceptional: he was described as generous and liberal, and old people fondly looked back to their youth when they had worked at Crosse Hall. Children had been a large part of the workforce, doing laborious and tedious tasks, but no-one condemned their old master. One account tells of a girl, aged seven, walking daily from Market Street to begin a day's work at Cowling.

Cobden and his partners were competent and successful businessmen, marketing printed cloth at cheap rates. Though the Sabden works fared well, Crosse Hall did not, perhaps due to Cobden's increasing commitment to the world of politics. Frederick Cobden was not as successful a manager, and was less astute than his brother, and the works faltered. Richard Cobden, however, kept the esteem of his people. One story tells of him riding into the mill yard, distributing copper coins among the mill lads. Wages at £2 a week were good. In 1905 Joseph Talbot, aged ninety-one, recalled that 'He had got that much work for em that he worked two sets of men, one at neet and the other in't day.'

In future years they all remembered the repeal of the Corn Laws, Cobden's triumph as an MP. His workpeople celebrated this event in some style in 1846. On a Saturday in July the works band headed a procession of 650 people through Chorley's streets and lanes. At the head they carried a portrait of Cobden; twelve men followed, each carrying a pole topped by a loaf of bread. This emblem, of freeing the poor from an economic straitjacket, was a potent image in political life for decades. Late in the century a slogan was used 'Vote for Lawrence and the Big Loaf.' In the week after the repeal Cobden treated his workers to a free rail excursion to Fleetwood – men, women and children in one happy throng. Banners rose and fell among the crowd, slogans reading 'Peace and Plenty,' 'God save the Queen,' and 'Cobden for ever!,' Fourteen hundred proud marchers each sported a crown-sized commemorative medal on a blue ribbon. At 8 a.m. they embarked from Chorley station, setting out for the seaside to be treated to a free meal – a day out at the coast which was to be the forerunner of so many more.

In 1847 Cobden bought the land on which the works stood from the Gillibrands. In that year, too, the Tory press tried to create a false dispute between Cobden and his workpeople, based on a revised pricing of costs; a works deputation scotched the issue in short time, a sign of Cobden's talent for man management. In 1852 the Crosse Hall Print Works, stated to be occupied by J. N. Sale as sub-tenant, were offered for sale in the *Manchester Guardian* and appear to have been bought by Messrs Heyworths who later built on the site.

CHAPTER SEVEN

The High Victorian Age

Market Street, markets and commerce

1822, June 25: by Cash for Cherrys sent to market and sold 3½pr £0 3. 9.

James Talbot's meticulous account book shows that he often sent produce, such as the cherries above, to Chorley market from the Bagganley estate. Other entries show that he also bought in the town's market – linen for the house, for example, or – from an Irish trader – a pig to be fattened up for slaughter. For seven hundred years the market has been at the heart of Chorley's life, literally and metaphorically. The markets, traditionally held weekly on Tuesday and Saturday are one of the town's most enduring features.

In the 1760s Market Street was said to be irregular in shape, with a shop built across the street, and was described as more like a field than a street. [Lancashire County Library]

It is unfortunate that the original charter for borough and market, granted in the 1250s by the de Ferrers family, disappeared long ago. The earliest document to mention Chorley market dates from 1498, when Lord Strange, Joan his wife, Sir Edward Stanley and Sir Richard Shireburne had to show by what right they claimed a market, fairs and other privileges. Locally, rival markets were chartered at Croston (1283), Charnock Richard (1284), and Euxton (1301), but the latter two did not prosper.

Early markets must have been held on the town's green (or Saint Thomas's Square), clustered around the market cross. Well into the nineteenth century the town's green kept a rural character: thatched cottages were interspersed among the shops, and there was a village pump and a duck pond alongside Mr Ince's farm (demolished in the 1850s to make way for a new police station) as well as the town stocks. A narrow lane led to Dole Lane while an equally narrow passageway squeezed between the Gillibrand Arms Inn and Market Street proper. These restricted access points allowed the market holders to control access and collect tolls. Around the green were pubs such as the Wheatsheaf and the Thatched House Tavern.

In 1826 Henry Hawarden Fazakerley, the lord of the manor, moved the market to a purpose-built site on the east of Market Street, approached by a broad new street bearing his surname. He also transferred the stocks and village pump, siting them alongside the fishstones in the new market place. The fishstones, a circular stone enclosure with four entrances, were in the centre of the square: on the flat stones fish and shellfish were displayed for sale. Shellfish came in from Banks, fish from the Lune and the Ribble. The new market place was a large open square, with stoops (or posts) to control access for traders. There was a rough earth surface and in poor weather the site was a quagmire. In 1865 the Improvement Commission heard complaints that it was 'in a very wretched state': the six approaches were frequently blocked and shoppers walked ankle deep in water.[1]

New shops, usually single-storied, grew up around the square. In 1829 the Fazakerley Arms opened its doors; later in the century the landlord collected the market tolls on behalf of the Fazakerleys. In 1828 the tolls were valued at £63 yearly. Another building surviving from the early period is the old Redmaynes, on the west side of the market, built in 1827. The Market Tavern was opened later still, perhaps in the 1840s. The Leach family recalled during this century that stalls were built for the market by their joinery firm – their piano and furniture business in Chapel Street was a familiar site into the 1950s.

The Market Square was used for events, such as a display of fireworks in 1848. In 1855, to mark the end of the Crimean War, a great bonfire was lit in the square: it went out of control, the fire spread to the stocks (which were destroyed to the relief of wrongdoers), and then damaged the fishstones.

Conditions for traders on the market are poorly recorded. A fine autumn day in 1845 saw a strong market with ninety-eight carts, in four rows, filling the Market Place by 10.30 a.m. one Tuesday morning: stalls then were almost unknown. Foodstuffs of all kinds were sold but most

A market scene from the early years of this century. Market traders such as this crockery dealer were frequent visitors from neighbouring towns and villages, some travelling from as far away as Warrington. [Lancashire County Library]

often locally grown vegetables and fruit. Tootell's diary records oats, potatoes and flour on sale in the 1810s, while one account recalled the scarcity of white, or American, flour.

A glimpse of protection for shoppers is seen in a receipt of 1807, when the new constable took over the town's regulated weights and measures – from yard lengths for cloth, to grain measures and a range of weights and ale testers. Customers at least may have fared well in one respect for two reports bemoan Chorley's local practice late last century of selling eggs and cabbages at fourteen to the dozen! Traders who stood more than one market complained of this unfairness. Among the traders some businesses have gone through several generations under the same names, such as M. Worden & Son (from the 1860s); the Burr family, who traded a century ago as fishmongers and fruiterers; and Tootells Tripe Stall, in business for more than a century.

In Fazakerley Street by 1851 there were two chandlers' shops, a brush manufacturer, bookseller, shoemaker, druggist and seed merchant. On the north side stood the Commercial Hotel, complete with a set of imposing pillars. At this date the businesses around the Market Square were geared to serving clientele from the country areas – there were the veterinary surgeon, harness maker and gunsmith for example.

The Improvement Commission made unsuccessful bids to buy the market rights along with the manorial rights in 1854 and 1873. In 1873 they offered £4,000 against the Fazakerley family's claim for £14,000.[2] After arbitration a sale price of £5,305 was agreed and the handover of these important privileges to the town came on 28 April 1874. Thereafter fixed stalls begin to appear on the square, there being fifty-five in 1889.

By the 1870s market traders were less likely to be producers than formerly. Two rival groups had appeared. Farmers from Euxton were said to buy in produce from their neighbours for resale on Chorley market. Other farmers bought fresh produce from their neighbours but sold door-to-door through the town. Market traders were especially incensed at the second practice since it undercut those who paid tolls and took out licences to trade. When Chorley Corporation came into existence in 1881, it found itself at odds with the traders. Chorley's tolls were high, but this was still an open market whereas larger towns were investing in handsome covered market halls.

One row began in 1913 when the tolls were increased. A meeting of sixty stall holders was held at the Shepherds' Hall in Chapel Street, and it resolved to found a Market Traders Association in protest. Significantly, many of these people were traders from other towns, Wigan, Manchester, Blackburn and Warrington among them. On 19 August 1913 they held a strike, a rare event in this sector of the community – it left shoppers with the only goods on show being perishable foodstuffs but the tolls stayed.

Any mention of markets must include Market Street itself. In the early 1800s markets were held in the open street: although the town's green was meant to hold the market the volume of trade resulted in a spilling-out along the street. In front of the Black Bull Inn (site of the Royal Bank of Scotland) pigs were customarily traded. Farmers' carts lined each side of Market Street from Mount Pleasant up to the present town hall. Farmers' wives were supposed to sell butter and dairy produce in the butter market, in a cellar beneath the 1802 town hall, but they often placed their wares on the pavement above. Farmers favoured the Anchor Inn at the top of Market Street on market days; within the dealers tasted the corn samples before purchase and the landlord did a fair trade in 'sixpennorth o' pratie pie' with the farmers. A butchers' market was held in front of the Gillibrand Arms, facing the Royal Oak, then a fine old inn with a thatched roof.

No tolls were levied for selling cattle in the street, but this changed after the removal of the cattle market to the site in 1874 which later became the Flat Iron. This market occupied the Dingle, which until the 1860s was a valley, well wooded and watered by a stream flowing from above the station area. Old people used to recall with fondness how this woodland was a good hunting ground for rabbits in the 1830s. In 1863 the Improvement Commission earmarked the site for a cattle market. The enormous hollow was filled in with builders' rubble, refuse, and butchers' offal! From 1874 the cattle market's regulated sales spared Market Street shoppers from the unpleasant turmoil of livestock trading.

This print of the Market Place, dated 1 May 1872, shows the brewers' drays from the Whittle Springs Brewery. It was probably taken during the May Day celebration when the town's carters paraded their decorated carts and lorries. [Lancashire County Library]

This market became a venue for large gatherings of all kinds. Fairs and circuses, musical recitals, the Grand Theatre, sporting events, political rallies were all staged here and, during the First World War, large bodies of troops, such as the Chorley Pals, for example, paraded. Why did it become known as the Flat Iron? The name only came into use after 1918. One explanation is that Manchester traders, using cheaply bought ex-Army lorries, could bring quantities of goods at small cost to markets like this. The Shude Hill Market in Manchester was nicknamed 'the Flat Iron' already and the name transferred to Chorley. Eventually the Flat Iron evolved its modern character, an extension of the Market Square with a wide variety of goods on offer.

Weekly markets apart, the seasonal fairs were ever more popular, colourful, noisy and exciting. The pattern was set in the Middle Ages, four fairs were held annually, on 26 March, 5 May, 20 August and 4, 5, 6 September. The first three were mainly cattle fairs, the last for the sale of toys, hardware, Yorkshire woollens and peddlars' goods.[3] Like the markets they also moved to the new Market Place from 1826. By the 1870s, at fair times, all the cattle market was given over to sideshows, rides, booths, stalls selling all kinds of sweets. Circuses such as Sangers or Barnum and Baileys were enormous draws: the millhand or ploughboy could try his hand in the boxing booths, gawp at the zebras, the snake-charmers, lion-tamers, dancing bears and scores of exotic animals. In the 1850s there were swing boats, fortune tellers and the bearded lady. A public holiday at the time of the September fair gave one and all their chance to enjoy the fun.

A popular fair with good weather attracted literally thousands of people, and with so many inns and taverns rowdy scenes were not unusual. Even the regular market day attracted the condemnation of Revd Gillow in 1875: 'Look to your streets on any market night . . . I have seen scenes of drunkenness and open profligacy'.

During Victoria's reign Chorley's shops took on a more prosperous appearance while Chapel Street subtly changed from a residential to a commercial centre. Likewise shops in Market Street expanded in size and number. Mangnall's Shoes (1831), E. H. Booth (1852), W. J. Sandiford and many more household names were side-by-side with rivals long gone. The best place to go for Chorley cakes in the 1880s was the Misses Corbett's shop in Chapel Street, these delicacies going for the price of 2d. each.

The higgledy-piggledy building and roof lines of the eighteenth century gave way to smart shop frontages bounded by paved footpaths, and street lighting improved the character of the thoroughfare.

Chorley's rate book for 1827 shows 133 numbered properties in Market Street: fifty-three of them were shops and ten were public houses. The 1863 rate book lists thirteen public houses, thirty-nine houses with other premises, four shops alone, and ninety-one houses with shops combined. Throughout the Victorian era Market Street and the town centre had a large resident population: many people lived 'over the shop' but the older, thatched cottages were cleared away in 1848 and 1882 as being slums out of keeping with Chorley's new image. The expanding trade and commerce of Chorley, and its larger population, encouraged the building of handsome new banks such as the Preston Banking Company (1886) facing High Street. Chorley Savings Bank opened in 1845 and moved to its premises facing St Laurence's in 1922.

On maps and plans before the nineteenth century the name Market Street is not used; the 1734 estate plan simply shows the name 'Chorley Town', and this accords with the use of the name 'Town's End' to denote the Big Lamp or Bolton Street-Pall Mall junction.

Reminiscences, though often dubious on dates, are nevertheless good on general impressions and Mrs Worthington, looking back to the 1840s from the year 1924, remembered Market Street being 'a funny street, more like a field', with thatched cottages and no buildings west of Market Street.[4] Fifty years on the picture of Market Street 'grown up' was preserved in Luke Berry's photographs, so very similar to the scene today.

Law and order

The constables' accounts of the eighteenth century are very mundane revealing little of the daily duties carried out by Chorley's amateur lawmen. In 1725, for example, the constables claimed expenses for accompanying prisoners to the sessions; they attended to wounded soldiers in transit; and they organised the building of new shooting butts for the militia. One task that year was the organising of a bonfire to celebrate the tenth anniversary of the accession of George I.[5] Thomas Breres was constable in 1733 when a new set of stocks was needed for the town's green. Adam Rigby and John Atherton were paid for five days work to make the stocks, though it is doubtful whether these were the same stocks which were fired by an out-of-control bonfire in the 1850s.

Highway robbery was a constant threat, whether to the postboy who was robbed at sword-point in 1799 or to citizens such as Henry Marsden, the miller of Crosse Hall, who was attacked and robbed by two men in 1764. The constables were sometimes required to imprison runaway apprentices, such as Robert Lee who in 1707 broke his articles with a Chorley tradesman, James Hall.

When the canal navvies rioted in Chorley in the 1790s the constables could not prevent them; likewise, the Plug Riots of 1842 saw large, disciplined crowds which were in no mood to listen to the law-keepers.

An advertisement was placed in the *Preston Chronicle* in 1833 for a deputy constable, 'whose character and qualification for this office will bear the strictest investigation'. A salary of £50 a year was offered. Two years later Robinson's directory shows that Chorley had one resident magistrate,[6] with visiting magistrates every three weeks, sessions being held at the inns. Punishment for crime in the 1800s was swift and severe; William Tootell records men being given a public flogging at the obelisk for riot. Three boys found guilty of stealing a goose in 1827 were transported, two for life, the third for seven years. A seventeen-year-old, Joseph Lee, earned a death sentence for burglary in 1821. Stealing four shillings in 1828 resulted in one boy of twelve being transported for life! In 1798 an association was set up to prevent croft breaking, the theft of bleached cloth from crofts. Fifteen of the signatories to the agreement were local firms.

During the 1850s Chorley came under the jurisdiction of the Leyland division of the county police force. The old dungeon which had served the town was superseded by a police station, completed in 1858, at the west end of St Thomas's Square. It was soon inadequate, and in 1869 a new station replaced the old, remaining in use until the 1960s.

The courthouse however was in High Street. Under the Lancashire Constabulary there were forty-four police officers of all ranks for the Leyland division. Chorley, in spite of its borough status and increasing importance, did not operate its own force.

Although the Chorley police officers were called on to deal with a wide range of offences from serious riots (as in 1868) to daily problems of drunkenness, petty theft and assault, their skills were challenged by characters like the blacksmith in High Street who was involved in cock-fighting, and who would hide the birds under the working forge when the constables checked his premises. With the turn of the new century a different kind of offence posed problems for policemen. Motoring offences were a novelty in 1909 when one motor vehicle exceeded the speed limit of five miles per hour between Adlington and Heath Charnock. Police constable Mitchinson had tailed the driver on his bicycle, the

When this photograph of Market Street was taken in the 1880s there still remained several thatched cottages, seen here on the left, with window shutters and rudimentary sanitation, though most were swept away under Victorian slum clearances. [Lancashire County Library]

vehicle having done one mile in 8 minutes and 2½ seconds. Speeding at 7 miles per hour earned a fine of ten shillings!

The inadequacy of the old police station was apparent during the 1960s – and it was agreed to demolish it and rebuild a new divisional headquarters for Chorley. After using the old Highway Hostel at Euxton as an interim headquarters, the force moved to the new, 60s style headquarters on the old town's green in 1966.

The demon drink

Throughout the last century a long-running battle was waged between the pubs and the temperance movement. The pubs fulfilled many roles: the Royal Oak, Gillibrands Arms and Black Bull's Head were staging-posts for the coaching network; some included coffee houses and newsrooms; the Royal Oak's Assembly Room was the only suitable venue for public events; inns and taverns were social gathering points for friendly societies, burial clubs, building clubs, sporting clubs, political meetings, and trades unions. Pubs only tended to settle into a purely recreational role when more avenues opened up elsewhere: the Reform Club and Conservative Club, for example, later became centres for political parties, while the churches grew in number and widened their activities to recruit interested young people. The Parish Church Institute and the various clubs attached to almost all the denominational churches encouraged sports and wholesome activities.

The temperance cause began in Preston under the leadership of Joseph Livesey of Walton-le-Dale. His message spread: Charles Robinson printed a tract in Chorley called *The Besetting Sin* in 1825. W. E. Moss of Blackburn recalled how he was introduced to the cause in Chorley at Revd Ride's Unitarian schoolroom in Park Street. Ride conducted a free night school for people like Moss. The latter began to organise meetings of the Blue Ribbon Army on the Market Place from 1882. Tough heckling did not deter the crusaders and the numbers of supporters grew. The Co-operative Hall in Hill Street was their headquarters for a time. Moss, a weaver at Fletchers' Mill in Brooke Street, met the renowned Mrs Lewis of Blackburn, 'The Drunkards' Friend', and became her temperance missionary in September 1888.

Some diehards would not change their ways. George Taylor, a carter and an old man, was brought before the magistrates in February 1911, accused of being drunk in charge of a horse and trap in Market Street. Taylor said the horse itself was drunk and blind, but would go wherever he was led. A police superintendent said this was Taylor's twenty-ninth conviction for such offences. He was wrong, said the old carter – this was the forty-second!

Coal in Chorley

Coal-mining was one of the core industries of the Industrial Revolution, but its story in Lancashire is much older: some records show coal being produced in the thirteenth century.

'Firestone or Seacole' was mined around Wigan in the reign of Elizabeth, and in 1563 the Shireburne Rental talks of Hugh Kingley's Cole field in Chorley[7] (though this may be charcoal), while Nicholas Heskin was getting 'cannel' in The Lane at Welch Whittle in 1590. The will of Robert Charnock of Astley, who died in 1616, refers to coal from the Charnock Colliery and in 1620 mining rights in Coppull and Charnock Richard were excepted by the terms of a lease.

An early clue to mining in Chorley is a reference to 'Thomas Greene, collier' who applied for relief in 1652–3. Forty years later Doctor Kuerden, in his *Itinerary*, described workings on Chorley Moor: 'passing over Chorley Moor you leave on the left a fair built Hall formerly the seat of Harington but now of Gillibrand of Chorley. Here are great quantities of Coal'.[8]

Early in the eighteenth century John Halliwell of North Tunley mentioned excellent quality coal coming from Burgh, Birkacre and Whetstone Valley. It was perhaps one of those mines which caused a dispute between Richard Clayton and Thomas Gillibrand in 1743: Halliwell and John Chadwick of Birkacre made an award concerning the disputed pit.

In 1712 Robert Patrick Lancaster was granted a lease by Richard Chorley, for three lives, of a coal mine at Charnock Richard, with 'a liberty to dig coal out of all mines and pits.' Lancaster was to pay Chorley 5d for every twenty-three baskets of coal he brought out. That kind of measure appears again in the account of Charles Waring, who made a deposition in 1780. He was, he said, born at Duxbury in 1750, and taken on to work

Duxbury Pit, *c.* 1910. The coal industry was a large employer of labour at this time, a fact easily forgotten today. Chorley's pits, however, were never as productive as those around Wigan, the heartland of the Lancashire coal industry. [Lancashire County Library]

for Thomas Chadwick of Duxbury in 1760, payment by results as follows: 'to draw in the bottom of his coal pits at 3d for 24 baskets for 40 yards from the bottom of the pit and for every 24 baskets more and so on in proportion till the sum amounted to 8d for another 24 baskets'.

Coal was worked in the heart of Chorley town long ago; in 1788, for example, Thomas Weld of Stonyhurst sold the 'mines, beds or veins of coal lying under Many Pits Field', which lay roughly across Gillibrand Walks and up as far as modern Avondale Road. The sale was to Roger Fishwick and John German, colliers of Charnock Richard, and limited them to 'putting down eye or eyes, pit or pits', and forcing them to shore up with adequate supports to avoid subsidence. Two points are relevant. First, the field abuts onto the Gillibrand estate, where coal was already worked, and second, the name of the field was already old by 1788, which implies that the area was well worked already, possibly using the bell pits common before deep mining began. Where seams cropped up near the surface bell pits were adequate and thus presumably profitable, requiring little investment of capital. At this period a pamphlet, promoting the Lancaster Canal, speaks of local mines, 'for coal is to that country from Chorley to Worsley of more value than gold. From Walton to Chorley is not eight miles farther. Mr Chadwick's coal near Chorley in different beds 7 feet thick, Mr Norris's 9, Mr Livesey's 9, Standish 16, Blackrod 20'.

The well-to-do and aspiring coal owners pressed for the line of the Leeds and Liverpool Canal to be diverted so as to serve their pits on its way north. Thomas Chadwick of Burgh, referred to above, was an entrepreneur in the eighteenth-century style; his ventures included coal, iron forges, land and farming, as well as ships, textiles and trade – all avenues open to a Catholic gentleman restricted in his scope for public affairs.

Colliers underground at the Duxbury Hall Colliery before the First World War. [Lancashire County Library]

As Chorley was situated on the northern edge of the Wigan coalfield, the area had less promising prospects than Wigan itself. Seams of Upper Mountain Mine coal are most prominent under Chorley. Cannel and Lower Mountain Mine also feature locally, roughly from 6 to 18 feet apart. Ninety years ago one writer said that the depths of the seams were: King coal, 127 yards; Bone, 242 yards; Yard, 195 yards; Smith, 266 yards; Arley, 331 yards; Mountain Mine, 215 yards. Mines 'crop out' on the banks of the Yarrow,[9] and in the other seams there are various fractures and 'steppes'. The great fault or 'upthrow' follows the course of the Yarrow from the Carr to Throstle Nest Wood. The different seams and their characteristics were very familiar to the old miners, as also were the fossilised beds of cockleshells found below the fields and woodlands of Chorley.

Fishwick and German, referred to above, were partners in coal-mining at various sites towards the end of the eighteenth century. In 1776, for example, they agreed with William Gillibrand of Gillibrand Hall to exploit the potential for mineral extraction on his land for twenty-five years. Mr Gillibrand negotiated an advantageous deal: Fishwick and German should supply all the domestic coal needed for the hall, provide slack for burning marl to be used for agriculture and hand over one half of all the profits annually to Gillibrand, expenses deducted. Despite the great things hoped for the pits, Fishwick got into financial difficulty, borrowed money from Gillibrand and traded away his gains. The backers of the scheme, including John Hollinshead (who had been responsible for much of the mine drainage), lost large sums. When Thomas Gillibrand died in 1789 his sons' guardians accused the colliers of negligence, saying the mines were £1,500 in debt. This apart, several sources show that the grounds of Gillibrand were exploited not just for coal: attempts were made to work iron and copper. The family was personally involved in its investments: in 1852 the heir to the estate, young H. H. Fazakerley aged nineteen, was killed in an explosion of firedamp at one of their pits.

Birkacre and Burgh Pits were extensively worked in the first quarter of the century, the former by James Anderton and the latter by Mr Heaton. John Gent appears in a directory of 1793 as auditor at the coal-mines but at which is not specified. Burgh Hall Pit was managed by the executors of Anderton in 1825, in which year there was another firedamp explosion in which two colliers died. The Burgh Pit had its own colliery railway running from the mine northwards, parallel to Burgh Lane, until it reached Plock Farm where it turned across Weldbank Lane, skirting Willow House and reaching Pall Mall at the weigh house, which still stands. Working people had their coal delivered from Burgh on the backs of donkeys: 'an old man and his daughter, covered with coal dust, driving half-a-dozen donkeys, with panniers, carrying from 2½ cwt to 3 cwt of coal each'.

Heaton was credited with putting an early railway engine on the line, replacing the muscle power of the past. At this pit during the 1840s the stationary steam engine used was the Sans Pareil, a contender with Stephenson's Rocket at the 1829 Rainhill trials. In Chorley itself two early pits were the Millstone and the Fellery (or Church) Pits, sunk by Thomas Whittle, dating from the 1820s. 'A Native', writing to the *Chorley Echo* in 1883, remembered an older pit, immediately behind the west side of Market Street: 'in the field behind the Brown Cow beerhouse, in Market Street. The coal was got in and sold by 'baskets', and they were hoisted from the mine by a 'gin-horse', a very primitive mode compared to our present system'.

The whim-gin or whimsey, horse-powered, was common at the old coal pits, hauling men, equipment and coal to the surface. The name occurred in two place-names in the last century: one in a yard off Standish Street, where the 'Old Whim' is shown on the Ordnance Survey map, the second, in Gin Bow, off Jackson Street. The Millstone Pit, started before 1829, was named after the Millstone Inn, near the site of the Cunliffe Street Primitive Methodist Chapel. The Fellery Pit was sunk to the east of Clifford Street (named Coal Pit Lane until the 1860s), roughly opposite the recently demolished swimming baths. Not far away a third pit was developed by Mr Darlington of Coppull. The Station Pit was just east of the railway station, on the site of the bowling green for the Railway Inn. Here a single track rail line went up Seymour Street, crossed Eaves Lane near the Seven Stars, then down the reverse slope to the loading wharf on the canal.

Chronologically the next pit was the Rangletts, situated on Chorley Moor behind Duke Street. Its workings connected with those of Station Pit. Mr Blundell managed the Rangletts until at least 1865. During this century the mine was prone to flooding and difficult to pump dry. Eventually the headgear collapsed into the pit. The Black Pit off Pall Mall dated from 1846 or earlier.

The most isolated local mines were on the east side of Healey Nab, where Nab Colliery was operated by Barnes and Nightingale in 1848: a seam of Mountain Mine coal cropped sufficiently well to be worked into this century.

Richard Benson Blundell (1793–1853), mentioned above, was an eminent figure in mining circles, running collieries at Orrell, Blackrod, Pemberton, Chorley, Wigan Mesnes and Amberswood. When the Whittle leases ran out Blundell took over in Chorley, leasing from the Cunliffe Grundy estates in 1846, Lady Hoghton, and the Fazakerley estates. At best his firm worked four mines in the town, Millstone, Station, Fellery and Chorley Moor. Production in 1845 stood at 28,600 tons, dropping to 14,852 by 1853. In 1851 at three of his pits thirty-two miners turned out one hundred tons of coal daily. However, by 1854 it was said that Blundell's Chorley Pits ran at a loss of £4 16s. od. per ton.

At Red Bank a cluster of mines was worked north of the Yarrow and Duxbury Woods. In the 1850s the Whittle, Standish and Cunliffe Grundy estates all had mining interests. Local pits were frequently plagued by flooding. Whittle's Mill Pit, Carr Colliery at Red Bank was so badly flooded in 1889 that it had to shut down. The workings had apparently cut into old flooded workings of the Burgh Colliery, and within days the pit was unusable and sixty miners were out of employment.

Chorley Library has the transcript of a diary kept by a pit brow lass from Chorley, from the early part of this century. Mrs Polly Holden started work aged thirteen for Duxbury Park colliery and worked there until she was twenty-three. Her home at Tincklers Barracks was not far from her workplace. Along the way she met ten pit brow lasses who walked from Chorley: 'I wore a red head wrap, tied around my head, to keep the coal dust out of my hair, then a nice shoulder shawl thrown over my head wrap. I wore a black velvet blouse, and a blue striped Pit Skirt. I made my own Pit Brats, out of Irish Linen. I wore a man's jacket to come home in, also pit breeches as well'.

Their wages were low – one shilling and twopence per day and they worked six days a week. Sickness pay was stopped at threepence per week, exactly the same sum Polly's mother allowed her to spend for herself: all the rest of her wages went into the family income. There was a strike in 1905. Duxbury Park Colliery kept working until a band of miners from Wigan turned up to shut down all work but pumping out water. Polly was covered by pay of five shillings weekly from the sick club during the strike.

When she turned eighteen her wages went up to two shillings a day, her spending money rising to sixpence. Her diary describes the hard work of the pit brow lasses, the environment of the mines and the characters it generated. Her diary concluded,

> I have often cried when I've seen the miners brought up Pit, dead, or wounded, . . . I think a miner should be treated in a proper way, he has to risk his life, besides having lumps knocked off him, while he is digging coal, for you to burn.

The period Polly Holden recalled was around 1900, a period when mining no longer took place near Chorley town centre. Chorley Moor Colliery worked on well into this century, and then the old workings were filled in, built over and largely forgotten.

The coal industry acquired a reputation for stormy industrial relations. Efforts to set up trade unions in the Wigan coalfields appear at an early date, as do records of strikes in local pits. A report was published in the *Chorley Standard* for August 1869 of a meeting addressed by agents of the Miners Association. Their theme was the reduction in wages prevailing in recent months. Wages ranged from two to three shillings a day.

Strikes took place in 1881, 1893, 1912, 1921 and, of course, there was the General Strike of 1926. Five weeks into the 1921 strike households were running short of fuel, and families gathered sticks from the woods. Where outcrop seams of coal could be tackled easily, desperate hands foraged for coal. Small boys dredged the canal with buckets and miners on strike stopped the transit of lorries with loads of coal when it was thought they were going to feed the mills or industry. In 1926 the miners, numbering two to three thousand in Chorley, Coppull and Adlington, came out on strike but avoided violent or unlawful activity. According to the 1921 census there were not large numbers of miners in Chorley itself; 1,228 men and three women worked in local pits, 468 of the men being 'hewers and getters.'

Since the skills of mining are valued worldwide it is not surprising that British miners worked on every continent. In the early years of the twentieth century colliers were recruited to work in North America, the Chorley miners being especially associated with the Union Pacific Colliery at Hanna, Wyoming.

Most of the men came home when their contracts expired, but a few stayed on. We know about this practice through a mining disaster which struck the pit in June 1903. An underground explosion trapped 248 and dozens were killed. Of the nine Chorley men there, six survived, and two of the dead were brothers from Pall Mall, named Clarkson. Still a few remained to work on at Hanna. Tragically, a second explosion in 1908 in the pit resulted in many more deaths, eight of them miners from Chorley. Robert Warburton from Bengal Street survived the first explosion but died in the second. Harry Nowell, however, from Hollinshead Street lived to tell the tale of both disasters. As the *Chorley Weekly News* said, 'There is quite a colony of Chorley miners at Hanna and only a fortnight ago a small party of miners from this district went out'. The common factor for these men was that all had been employees of Chorley colliery in Pall Mall.

In time all of the Chorley pits were closed down, mining moved out of the town, to Coppull and Adlington, and particularly to Ellerbeck where extensive open-cast mining was undertaken in the 1980s. The industry, like cotton in its day, faded away leaving few traces of its presence.

Local government

> And this Jury . . . do order that James Tomson: Evan Foster: Lawrence Jacson: Henry Riding: Mrs Edmundson and Edward Blackledge . . . remove their dung and wood out of ye streets in Chorley

That directive by the manor court leet was issued in 1726, but a similar order could have been made in 1626 or in 1826. Keeping the streets clean was not just a public health issue but also involved civic pride. For centuries Chorley's 'local government' was a court made up of jurymen acting under the lord of the manor. Rates were collected to pay for roads, disputes were settled and trespasses regulated. Until the county police force began in the 1840s Chorley's law and order was under the control of a sole constable. While the town was of limited size the manorial court (or court leet) was able to cope with its administration.

By the end of the eighteenth century many local issues were dealt with by the parish vestry, the meetings of which were recorded in the Town's Book (1781–1823). Early in 1787, for instance, 'a dungeon or small prison' was to be built at the Town's End; 1817 saw the vestrymen debating whether to pave the towns' green, then a busy market place – they resolved to settle for gravel. A well-known entry from 1803 explains how some street names originated, 'That all the public streets within the Township of Chorley be named and all the Houses numbered in each street and that the same be done by Mr William Bibby and Mr Thomas Somner'.[10]

This produced street names such as Pall Mall, Holborn, Cheapside, Fleet Street and possibly Chancery Lane. In 1821 two men, Henry Newton and Edward Eccles were paid £20 a year to destroy moles. Humans who might become a burden were also dealt with – in 1781 the overseer demanded to see settlement certificates or enforce eviction on those not legally settled in Chorley.

Economy in local government is nothing new: the vestry ordered in March 1788 that no liquor be allowed in future to workmen; the vestry's own meetings however were held in rotation in the towns' pubs and usually included a bill for refreshments.

Although many topics were trivial, some were vital to the townsfolk; one was the sinking of new wells, another the new workhouse and a third the town hall of 1802. This, a more modest affair than its successor of 1879, was a gift from John Hollinshead. The basement held a butter market, while the upper rooms were used for administration. The building also contained Chorley's lockup, a cell 8 feet by 7 feet by 10 feet high, with a small round hole for ventilation and no bedding at all. It was the last place Joseph Ainsworth of Rivington ever laid his eyes on. Arrested for robbery in 1833, he spent nine days in the cell before hanging himself from the ceiling. The townspeople, outraged at the official attitude which said he should remain there, removed his body to the Gillibrands Arms prior to burial.

The court leet met until 1828, the vestry meeting in one form or other until mid-century. The system of a parish constable, local magistrates, and the overseer of the poor worked tolerably well. In 1835 one constable and one magistrate were resident, while the larger body of magistrates came every three weeks, holding session at the Gillibrands Arms. It was here men met to discuss the incorporation of the town at the time of the Great Reform Bill but Chorley had to wait another fifty years before it achieved borough status. Even in Victorian times it was argued that this held back progress and prosperity.

A Political Union had started up in 1830; legislation to improve industrial conditions was hotly discussed and Chartism was active. In 1839 *The Preston Chronicle* described a rumour that local smiths were turning out pikes to arm Chartists, and 400 special constables were appointed, with fifty troops sent to keep order. Local issues remained more important, however, and there was growing pressure for administrative change. Hotly debated subjects included the poor maintenance of the streets, the removal of night soil, and gas lighting. In 1845 there was an unsuccessful move to petition for a Chorley Improvement Act for remedying these problems.

One man with a strong local link was to become the instrument of change. Robert Rawlinson, a civil engineer and specialist in public health, was instructed by the General Board of Health to conduct a public inquiry into sewerage, drainage, water supply, burial grounds, paving, lighting and the town's sanitary condition. His report, published in 1853, is one of the landmarks in Chorley's history, notable for its impartiality and its use of statistics comparing Chorley with other towns.[11] Naturally, Rawlinson supported the adoption of the Public Health Act of 1848, which he estimated would cost the town £100 as against the £1,000 it would take to promote a private act. He made comparisons with Chorley's Improvement Bill, highlighted the common features, citing the omissions from the Bill which were meant to keep rates low for large property owners.

Sanitary conditions in Chorley of the early 1850s were alarming: sewerage was almost non-existent (the River Chor took all the effluent); cesspits and middens were commonplace (solid matter was sold to farmers as a fertiliser); graveyards overcrowded from centuries of burials. There was a primitive water supply from wells and springs. In warm weather parts of the town endured an appalling stench. Rawlinson's skill in public health and civil engineering taught him that resolute, if expensive, schemes could remedy the faults. Using Ulverston as a comparably sized town, he showed that the average age at death in Chorley for 1841 was 24 years 10 months, while the equivalent for Ulverston was 41 years 8 months. Infants, in particular, died young in Chorley. The areas most prone to disease were Bolton Street with its adjacent streets, and Water Street and Bengal Street. An outbreak of typhus in 1847 confirmed his

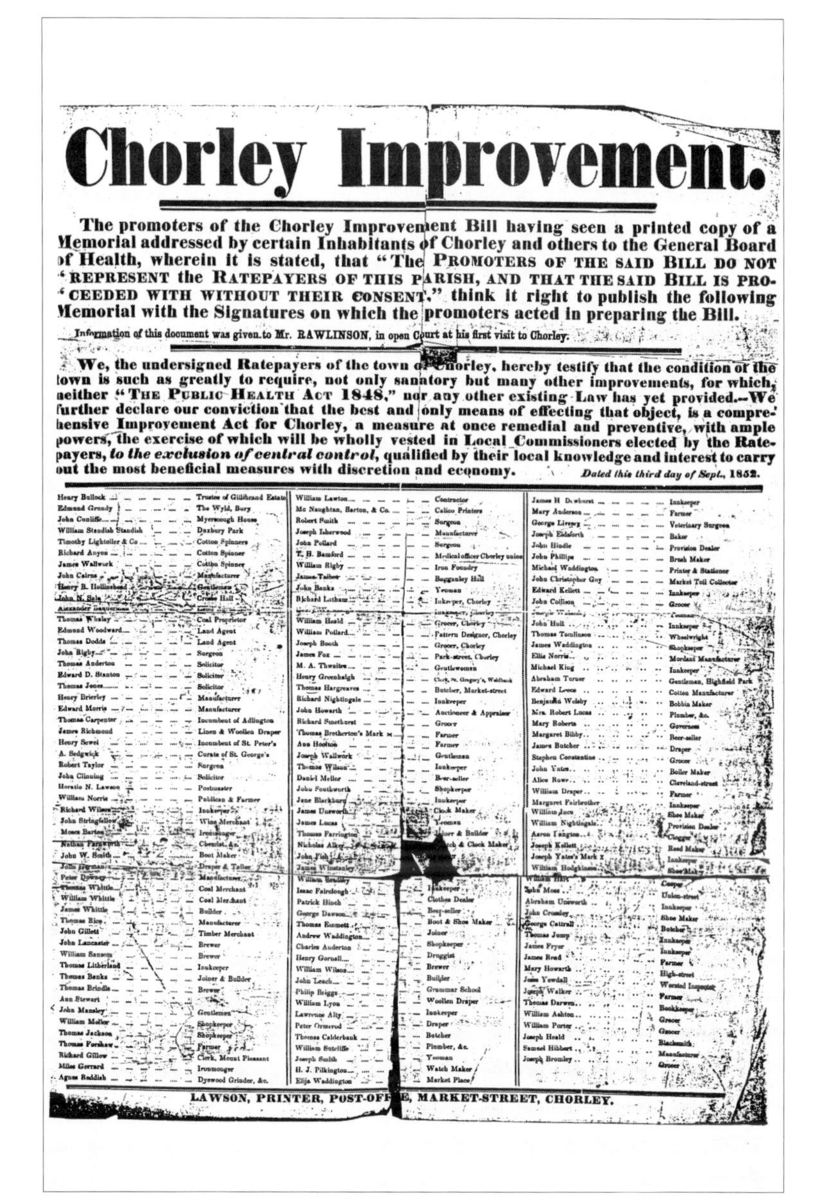

Chorley Improvement.

The promoters of the Chorley Improvement Bill having seen a printed copy of a Memorial addressed by certain Inhabitants of Chorley and others to the General Board of Health, wherein it is stated, that "THE PROMOTERS OF THE SAID BILL DO NOT "REPRESENT the RATEPAYERS OF THIS PARISH, AND THAT THE SAID BILL IS PRO-"CEEDED WITH WITHOUT THEIR CONSENT," think it right to publish the following Memorial with the Signatures on which the promoters acted in preparing the Bill.

Information of this document was given to Mr. RAWLINSON, in open Court at his first visit to Chorley.

We, the undersigned Ratepayers of the town of Chorley, hereby testify that the condition of the town is such as greatly to require, not only sanatory but many other improvements, for which, neither "THE PUBLIC HEALTH ACT 1848," nor any other existing Law has yet provided.—We further declare our conviction that the best and only means of effecting that object, is a comprehensive Improvement Act for Chorley, a measure at once remedial and preventive, with ample powers, the exercise of which will be wholly vested in Local Commissioners elected by the Ratepayers, *to the exclusion of central control*, qualified by their local knowledge and interest to carry out the most beneficial measures with discretion and economy.

Dated this third day of Sept., 1852.

Henry Bullock	Trustee of Gillibrand Estate
Edmund Grundy	The Wyld, Bury
John Cunliffe	Myerscough House
William Standish Standish	Duxbury Park
Timothy Lightoller & Co	Cotton Spinners
Richard Anyon	Cotton Spinner
James Wallwork	Cotton Spinner
John Cairns	Manufacturer
Henry B. Hollinshead	Gentleman
John N. Sale	Crosse Hall
Alexander [illegible]	[illegible]
Thomas Whaley	Coal Proprietor
Edmund Woodward	Land Agent
Thomas Dodds	Land Agent
John Rigby	Surgeon
Thomas Anderton	Solicitor
Edward D. Stanton	Solicitor
Thomas Jones	Solicitor
Henry Brierley	Manufacturer
Edward Morris	Manufacturer
Thomas Carpenter	Incumbent of Adlington
James Richmond	Linen & Woollen Draper
Henry Sewel	Incumbent of St. Peter's
A. Sedgwick	Curate of St. George's
Robert Taylor	Surgeon
John Clinning	Solicitor
Horatio N. Lawson	Postmaster
William Norris	Publican & Farmer
Richard Wilson	Innkeeper
John Stringfellow	Wine Merchant
Moses Barton	Ironmonger
Nathan Farnworth	Chemist, &c.
John W. Smith	Boot Maker
John [illegible]	Draper & Tailor
Peter Downey	Manufacturer
Thomas Whittle	Coal Merchant
William Whittle	Coal Merchant
James Whittle	Builder
Thomas Rice	Manufacturer
John Gillett	Timber Merchant
John Lancaster	Brewer
William Sanson	Brewer
Thomas Litherland	Innkeeper
Thomas Banks	Joiner & Builder
Thomas Brindle	Brewer
Ann Stewart	[illegible]
John Mansley	Gentleman
William Mellor	Shopkeeper
Thomas Jackson	Shopkeeper
Thomas Forshaw	Farmer
Richard Gillow	Clerk, Mount Pleasant
Miles Gerrard	Ironmonger
Agnes Reddish	Dyewood Grinder, &c.

William Lawton	Contractor
Mc Naughtan, Barton, & Co.	Calico Printers
Robert Smith	Surgeon
Joseph Isherwood	Manufacturer
John Pollard	Surgeon
T. B. Bamford	Medical officer Chorley union
William Rigby	Iron Foundry
James Talbot	Bagganley Hall
John Banks	Yeoman
Richard Latham	Innkeeper, Chorley
[illegible]	Innkeeper, Chorley
William Heald	Grocer, Chorley
William Pollard	Pattern Designer, Chorley
Joseph Booth	Grocer, Chorley
James Fox	Park-street, Chorley
M. A. Thwaites	Gentlewoman
Henry Greenhalgh	Clerk, St. Gregory's, Weldbank
Thomas Hargreaves	Butcher, Market-street
Richard Nightingale	Innkeeper
John Howarth	Auctioneer & Appraiser
Richard Smethurst	Grocer
Thomas Bretherton's Mark ×	Farmer
Ann Hoolton	Farmer
Joseph Wallwork	Gentleman
Thomas Wilson	Innkeeper
Daniel Mellor	Beer-seller
John Southworth	Shopkeeper
Jane Blackburn	Innkeeper
James Unsworth	Clock Maker
James Lucas	Yeoman
Thomas Farrington	Joiner & Builder
Nicholas Alker	Watch & Clock Maker
John Fish	[illegible]
James Winstanley	[illegible]
William Bradley	[illegible]
Isaac Fairclough	Innkeeper
Patrick Hinch	Clothes Dealer
George Dawson	Beer-seller
Thomas Emmett	Boot & Shoe Maker
Andrew Waddington	Joiner
Charles Anderton	Shopkeeper
Henry Gornall	Druggist
William Wilson	Brewer
John Leach	Builder
Philip Briggs	Grammar School
William Lyon	Woollen Draper
Lawrence Alty	Innkeeper
Peter Ormerod	Draper
Thomas Calderbank	Butcher
William Sutcliffe	Plumber, &c.
Joseph Smith	Yeoman
H. J. Pilkington	Watch Maker
Elija Waddington	Market Place

James H. Dewhurst	Innkeeper
Mary Anderson	Farmer
George Livesey	Veterinary Surgeon
Joseph Eidsforth	Baker
John Hindle	Provision Dealer
John Phillips	Brush Maker
Michael Waddington	Printer & Stationer
John Christopher Guy	Market Toll Collector
Edward Kellett	Innkeeper
John Collison	Grocer
[illegible]	Yeoman
John Hull	Innkeeper
Thomas Tomlinson	Wheelwright
James Waddington	Shopkeeper
Ellis Norris	Mordant Manufacturer
Michael King	Innkeeper
Abraham Turner	Gentleman, Highfield Park
Edward Leece	Cotton Manufacturer
Benjamin Welsby	Bobbin Maker
Mrs. Robert Lucas	Plumber, &c.
Mary Roberts	Governess
Margaret Bibby	Beer-seller
James Butcher	Draper
Stephen Constantine	Grocer
John Yates	Boiler Maker
Alice Rowe	Cleveland-street
William Draper	Farmer
Margaret Fairbrother	Innkeeper
William Juce	Shoe Maker
William Nightingale	Provision Dealer
Aaron Tangton	Clogger
Joseph Kellett	Reed Maker
Joseph Yates's Mark ×	Innkeeper
William Hodgkinson	Shoe Maker
William [illegible]	Cooper
John Moss	Union-street
Abraham Unsworth	Innkeeper
John Cromley	Shoe Maker
George Cattrall	Butcher
Thomas Jump	Innkeeper
James Fryer	Innkeeper
James Read	Farmer
Mary Howarth	High-street
Jesse Yewdall	Worsted Inspector
Joseph Walker	Farmer
Thomas Darwen	Bookkeeper
William Ashton	Grocer
William Porter	Grocer
Joseph Heald	Blacksmith
Samuel Hibbert	Manufacturer
Joseph Bromley	Grocer

LAWSON, PRINTER, POST-OFFICE, MARKET-STREET, CHORLEY.

The Chorley Improvement Act of 1853 had a stormy passage. This poster, dated 3 September 1852, bore the names of all the townspeople who actively supported the Bill. They range from cotton merchants and the landed gentry to clergymen and individual townspeople. [Lancashire County Library]

verdict, devastating Club Street (or Standish Street), as well as the Duke of York area. That November cholera added to the agony.

The Chorley Improvement Act, passed in 1853, resulted in the establishment of an Improvement Commission, made up of twenty members, one-third retiring each year. The franchise was limited: voters had to be owners of property with a rateable value of £6 annually. Voting took place at the town hall on one afternoon in July – elections were thus select gatherings. The commissioners were usually from the new elite, rather than the old land owning gentry. The presence of the Lightollers, Healds and Smethursts showed that the captains of industry and commerce were now at the wheel and it has been said that their decisions reflected their own self-interest and a penny-pinching pursuit of expedient solutions. Two enduring relics of their tenure still survive; the town hall of 1879 and the sewage and drainage improvements of the 1850s. Rawlinson, no less, instigated the latter works, following his separate report on sewerage and drainage, published in 1857.[12] One feature, his brick sewers, egg-shaped in section, was uncovered in recent years in Market Street. These sewers, built at the end of the 1850s, still functioned and stood up to the pounding of decades of motor traffic. Slowly the town's health improved due to these efforts.

Near the end of the Improvement Commission's life the town hall was completed. It was perhaps a curious choice for the commission, given its dislike of expense. In 1870, when the Gillibrand Arms and parts of the Fazakerley estate were on the market the commission bought them up, ostensibly to widen access to St Thomas's Road and the town's green. 1871 brought a new Improvement Act and in 1872, when there was said to be public demand for a large public hall for concerts, theatre and public meetings of up to 1900 people, the town hall project assumed a new prestige and importance. Plans were invited and sixty submitted. Many involved shopping arcades, ornamental gardens and offices. Ladds and Powell of London were eventually chosen as architects, with a target cost of £14,000. The site was cleared, contracts were issued in 1874, and the corner stone laid in 1875 but building took four years. The Italianate design incorporated the clock tower (120 feet high) based on a Venetian campanile. The cellars contained a butter market, entered from Meal-house Lane, and there was also a great public hall, 104 feet long. Offices for the staff took up the remainder, with rooms for the political parties and freemasons.

When the town hall was officially opened in August 1879 the day was a public holiday; sunny weather smiled on the procession through the town, led by the artillery band and 6,500 medals to commemorate the day were presented to schoolchildren.

The public hall fulfilled expectations. Travelling theatre groups, political meetings, musical concerts, First World War recruiting drives, women's suffrage, even a rally of Sir Oswald Mosley's Fascist Blackshirts in 1935 – all were held there.

Long before it became a borough in 1881 Chorley had several 'mayors'. Good-natured, tongue-in-cheek amusements, and usually staged in a particular pub these concluded in the election of mock officials. April 1869 saw the standing-down of William Brindle, alias Pummell, 'mayor' of Botany Bay for five years. The 'elections' featured two rival candidates; processions, party colours and grandiose speeches, with plenty of refreshments to add to the fun. In 1875 there were two of these elections, held between tacklers, one at Crosse Hall in October and a second at Weldbank in November. Two aspects of these events are noteworthy: the first is that each took place in a district which had taken on a distinct community identity; the second is the mocking of the limited suffrage under the Improvement Commission.

The latter issue is certainly important. There was growing popular agitation for democracy, and the time was ripe to turn away from the benevolent paternalism of the commission.

From May 1880, meetings, both public and private, thrashed out the question of incorporation; it turned into an undignified squabble. An often-quoted anomaly was that some ratepayers had six votes on the strength of rateable values, and some even more but an estimated 1,656 householders had no votes at all! A petition to the Improvement Commission resulted from one public meeting, though it was soon rejected. A second town's meeting was called, giving unanimous approval to the petition, but still the Commission would not bow to public opinion. In the end an independent petition, signed by 2,362 people was sent to the Queen, begging that Chorley might be incorporated. The government held a public inquiry. Having heard a mass of detailed, often conflicting evidence, the inspector ruled in favour of the petition.

For the second time in its long history Chorley became a borough. The 1881 census showed the population had reached 19,478, an increase of 3,500 on 1871. By the new royal charter there were to be four wards, eight aldermen and twenty-four councillors in all. Richard Jackson was appointed the first town clerk, while the honour of becoming the first mayor fell to Augustus William Smethurst of Rookwood, a cotton manufacturer, long established in Chorley, of comfortable means, and an active supporter of the incorporation. A Liberal and Anglican, he was also said to be

Construction work under way on Brownley's Victoria Arcade dates this photograph to 1893. The open aspect of the Market Place, showing few covered stalls, looks unfamiliar, as does the rural vista beyond the rooftops of St Laurence's. [Lancashire County Library]

tolerant on religious issues and generous to the needy. Along with the borough Charter the town acquired a handsome coat of arms, incorporating the cornflowers of the Chorley family's coat of arms, yet the motto chosen excited much curiosity: "Beware" had no precedent in local life and seemed forbidding. The Latin tag "proposite tenax", used by the Chorleys, was later adopted by the grammar school, and in 1922 Alderman Fearnhead declared that a solution to the continuing puzzlement should see the motto amended to Be aware, the form later adopted in the 1980s.

New matters came to the fore, as Chorley Corporation began its work. The public library was opened in 1899, Edward McKnight being the town's first librarian. Sewage disposal works were constructed in 1894 at a cost of £20,000, and the destructor works in 1904. In the year following the First World War and up to 1936 the Chorley Corporation built 540 houses as rented council property, while 597 houses were built by private means.

Fire-fighting had been an issue tackled by the Improvement Commission, with the Corporation Yard area behind the Big Lamp as their depot. New buildings were erected in 1900. Gas lighting, begun by a private company in 1819, had grown appreciably in the last century. Two hundred street lamps lit the town in 1854; in 1871 the plant was bought by the Improvement Commission and a number of technical advances followed. A new retort house was built in 1875, and a gas holder with a capacity of 750,000 cubic feet of gas was erected in Bengal Street in 1897–8.

In 1932 the corporation acquired Duxbury Hall, with 540 acres of parkland and woodland. The hall was intended to be a social centre, with plans to develop housing for the parkland.

In 1894 an inquiry was held on the question of forming a rural district council for the Chorley area. Elections were held in December of that year, the first offices being in High Street, though a move was made in 1936 to Gillibrand Street in the old hospital building. Three urban district councils came into existence in 1895, for Adlington, Croston and Withnell. The framework was now fixed for a pattern of local government provision which served the Chorley area until the reorganisation of the whole structure of local government was carried out in the early 1970s. The new Chorley District Council began its work on 1 April 1974.

Education in Chorley

Chorley Grammar School was the earliest school in the town (1611), though its intake was limited to boys (and few of them). The dame schools, of the type funded by the Crompton family, were more open and a range of private schools formed an important part of education provision until about 1900. References to schools seldom appear before 1800 although the Papists List of 1766 names Hannah Edgar (40) as a schoolmistress. The *Blackburn Mail* in 1795 printed an advertisement for a schoolmaster: 'a Master who is of the Church of England, properly qualified to teach

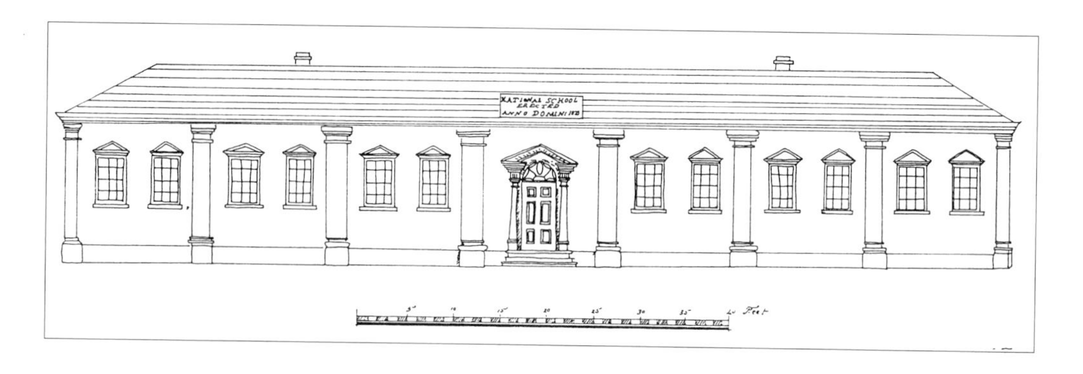

Edward Tootell's drawing of St George's National School of 1825, complete with a truncated classical façade for the old school which was situated at the Big Lamp. [Redrawn by the author]

children to read, cast accounts and Grammar. The school is not free – the customary fees and salary due to the School may be known by application to the Revd Oliver Cooper . . . of Chorley'.[13]

The long running friction between Chorley and the mother church at Croston had embraced the grammar school as well as the chapel. When the curate resigned in 1791 the Rector of Croston threatened to send 'an unintelligible Welshman' in his place, while a 1793 directory lists Oliver Holding as a teacher of classics and mathematics. Four years later the school was in a doldrums, having only six pupils. In that year Henry Brierley, Curate of Euxton, took over as master. By 1824 the school had sixty pupils and there was an emphasis on teaching commercial subjects rather than classics. During the winter of 1823–4 the old building in the churchyard was taken down, the tithe-barn demolished and a new school built. Now encased in the Union Street boundary wall of the church is the school's date stone, rescued when the old building was in its turn demolished in 1933.

For many children and adults the main opportunity for learning the basics of the 'three Rs' was the Sunday School – in 1824 1039 children had free places, while there were 120 day pupils at the charity school in Bengal Street. The adult school, started in 1817 but closed in 1825. For a time branch schools were opened at White Coppice and Heath Charnock. The charity school built a schoolhouse and £600 was raised in 1824 to aid this. A school at Weld Bank for parishioners of St Gregory's was started in 1818 and soon thrived. James Kirkley was schoolmaster here in 1824. In Park Road, Revd William Tate ran a school aided by the Cromptons. In St Thomas's Square James Stevenson kept a small private school, as did James Leach for Catholic pupils in Market Street.

By the late 1820s more schools were springing up. Henrietta Brierley's 'ladies boarding school' was in Park Road, Mrs Yates' ladies' day school in Water Street. The better-off had more choice: William Talbot of Bagganley Hall was one of the pupils at Revd Brierley's school from 3 August 1818, as his father recorded: 'My Son William began to go to school to Mr Brierley to lern to reed at Chorley this day'. The boy moved on to Wigan in 1821, learning reading and writing from Mr Harrison, and then to Mr Price at Standish for thirty guineas a year. A few extras arrived

Important to Parents.

MORAL AND INTELLECTUAL TRAINING.

The Inhabitants of CHORLEY and the Neighbourhood are respectfully informed

THAT

DAY SCHOOLS

FOR BOYS AND GIRLS,

Will be opened in the SCHOOL ROOMS of

THE ST. GEORGE'S-STREET CHAPEL,

On TUESDAY, JULY 3rd, 1849.

The School Committee are happy to inform the Public that with the view of rendering the Schools worthy of support and confidence, they have secured the services of a

MASTER AND MISTRESS FROM LONDON,

Of first-rate ability, and of considerable experience in the art of Instruction.

These Schools are intended to impart a superior English Education, Religious in its influence, *but without any sectarian bias.*

The Course of Instruction will comprise Spelling, Reading, Writing, Slate and Mental Arithmetic, Book-keeping, Land-Surveying, Geometry, Algebra, the Elements of Natural Philosophy, Drawing, English Grammar, Etymology, Composition, History, Geography, Natural History, Astronomy; in addition to which the GIRLS will be taught Plain and Fancy Needle-work, and Vocal Music.

THE TERMS--

Payable in advance (either weekly or quarterly) will range from *two-pence* to *six-pence per week!* A small additional charge will be made for Instruction in *Greek, Latin, French,* or *German.*

N. B.—Parents wishing their Children to attend, are requested to make early application to MR. C. MAYSON, *Park Road;* to MR. JOHN HODGKINSON, *High Street;* or to MR. BURROWS, the Master, who will attend at the *School-Room* from Nine to Twelve o'Clock each day, to afford any information that may be desired.

THOS. WATTS, Chairman.

HOUGHTON, PRINTER, CHORLEY.

Although the introduction of state education had to wait until the 1870 Education Act, a number of local initiatives from 1817 onwards saw several private schools open, of which this is an example. [Lancashire County Library]

via the housekeeper – a silver spoon, a pair of shoes, a jacket and waistcoat and four nightcaps. In 1830 he was apprenticed to Mr Welch at Wrightington to learn the science of surveying.

Many boys and girls were taught in one-room establishments. A future mayor, J. Sharples, learned his basics at Mrs Thomas Smith's on the Duke in the 1860s, while Councillor Leach was taught by Bobby Johnson at his cellar in Bolton Street.

In 1825 St George's National School was built at the junction of Pall Mall and Bolton Street. The National Society provided £200 of its costs, and other money came from local charity. Lessons were limited at first – reading, writing and arithmetic for all, with sewing and knitting as extras for the girls. Robinson's 1835 directory lists sixteen schools. Denominational schools still had a key role: one Unitarian school was run by Maria Clark in Park Street (1851) and Chapel Street Catholic Chapel had a school in the same year. In 1844 the grammar school had seventy pupils on its books.

The handsome Parochial School in Parker Street was opened in 1835 on land given by Robert Townley Parker. Here, too, charitable funds helped to defray the costs. A room in Water Street was taken over for teaching adults. One of the pupils at the Parochial School was Edward Carter, born in 1853: 'The headmaster i thoose days weer a chap named Mester Ivans, and he weer a Kriceter, and we used to ged hauf a day every wick to watch um practice. I can remember me an' my brother geddin' a new suit apiece, and when we went to schoo in um they coad us Workhouse Lads.'[14] The workhouse committee had decided as early as 1826 to pay 1d each week for each child to attend the denominational school of their affiliation.

Church schools increased in number: St Mary's on Mount Pleasant from the 1850s (infant school 1860); St Peter's (1861), St James' (1873), Heapey Road St Mark's (1895); Sacred Heart (1891), All Saints (1900), St Joseph's in Harpers Lane (1914). Hollinshead Street Sunday School opened in 1836. In the new century the first council school opened at Duke Street in 1915, followed by Highfield (1923). Market Street Wesleyan Methodist School was condemned in 1911 and closed 1915. Much later came the boom in the second half of the century: a new school for St George's (1974), Gillibrand CPS (1974), St Laurence's (1969) and several new secondary schools: Parklands, formerly the Grammar School (1962), St Alban's (later Albany) in 1960, Southlands (1956), St Hilda's (1963), St Augustine's (1959) and St Michael's (1965).

No establishment changed so much as the grammar school. In spite of the tribulations of the early 1860s the churchyard school was abandoned in favour of a new school in Queens Road, once more on Townley-Parker land. The Trustee Saving Bank's predecessor took over the old school from 1868. There were eighty pupils in 1886. One recollection of this era talks of the boys leaving school to pester Old Todger, a disreputable old character who spent much of his life in the stocks. The teachers meanwhile passed into legend: one, Mr Cheetham, was noted for strictness and immortalised in rhyme.

Lord have mercy upon us,
And keep old Cheetham from us.

A good picture of the late Victorian schools is given in the school attendance officer's report for 1893–4, in which he noted the number of families leaving the town after the completion of the Thirlmere Aqueduct.

From November 1892 to September 1894, he said, 440 children had gone to work as half-timers.

School Attendance, 1893–4

	Name of school	On registers	Average	Accommodation
1.	Heapey Institute	107	89	166
2.	St Peter's	341	267	394
3.	Parochial	551	429	792
4.	St Mary's	636	519	761
5.	Wesleyan	541	389	763
6.	St George's	1062	763	1000
7.	St Gregory's	276	214	280
8.	Sacred Heart	557	451	650
9.	St James'	735	502	761
10.	Hollinshead St.	441	357	550
11.	Private Schools	200	150	—
	Totals	5447	4130	6117

It would have been revealing to hear his comments about the disparity between the register figure and actual attendances.

Relatively little is said nowadays about the part played in education by Sir Henry F. Hibbert (1850–1927). He served on the town council, the county council (from 1891) and was MP for Chorley from 1913 to 1918. Education was dear to his heart – and especially sport, for as a boy he had been severely ill and regained his health partly through rigorous sporting activity. He had a key role in the 1902 Education Act and was knighted for his education work in 1903.

Hibbert was chairman of the County Council Education Committee in 1903 and, despite his resignation from the Technical School Committee, he was able to press for Chorley to be given a new secondary school. Long before 1900 forward thinking politicians realised that the key to Britain's prosperity and standing would be an education system across all social classes with better technical education. Hibbert had been a pupil in one local technical class and in 1885 started the Gilchrist lectures in the town hall. The scheme succeeded where the Mechanics Institute had failed. Evening classes in 'scientific and technical subjects' were held in the old butter market, then in the board room in High Street, later moved to the old drill shed in St George's Street. The technological school was popular with students: in 1887–8 there were 120, in 1888–9 150, in 1890–1 372. Hibbert next tried unsuccessfully to get the council to adopt the Technical

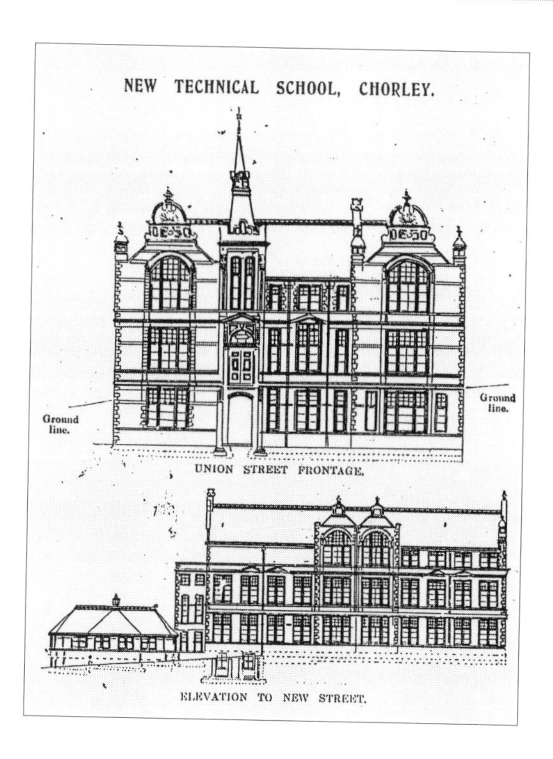

The present location for Chorley's central library started life as a technical school in 1906, with facilities for secondary and technical education. [Lancashire County Library]

Instruction Act. By the 1890s the school was housed in the Old Post Office building at the corner of the Market Square, now with 935 students.

After much wrangling the county council devolved power to Chorley Borough Education Committee, under the 1902 Act. The original plan for a technical institute in Union Street was amended to a combination of secondary and technical school. When the building opened in 1906, thirty boys from the old grammar school moved across from the Queens Road site.

The new building was a fine Edwardian achievement. Second only to the town hall in splendour it cost £12,500, together with £750 for the land which was bought from Colonel Silvester. Its facilities and curriculum included a weaving shed in miniature, cookery classes, cotton spinning, plumbing instruction, physics, chemistry, art classes – a broader curriculum than any taught before in Chorley and one which was open to girls as well as boys. The grammar school was managed by a board of trustees from the 1890s until 1905 when Chorley Education Authority assumed responsibility. In 1907 the school moved to Union Street, where it stayed until April 1962.

A contemporary technical centre for the 1890s was the Chorley Polytechnic Ltd., situated in the old mill at the corner of Fellery Street and Hollinshead Street. Originally built in 1762 this was a commercial school, modelled on the London Polytechnic, with fixed principles – it was non-political, non-sectarian, and served for the instruction of the people and moral and physical development. For amusement, billiards, chess and newspapers were provided. One hundred and twenty members were enrolled by November 1892, including A. G. Leigh, R. T. Ditchfield, the rector and several councillors.

Little Ireland

It was inevitable that Lancashire was usually the first contact for Irishmen emigrating from their homeland. Even before the famine of the 1840s emigration was common, and by the 1860s most Lancashire towns had an Irish community. Chorley's Irish area was centred on Standish Street, nicknamed 'Little Ireland' or 'Club Street' in local folklore. Before 1800 the district was farmland, but in 1802 Robert Lightoller and William Anderton, cotton spinners, rented a plot of land to build a cotton mill.

This 'Old Mill', completed in 1807, was mentioned in William Hall's account of the spinners' dispute of 1826. Burned down in 1829 and rebuilt on the same site, it was one of two mills owned by the Lightoller family.

In the lee of the mill, cottages were built, with courts and entries off Standish Street – Sizehouse Entry, Engine Yard, Preston's Yard and Thistleton's Yard. The cottages were not all owned by the mill; the valuation list of 1826 shows thirteen cottages owned by the Lightollers, while scores more were owned by individuals in groups of ten or less. The same picture emerges for 1863 when the family owned seventeen properties, Messrs Collyer and Ormerod fifteen, with others in the same proportion as in 1826. Not far away a triangle of properties was erected in 1808, perhaps for speculation investment, in Bolton Road. This 'club' principle may account for Standish Street's nickname. In time cottages, shops, pubs all clustered around the mill, the earliest in this part of Chorley.

What evidence is there for Irishmen in Chorley? The 1841 census gives the first clue to a sizeable, transient group when 2,000 of the 13,139 population were described as labourers working on the Bolton to Preston railway. After the late 1840s more Irish people arrived, victims of the Potato Famine. Chorley's relieving officer said in 1848 that he had given relief to 2,338 'vagrants' in six months alone: 'a great majority of these vagrants consist of Irish men, women and children wandering about as they say in search of work – tramping begging and imposting'. His answer was to put families into lodging houses in Chorley, each individual costing the ratepayer 2d a night.

The 1851 census gives us a clearer picture – just under 50 per cent of all families in Standish Street were Irish. The majority of adult males are shown as farm labourers, probably echoing their last occupation.

One man, Patrick Higgins, living in nearby Albion Street, had eleven people resident in his house, all born in Ireland, yet by 1861 all had moved away.[15]

Patrick Higgins	Head	Mar.	45	Ag. Labourer	Ireland
Sarah Higgins	Wife	Mar.	34	Care of house	ditto
John Higgins	Son		16	Ag. Labourer	ditto
Patrick Higgins	Son		15	ditto	ditto
Ann Higgins	Daughter		10	Factory worker	ditto
Thomas Higgins	Son		8	School	ditto
Mary Higgins	Daughter		6	School	ditto
Honora McDonald	Lodger		60	Care after family	ditto
Bridget McDonald	ditto		25	Hawker of small ware	ditto
Ellen McDonald	ditto		16	Factory worker	ditto
John McDonald	ditto		15	Labourer	ditto

The 1871 census shows eighty-four Irish families in Standish Street, thirteen of them running lodging houses though many more had up to three boarders. The question of lodging houses was a vexed one. When Robert Rawlinson's report on Chorley's health appeared in 1853 lodging houses were a current issue after the passing of the Common Lodging Houses Act. One proprietor in Standish Street thought it a bad law, limiting the number of lodgers: 'I am sometimes obliged to separate families, because I may not put all the children into the same bed as their parents'. A police officer said that the charge for half a bed was between 2d and 3d a night.

The report also records water supply and quality, since Standish Street had a private pump which cost 1d per week to use. Whether this contributed to the area's poor health and lack of resistance to disease is not clear. The inspector of nuisances for the town described how one privy might be used by six or more households. Paths, alleys and passageways were disfigured with human filth. He attributed this 'to the dirty habits of the Irish.' Rawlinson, however, disagreed with his assertion.

Later censuses show that the sons and daughters of the original settlers were as likely to be mill workers as their English contemporaries. Hugh Fallon, for example, a boy of nine, was killed in 1869 when he fell from a hoist at Nixon & Killick's Mill. Skilled occupations began to appear among the jobs described.

Attitudes towards the Irish community in Chorley and elsewhere were often hostile. There were no precedents for the assimilation of a large group of newcomers who spoke a different dialect, were predominantly Roman Catholic and who might be conspiring to do violence for political reasons. Riots occurred in 1850 and 1864 in Standish Street, although these had no obvious political background. Nevertheless, the shooting of Sergeant Brett by Fenians at Manchester in 1867 alerted the authorities to the danger of armed Irishmen plotting rebellion. The Irish Republican Brotherhood was active in Lancashire and popular opinion seems to have grown more frenzied. In December 1867 Richard Wood was arrested at Church Brow for threats to blow up the Irish – he was locked up for his own safety. Writing in 1865 Arnold said that 'a large majority of the pauper class are Irish, for whom the native population of Lancashire has no very great esteem'.

In Chorley the issue boiled up in November 1868. A parliamentary by-election was held for West Lancashire, contested by Lord Stanley, Lord Hartington and Patten. Public interest was heightened because of an extension of the franchise, giving more men than ever the vote. Excitement was intense on election day. The Royal Oak was the headquarters of the Tories, the Red Lion that of the Liberals. Hundreds of people were on the streets, for the mills were closed. A rumour went round that a large gang of navvies and Irishmen were planning to cause a disturbance. The *Chorley Standard* reporter said that this proved false: 'So far as we have observed, the Irishmen were very well conducted, and deserve much praise'.

At about 3 p.m. a mob of three hundred young men, wearing orange and blue favours, stormed into Standish Street from Market Street, where they rained bricks and stones on the houses there. Two cottages especially were badly damaged. In retaliation a body of Irishmen turned out to protect their homes. By this time the police, reinforced to thirty because of the election, had four officers tackle the mob. The ringleader was arrested and the remainder retreated. Thomas Wilcocks, recalling the election, in 1929, described how the disputes in Market Street escalated. Superintendent Bentham formed his constables into four ranks across Market Street and then armed with cutlasses, the police advanced down the street until the crowd was dispersed. It was rare for the Riot Act to be proclaimed in Chorley, but it was then read from the Wheatsheaf Hotel. The election was won by Stanley.

In July 1869 there was another disturbance, when a crowd taunted Irish families with jeers and waved orange and blue ribbons. The police controlled the incident but the colours remind us that the Orange Order was very active in Chorley in the last century. Indeed, Dr Frank Neal has pointed out that the Sylvester family of Chorcliffe House were important leaders of the national movement.

In 1863 the Association of Loyal Orangemen of Chorley met for a supper at the Eagle and Child Inn. This was reported as a social gathering with patriotic and laudable aims, but thereafter reports on the Order vary in style.

One meeting at the Townley Arms in 1876 was preceded by a parade with the artillery band. On one banner was the image of King William III, on another Revd George Marsh (the Protestant martyr). Orangemen carried drawn swords and provocatively marched past Standish Street. Ceremonial parading around Standish Street by the Order became an institution. In 1889 the Orangemen were celebrating the bicentenary of the Battle of the Boyne; Chorley's parade comprised 450 people, men, women and children all taking part. On this occasion the Orange Order were praised for their tolerance in facing angry women in Club Street who jeered them and waved green ribbons to taunt them. It may be that the stern instruction to youngsters, even in this century, to stay away from Club Street, stems from old conflicts in Little Ireland begun in the 1840s.

Standish Street had a notorious beerhouse, the Hare and Hounds: popular legend claimed that its nickname, the War Office was due to the frequency of drunken riots there. That attribution has been challenged in 1993 – the real background to this name being the activities of Seamus Meakin, who assisted ex-servicemen to claim their pension rights during and after the First World War. The pub was his base – hence Seamus' War Office.

As time passed the character of Standish Street changed, the old issues blurred. The second and third generation Irish became entirely assimilated into Chorley's life, making as positive a mark on the community as the many other immigrants who were drawn here over the last century.

Cellar dwellings

The quality of Chorley's housing of the last century was a barometer of wealth and rank. Large, comfortable and individual houses were built in Park Road in the 1820s, and others along Southport Road from the 1890s for prosperous mill owners and merchants. At the other extreme the artisan class was housed in characteristic rows of redbrick, slate-roofed housing, archetypical of Lancashire. Some people still lived in the thatched, single-storey cottages found in the town centre as late as the 1880s. These cottages, lacking glazed windows, cold, damp and unhealthy, could be seen in Market Street, Back Mount, the top of High Street and Town's End. Yet even these were considered better than the cellar dwellings at the bottom of the social heap.

How and why these developed is a matter for speculation. Some were undoubtedly former handloom weaving cellars, where the dampness of earth floors assisted the working of the cotton. Once the need for weaving space was past, a 'room to let' could be turned to financial advantage.

A valuation list for 1827 shows 211 cellars though only seventy-nine were occupied then. They were not concentrated, but spread across twenty-nine locations in Chorley; Water Street had forty-four cellars, Knowley twenty, Market Street eighteen and Bolton Street twelve.

The best surviving examples are found in Parker Street and in Chapel Street (opposite St Georges). The latter show one flight of stone steps leading to the 'house', and a separate flight down to the cellars which were used for weaving in the 1840s. A similar system was seen in Bolton Street, all the cellars 'up t'Duke to the Albion' being weavers cottages in the

A rare photograph of the 'up-steps' cottages at the junction of Eaves Lane and Harper Lane. The old parish club belonging to St Peter's stands alongside the Talbot Arms, which sold the noted ales of Mercer's Brewery. [Lancashire County Library]

1860s, while in Water Street William Crook still plied his trade as late as 1881. Occasionally cellars were used for other trades. Peter Turner, for example, offered his cellar for let in 1886, 'with a good clogging connection'.

Robert Rawlinson first questioned the health record of the cellars. His 1853 report said,

> in these the evils of defective ventilation and imperfect drainage are peculiarly oppressive. In several cellars the poor people have placed bricks under the feet of their beds to raise them off the damp floor.

The rents were cheap (1s 6d per week) but a decade later the Improvement Commission resolved to clear them away. Under the provisions of the Chorley Improvement Act, cellar landlords had to obtain a certificate of worthiness from Dr Rigby, Medical Officer of Health, or cease to let the cellars. A deadline was set for December 1867, which allowed time for opposition. An impassioned opposition from some of the landlords claimed that their income from rents was low and they were living in near poverty themselves. Mrs Yates claimed in December 1866 to receive only 2/6 per week from rents.

This can be compared with the earlier position of the Waterloo Mills, which had forty tied cottages in the 1840s and whose cellar rent book for 1842 shows that individuals paid one shilling, three or four shillings for their cellars under their terms of employment with the mill.

In 1866 there were 173 occupied cellars in Chorley, and twenty-nine unoccupied. In them lived 298 people, the worst had nine people living in one room. Dr Rigby pursued the health factor and was attacked in the press for his pains. 'Chancery' said that no cellar dwelling was as unhealthy as Cannon Street, but Dr Rigby in the *Standard* for May 1867, defended his assertion that Chorley's death rate was the highest in England.

The campaign did succeed. Cellar dwellings were phased out, but it was slow progress: a report to the town council in 1908 said that twenty-nine cellar dwellings were still in existence, 'most of them unoccupied', though this may mean that they were used other than for housing. Dampness, inadequate light and ventilation, cramped conditions, lack of water – all meant that their survival was indefensible.

The railway comes to town

Among the onlookers at the celebrated trials for locomotives which took place in 1829 at Rainhill were two men who played an active role in bringing railways to Chorley: Richard Smethurst (of North Street Mills) and John Hargreaves of Preston (a carrier and agent). Later, when Stephenson was working on the line across Chat Moss, Smethurst and a number of interested colleagues approached him to build a line from Bolton to Preston. Pleading pressure of work, Stephenson declined but recommended a surveyor named Rastrick who carried out preliminary

Chorley railway station in a famous print from the 1880s. The bridge seen here was later replaced by the subway which is still in use today. It has been said that the town's motto 'Beware' was taken from the sign 'Beware of the Trains' displayed on the gates of the level crossing. [Lancashire County Library]

work on a possible line. He learned that a rival line, surveyed by Vignoles, would run north from Newton-le-Willows to Wigan and ultimately to Preston. Hargreaves' local knowledge was intended to help Rastrick but the first route chosen was very different from the final choice. Crossing the Yarrow at Duxbury it would have gone across the Lighthurst farm, and swung west to meet Pall Mall at the Burgh Colliery line. Beyond Pall Mall the line would have gone across Gillibrand Fields and Southport Road before passing through Astley Park to join the Preston line at Farington.

Smethurst reputedly scotched the plan when he pointed out that Lady Hoghton and Sir Frank Standish would not see their estates spoiled, nor could the company afford the compensation. The mill owner advised a simpler and cheaper line north from the Yarrow, crossing Harpers Lane and swinging west from Hartwood. Vignoles, meanwhile, aimed to get the Newton–Wigan line to Preston first and negotiated for a station site. In 1830 Rastrick's survey was complete, involving a line close to the present route but going across Lyons Lane at a higher level than the route as built. His efforts were wasted, as the Parliamentary committee turned down the line. In 1834 Vignoles considered a line off his Wigan-Preston line, to run from Euxton to a terminus at Chorley. This plan would also have meant disrupting the tranquillity of Astley Park.

Two years later Rastrick returned, to survey a line from Chorley through Whittle to Preston using the Old Tram Road at its northern end. Despite receiving approval from Parliament this was never built, as it was more expensive than the ultimate choice. The Bolton and Preston Railway Company would not give up. In 1838 Rastrick and Vignoles negotiated further use of the section of the line from Euxton to Preston and at last it was possible to begin work. Construction began at Bolton and made good progress; by July 1839 the line reached Rawlinson Lane in Heath Charnock; next the Black Brook was spanned by a viaduct and the line driven on. The line to Chorley Station was let in 1840 and from the junction with the Wigan line at Euxton work proceeded eastward to Chorley. The line's biggest obstacle would be Hartwood, where a tunnel 352 yards long was proposed. The navvies started on the tunnel in 1841; in May two steam engines were pumping water from the workings, but the enemy was quicksand. November saw seven steam engines at the site and an army of men toiling. Seven men, so the persistent legend runs, died in one day when the tunnel collapsed under the quicksand. In later life Alderman Saville recalled working on the tunnel construction, one of thousands of men on the line who swelled the 1841 census returns. A drastic solution to the subsidence was sought. In July 1842 the tunnel works were opened out into a lengthy cutting, opposed by the landowners who, it is said, were paid £13,000 in compensation for loss of land.

A road bridge was built over a length of 100 yards of the line and a series of flying arches were constructed on the western exit from the tunnel to buttress the slopes on either side.

From February 1841 passengers were carried by rail from Bolton as far as Rawlinson Lane; here coaches enabled travellers to get to Preston. The service was popular, 47,000 people using it in the first six months. Chorley station opened on 23 December 1841 but not where it now stands. The first station stood further down the line, on land where the goods yard later took its place. The line was finished in 1843 and opened on 22 June. Passengers on the Bolton and Preston Railway line were charged an additional fee of one shilling each by the North Union Railway for the stretch from Euxton to Preston, but the extra toll was removed when the companies merged.

The benefits brought by the opening of the railway were enormous. Businessmen could travel quickly and comfortably to the Manchester Cotton Exchange. Freight began to move by rail and developed extensively. Another major benefit was a social one. Chorley folk quickly appreciated the freedom of movement which railway travel gave them. Cobden set the pace when he organised his workpeople's trip to Fleetwood in the 1840s. Thereafter working people grew familiar with the delights of the seaside.

When the mills began to provide holidays, locals took part in the annual stampede of wakes weeks. In 1899, 6,788 people travelled from Chorley Station, their holidays paid for by savings and 'go-away' clubs. Not surprisingly, Blackpool was the favourite destination, with 1,415 on one day alone. Southport, Morecambe, Douglas and Scarborough also attracted large numbers. Chorley holidays of 1924 were quieter than usual, but even so 2,000 left Chorley for Blackpool. A typical scene was this, from 1924

> The great trek to the railway station started on Friday night. Not until a late hour did the stream of trunks, handbags, tennis rackets, walking sticks, spades and buckets leave, and early morning brought

a renewal of the hurrying line of holiday-makers. So it went on throughout the day, and although the keen eye might perceive a slight slackening, Saturday's crowd in the town seemed little smaller than usual.

Few issues divided Chorley so lengthily and vehemently as that of the railway crossing. The first station of the Bolton and Preston Railway was midway between Lyons Lane and Steeley Lane, later the site of the goods yard. Nearby an ancient road, Steeley Lane, crossed the line. At first no gates were provided. Wicket gates came later and for decades the gates were opened only for short periods or for people on foot. The long detours for other traffic were resented and many took a chance in crossing the line when trains were near. One account said fifty people had died at the crossing, a much exaggerated figure but indicative of the way tempers flared over the 'loss' of the right of way.

The new station was opened in 1863 and henceforth Steeley Lane crossing caused much argument. A bridge was built over the line to assist foot travellers but in 1873 a crowd forced the crossing gates open in defence of their rights. Public opinion and the Improvement Commission opposed the railway company, and fines were imposed on the trespassers. In 1874 the railway company closed the crossing to all but people on foot, and even the new town council after 1881 failed to resolve the problem.

The elderly are said to have found the footbridge difficult, and in May 1890 Annie Gent, a widow, was killed by a train when she opted for the crossing in preference to the bridge. One year later a subway was built, there to this day and never seen as a satisfactory solution to the division of Steeley Lane.

Further up the line a similar row raged over the loss of the footpath from Union Street across the Fellery. This was said to be a boon to anyone heading for Heapey and Eaves Lane. Today a detour around Steeley Lane is an inconvenience long accepted but the division of Chorley into two parts, east and west of the railway, has been a burden which need never have happened.

Coal built the railway to Blackburn from Chorley. A rail link to east Lancashire was first mooted in the 1840s, but was laid aside in favour of more urgent projects. In 1864 the plan resurfaced when the Wigan coal owners saw the line as the best way to get coal to Blackburn, which was growing fast and demanding fuel. The mine owners vowed to put £200,000 into the cost of building and, following some negotiation about the course of the line, work began on the railway from Blackburn to Chorley, a scheme which cut the previous distance between the two towns from twenty-one miles to nine and a half. Despite the fact that much of the terrain was moorland the work was completed in December 1869. It was claimed at the time that the line was unique in having steel rails along all its length. More importantly, the Mayor of Blackburn said it would save one shilling off the price of each ton of coal, saving Blackburn £20,000 a year. The line cost £530,000, well over budget.

The line was closed in the 1960s, a victim of the Beeching cutbacks.

In the late nineteenth century Chorley had three busy works constructing railway wagons. The first and largest of these, John Whittle's Railway Wagon Company, was established in 1861. By 1873 it was known as the Union Railway Waggon Works, owned by Whittle and Rushworth, though Whittle later became the sole owner. The works was impressive, extending from Albion Street to Railway Street, along the line of George Street. Furnaces, joinery shops, steel storage sheds and office blocks occupied 12,000 square yards. In 1873 thirty-five wagons each week rolled off the production line destined for coal mines up and down the land, especially in South Wales, the North East and Glasgow.

The second wagon works, Baxendale and Heald's, lay across the tracks, in Steeley Lane, opposite Anyon's Mill. The firm started up in 1866 and also produced large coal trucks, about twenty-five each week. Simon Leach owned the third company, which was also in Steeley lane, with an entrance off Lord Street. A report from 1873 says that the axle boxes were made in Heald's foundry nearby. Leach's was a much smaller operation, thirty-five men producing up to ten wagons weekly. In national terms all these were small undertakings and by 1890 only Whittle's works still survived.

The Chartists and the 1840s

Folk memory recalled 'The Hungry Forties', when hardship and hunger went hand in hand with the decline of handloom weaving. In Chorley 50 per cent of the operatives in 1842 existed on hand-outs from those who were in work. Weavers had very little work, the calico printers none. On a spring morning in May 1842 five hundred men paraded the streets, seeking support; charitable neighbours gave bread, bacon, cheese and enough money to give each 1s. 2d. Lancashire as a whole was in the same plight, but there were aspirations for change, seen in the local support for the Chartist cause. Preston's Richard Marsden, a national leader, spoke on several occasions in Chorley and support for him appears from 1839 onwards. He may have been at the meeting in April 1842 which ended in a serious accident. The second floor of the building which housed Nelsons Smithy near the Market Place was the venue. The floor gave way and dozens of people were injured, much to the delight of their opponents.

Marsden addressed several Chorley meetings in August 1842 and it is possible that this sparked the so-called Plug Riots, named from the practice of stopping mills by striking out the boiler plugs. On Tuesday 16 August a crowd, two thousand strong, came from Wigan to Chorley, to join a local crowd assembled in a croft off Elbow Street. Chorley's constable, with no police and no troops available, left the rioters well alone. They closed all the mills, smashed the boiler plugs (including that at Red Bank Pit) and commandeered food from the shops. The next day the Chorley mob, five hundred strong, went to the railway workings at

Hartwood Tunnel to enlist the navvies – who declined to help. The mob went on to Leece's mill at Whittle-le-Woods, then to Leyland, Bamber Bridge and Walton. John Waring, aged twelve, and Jethro Rigby, aged ten, were pressed recruits and watched their colleagues, armed with pikes, advance to face the army regulars. One volley of shots changed their plans, the mob ran, and all hopes of Radical politics evaporated.

Falling back to Chorley the rioters took over Duxbury Hall where a carnival atmosphere prevailed. Eventually the Yeomanry turned out and restored law and order. A detachment of the 60th Rifles was garrisoned in Cairn's warehouse in Queens Road to prevent more trouble. Soup kitchens were opened near the White Horse and in High Street.

The Chartist cause survived in Chorley. In March 1846 striking powerloom weavers gathered in a field off Fazakerley Street, with a military style precision, playing fife and drum and marching to formal drill. They were, however, exhorted to use only peaceful actions to win the strike. Two years later, in April 1848, Denham Hill at Brindle was the venue for a large north Lancashire Chartist meeting, five thousand strong. Chorley's Chartists used four newsrooms in the town to keep abreast of national news and political debate. When the Great Charter was sent up to London, there were 6,512 signatures from the town to back it. One Chorley Chartist, Thomas Halsall (1798–1873), took advantage of the Chartist Land Plan, farmed in Cambridgeshire from the 1850s and died there.

Park Road: a century of change

The history of Park Road spans a century. Before the 1820s the road did not exist and the highway from Preston turned left at the spot where the Parkers Arms was later built. The road followed Water Street to Chorley Bottoms, where it crossed the River Chor before climbing the short stretch of Church Brow into Market Street. Stagecoaches, farm carts and carriages used this ancient route for centuries. Travellers on foot, however, had a simpler option – ascending Chapel Steps took them along a footpath through the fields of the Chorley Hall estate until it joined the highway in front of the Hartwood Green toll bar. The footpath followed the same line as the later Park Road; a plan of Chorley Hall estate during the 1730s shows this path and an old resident recalled its use in 1882.

In August 1821 the commissioners of the Wigan and Preston Turnpike Trust held a meeting to press for alterations in the highway, including a plan to take the road in a diversion from Chorley Hall well to the east of the town, rejoining the old road near Yarrow Bridge, another at Whittle Hills, and another which resulted in the building of Park Road. At the northern end the road followed the estate footpath but it reached Market Street over an artificial embankment, incorporating a culvert for the River Chor to reach Astley Park.

At the southern end another diversion bypassed Red Bank Brow with

Park Road or 'North Entrance' to Chorley, reads the caption to this 1910 postcard printed by Hildenheimer of Berlin. It gives a particularly good view of the parish church. [Author]

a direct line to the Yarrow. The necessary Act of Parliament was passed on 3 April 1822. A plan of the diversions, dated 1821, was made by William Miller and shows how the embankment forced the demolition of houses near the parish church. R. H. Blackburn, in his biography of Sir Henry Tate, links the demolition with the loss of Terrace Mount, where Tate was born in 1819.

The *Preston Chronicle* for 20 April 1822, included an advertisement inviting tenders for the building of the stone culvert, five feet in diameter, as well as the stone retaining walls on the east side. The embankment involved moving forty thousand yards of earth and once completed it altered more than just the highway: it changed the aspect for residents of Chorley Bottoms.

This culvert accounts for one of Chorley's legends. People today still speculate about the tunnel, said to run from Astley Hall to the parish church which was supposed to have kept the Charnocks dry on their way to worship. The legend has circulated for a century or more and seems to relate to the culvert, tall enough for a man to walk through to Astley Park, but not to the hall!

There is a tradition that the first person to use the new Park Road was Lady Hoghton of Astley Hall, whose carriage passed this way to the Preston Guild of 1822. The new road swept through fields and farmland, with Chorley Hall to the north and the Unitarian Chapel to the south east. New houses soon began to be constructed along the road. Like Hollinshead Street in the 1750s the new Park Road was highly attractive to the town's elite. The 'old' Rectory, built in 1823 was the first house, two more being built in October 1823 for Lee Lee, cotton manufacturer, at a cost of £2,600. By 1826 twenty-six houses are recorded in Park Road, though

Lee's seems to have been the grandest and most expensive. About this time Mr Crompton had a stone wall built on the west side of the road, some 8 feet high and extending beyond the frontage of Chorley Hall.

The Parkers Arms was built at the top of Preston Street before 1846, when the Ordnance Survey plan shows buildings occupying all the frontages from the rectory as far as Commercial Road. Park Road Wesleyan Methodist Chapel was built in 1842 and the streets behind Park Road began to develop as housing for working people.

By 1863 some forty-two houses were to be seen, many occupied by the cotton men – Hibbert, Smethurst, Lightoller, Widdows and Cairns. During the 1860s, however, the Cotton Famine broke and the mill owners were temporarily short of cash. When times improved new houses were sought, more in keeping with High Victorian taste. Park Road continued to expand northwards but now in more economical terraces. Before the end of the century the road was beginning to house artisan families rather than the leaders of the town. The western side of the road was not developed until after 1900, when the Chorley Hall estate allowed such development. Comfortable large new houses appeared, mostly with trim gardens to the front. They incorporated beautiful terracotta brickwork from the Withnell Brick & Tile Company of Abbey Village. It had taken little over one hundred years to plan, build and complete Park Road and consequently there were many variations in its social structure.

The Poor Law and the workhouse

> Fortunately for England a spirit of independence still remains among the peasantry. The poor laws are strongly calculated to eradicate this spirit. [Malthus, 1798]

The virtue or evil of the poor laws depended upon the standpoint of the observer. To the recipient of relief it was given grudgingly and in a demeaning fashion; to the people who paid the poor rate it was excessive and given to many of dubious need. For centuries the authorities in Chorley, like those everywhere else, assessed cases of hardship and paid out what relief could be given.

In December 1824, for example, the vestry decided to assist Henage Hodkinson, who was to be 'allowed 2 shifts, 1 under petticoat, 1 top petticoat, 1 brat, one pair of clogs, one pair of stockings for a little girl which he has adopted the girl having been left (by some person) on the township'.

In 1694 the township residents were assessed for poor rate, from Richard Brooke of Astley who paid £1 18s. 6d. to James Kelly who paid 2d., the whole assessment standing at £13 8s. 11d. The poor rate was the chief source of relief paid in Chorley, and was levied on all households except, of course, the poor themselves. A regular issue in the township papers is the need to restrict relief to genuine and local residents, evicting outsiders of dubious origin. In 1647 the manor court jury presented John Hodgeson for bringing in a couple to his house, 'strangers as inmates contrary to the statute'. He was to send them packing or pay a fine of 6s. 8d. weekly after the fixed date.

In 1731 William Sharrock was a defendant before the court because he was said to have 'taken into his charge privately a Bigg bellyed woman who had since been delivered of a child supposed to be a Bastard Child and likely to bring a charge upon the Town'. His actions, whether charitable or not, resulted in a fine of £1 19s. 0d. Fear of illegitimate children becoming the responsibility of the town was a powerful force. A century later the official view had not altered. The Town's Book for 1781 records 'that the Overseer of the Poor for Chorley, give notice to all Persons residing within and not belonging to the Township of Chorley to bring Certificates for Acknowledgement from the Towns they belong to, otherwise the Overseer to remove them and their families'.

The Town's Book shows that Chorley paupers were housed in the Westhoughton Workhouse in 1787, the town paying a one guinea subscription. Twelve months later the Vestry Committee decided to build its own workhouse on the Poor's Land at Eaves Lane. James Thompson drew up plans for a building '17 yards by 7 yards' and three storeys high. The workhouse minutes record that handlooms were used to keep weavers at work during their time in the workhouse. The Charity Commissioners reported in 1826 that the workhouse was a large building, in fair condition, but likely to make heavy demands in upkeep during future years.

The question of what to do with itinerants, vagrants or tramps, exercised the minds and ingenuity of the authorities at all times. The vestry determined on a simple solution in 1787 – to warn them off: 'the Constables provide and get painted two Boards to be affixed one at each end of the

The 'new' almshouses in Ashfield Road were built in 1888 to replace a row of seventeenth-century almshouses erected in Pall Mall under the terms of Hugh Cooper's Charity and provided housing for six aged persons of the parish. [Author]

the Town proposing and offering the Reward [as the law is directed] for the apprehending of Vagrants and bringing the same to conviction'.

During the last century Chorley's situation on a main highway meant that it saw many passing travellers. The Hungry Forties saw large groups on tramp and appeals for relief grew. Ireland's disaster of the Potato Famine brought thousands of people to England, some for work, some to emigrate via Liverpool. Some settled locally, mainly around Standish Street, giving rise to the epithet 'Little Ireland'.

From time to time conditions in the workhouse were attacked in the local press: since reporters were banned from board meetings, it was easy to claim that ill-treatment was rife. In June 1862, during the Cotton Famine, Betsy Blackledge, who had one five year old and one infant, had left Chorley workhouse for Bolton.

> In the room we had to be in in Chorley workhouse from morning till night, locked up, we had no fire before from 10 to 11 o'clock in the forenoon for females and children in that room from a few months old up to 5 or 6 years of age. The room was very dirty, and no brush of soap or anything else to clean it with and no one dared ask the Governess for anything to clean the room with . . .
>
> We had a small piece of common soap given us to wash ourselves with about 2 or 3 ounces in weight, for a week. There were 8 females and children in the room who had to be washed. The soap was used up by Tuesday morning . . . As regards the meals they are spoiled in cooking. For breakfast we had ¾ of a tin of thin gruel and a small piece of brown bread. For dinner the day we had rice boiled and sweetened with treacle we could not eat it, being so badly cooked. When we should have had potatoes, we had small chats, dirty and not half washed, and a small piece of meat.

Conditions of Dickensian squalor were reported. Some years later, in contrast, when the guardians were reported in the press by 'A Looker-On' as dining on the best food at the workhouse at public expense, 'fresh laid eggs, fish and fowl, choice joints of both beef and mutton, cow heel and tripe, . . . Bass's bitter beer, brandy and milk'. The absence of Messrs Lawrence and Richmond from the board was supposed to have allowed these 'abuses' worthy of Oliver Twist.

The size of the workhouse was clearly inadequate. A report as early as 1841 said that there were 173 people within its walls, while twenty women and thirty children slept in fourteen beds in a single room measuring 28 feet by 24 feet. 'The smell from the men's room was appalling'. Suggested remedies included bringing the number of inmates down to 120 and regular whitewashing of the sick room and outbuildings.

Chorley Poor Law Union was created in 1837, with twenty-six parishes and a population of 38,836. Meetings were held from 1838 at the old town hall in Market Street. The Brindle workhouse, built after 1790, was taken over by Chorley in 1842.

A new workhouse for Chorley was agreed upon, and in January 1869 Leigh Hall, architect, advertised for two million bricks for the building. Messrs R. Pickup of Chorley were the builders and the new workhouse opened in January 1872. Brindle inmates were transferred in December 1871, ninety sick and elderly in carriages and the rest on foot. The 1872 workhouse is now Eaves Lane Hospital, and it retains much of its original external appeareance. It was more advanced in concept than its predecessor: for example, the hospital facilities were more carefully designed, while the kitchen and dining rooms were much improved. Workshops and yards still, however, retained the work ethic.

In 1904 a government inspector found things running smoothly. When he visited the dining room the children were served 'scouse'. Mr W. W. Burwell served as a poor law guardian for many years and recalled that in 1915 the number of inmates had increased from 192 to 214, though the outdoor relief cases had fallen from 600 to 327 over the previous thirty years.

The best known Chorley charity was Cooper's, which provided almshouses under the terms of his will of 1682. The houses, built in one block, were situated behind the old St George's School on Chorley Moor. They formed a long row of six cottages, built of stone and brick and roofed with grey slates. Fitted with oak doors, four had upstairs bedrooms, but two had only one room, a combined kitchen and bedroom. The occupants were poor widows or single women, who could use the gardens behind their cottages for vegetables or for horticulture. Each year they were to have a grey russet coat or gown. In 1865 they enjoyed a tea party at the Eagle and Child, complete with entertainments and a drop of the 'crater'. By 1882, though, the trustees decided to demolish the building and new almshouses were built in Ashfield Road.

The charities which provided for relief to be given to the poor dated back centuries. On St Thomas's Day (21 December), at the Royal Oak, what was called the 'dole' was distributed. In 1847 hundreds of local families lined up to collect their bounty in coals and clothing. Other accounts speak of the dole taking many hours. Ultimately the Chorley Consolidated Charities took over the role of the separate charities.

As well as the poor law relief and charitable provisions there were numerous friendly societies, especially in Victorian Chorley. Some collected small sums from their members and devoted the money to the burial fees or sickness payments. The Mechanics' Society dated from 1757, while Princess Amelia's Friendly Society was active around 1800.

Charles Robinson printed a self-help tract in 1826. Written by 'A Sincere Friend' and called *A Friendly Address to the Poorer Classes, on the Important Points of Economy, Cleanliness, Industry, Honesty, Religion, etc*, it had twenty-four pages and cost 2d. The author was perhaps a clergyman, for it has a severe, moral tone. His readers were exhorted to be thrifty, sober, clean and diligent, yet practical hints, such as combining to buy coal, potatoes and provisions in bulk, anticipate the co-operative movement.

St George's Parish Church started life as a 'Waterloo' Chapel, funded from war reparations paid by France after the Napoleonic Wars in the 1820s. [Lancashire County Library]

It is surprising to find the author's attacks on 'shopping', or buying goods from one shopkeeper only on credit terms. Similarly, the pawnbroker came in for attack, as did 'Scotchmen' (buying on club terms) and quack doctors. The perils for the working man and his family were, it said, only avoidable through a religious life and careful economy.

St George's Parish Church

After Waterloo the French paid reparations for war damage. The money was distributed, under the terms of the 'Millions' Act, to build new churches in growing industrial areas, a status which Chorley claimed. On 10 September 1822 the foundation stone of the future St George's Church was laid on land acquired from the Leigh estate. The architect was Thomas Rickman and St George's reflects his preference for the Gothic revival. This 'Waterloo' church dominated St George's Street and had a tower 100 feet high.

The builder, Mr Rich of Wigan, fared badly from the project. When the walls were almost completed a severe storm blew down the east wall and some of the arches on the south side. Rich's contract price (£13,707 16s. 9d.) underestimated the final budget by almost £3,000 – poor Rich was rendered bankrupt, but his work is still impressive. By contemporary standards, the chapel (as it officially remained for years) was enormous; compared with St Laurence's (capacity 450 sitting) the new chapel could seat over 2,000, 1,200 of these were free places. St George's, erected at a period of great change and uncertainty, was a testament to faith and hope.

It was consecrated in 1825, divine service being held for the first time on 9 October. In 1831 a district was assigned to it and a parish was formally created in 1856. This was divided, to create St James, in the 1870s. Alterations were made in 1892 and again in 1957.

When Edwin Crew attended a service in the 1880s he described the congregation as largely middle class, perhaps appropriate to a church so close to the commercial heart of the town. Among St George's many distinguished clergy the most prominent was Thomas Cruddas Porteus, the noted antiquarian who ministered here from 1934 to 1946. The parish grew in other respects; the National School (1825) was built at the junction of Pall Mall and Bolton Street. The first school had separate rooms for boys and girls and was extended in 1848 and again in 1888. Five hundred pupils attended the school in the 1860s. St George's also entered the self-improvement movement, so popular in late Victorian times. Evening classes for working men started in 1863. Although originally aimed at wholesome education the centre gradually became a social club.

Just as St George's emerged in response to the town's growth in the 1820s, so new churches were built to keep pace with the expansion of Victorian Chorley. St James' parish was created out of St George's and a handsome new stone church was built in 1878.

St Peter's Church grew out of a Sunday school, which was started in a small schoolroom at Botany Bay by Canon Master in 1841. Several years later the schoolroom was used for services by Revd Henry Sewell and the next step was a new church. Lady Hoghton of Astley gave land in Harpers Lane, and the foundation stone was laid in 1849. St Peter's, designed by Charles Reed of Liverpool, had seating for 800 and was built in the Early English style. The church was consecrated on 25 April 1851 and a new parish assigned to it in 1852. In contrast with St Laurence's, 600 of the 800 seats were free from the start, and eventually all of them. In 1886 St Mark's chapel, with seating for 100, was built at Knowley.

Roman Catholicism

Catholics have always formed a substantial element in Chorley's population. There were at least 200 in 1766, and 8,000 in 1902 – one-third of the population. During the penal years it was said Chorley's Catholics travelled to Euxton, Wrightington, or South Hill to worship. The first post-Reformation chapel in Chorley was not built until 1774 at Weld Bank. Between 1755 and 1770 Father John Chadwick – one of the Chadwicks of Burgh – celebrated mass in the chapel at Burgh Hall one Sunday each month. From 1770 he lived at the hall and raised the money to buy land on Thurston Hodson's farm at Weld Bank.

Chadwick died in 1802. His successor, Father Richard Thompson, a Manchester man, was responsible for the extensions to the chapel: one

St Mary's Arch, 1912. The monument was set up in memory of Father Crank, a much-loved priest of St Mary's parish. One critic unkindly called the arch 'a piece of medieval mockery'. [Lancashire County Library]

phase was finished in 1813, while a second in 1829 included adding a tower and aisles. The church was dedicated to St Gregory. A school was built in 1817. The church was always well-attended, with a congregation of 1,800 in the 1920s.

After 1800 the influx of new families, especially of Irish in the 1840s, meant that a parish in embryo was created. Father George Gibson opened a chapel in 1847, in the former Wesleyan chapel in Chapel Street. His successor, Father Gillow, decided to build a chapel and school, St Mary's. The Mount Pleasant estate was bought from the Harrison family in 1851 for £2,800. This property, originally owned by the Shireburnes, and later by the Welds, included what was to be the presbytery, a former farmhouse on one of the medieval burgage plots. The new church, designed by Joseph Hansom, opened for worship in 1854. Church and school were housed under one roof, with two floors for school purposes and one for the church. Galleries were placed above each other in the church, earning it the nickname of 'three-decker'. The schools were moved to a new building in 1860 and the church extensively altered by Pugin and Pugin in 1909. The tower with spire dates from 1894. The archway onto Market Street, dating from 1913, is a memorial to Father Crank and has suffered badly in recent years from the effects of pollution. Sacred Heart Church in Brooke Street was constructed in 1875 as an iron school-chapel and rebuilt in stone in 1894. St Joseph's, in Harpers Lane, was built in 1910.

Methodism

Nonconformists played an active part in Chorley's religious life. Methodism arrived in the latter part of the eighteenth century, when Chorley was a small component of the Haworth Circuit. This vast 'parish' was superintended by a native of Brindle, Revd William Grimshaw. After 1776 Chorley was included in the Colne Circuit and it is known that John Wesley preached here in 1780.

> Mr Wesley was announced to preach at Chorley one week-day. Martha Thompson [the first woman Methodist in Preston] thought it was a capital opportunity for her friends to hear this wonderful preacher . . . She packed up a hamper of provisions, with some of Mrs Walmsley's ale, and prayed for the conversion of her friends.

Wesley made converts to Methodism in Blackburn in the same year and Mr Walkden, well known for his preaching skill, was persuaded to come from Blackburn to Chorley. A Methodist Society began, meeting in a cottage situated where the Albion Hotel in Bolton Street now stands, in 1786. As elsewhere Methodism was well-received among working people, but it also had one influential supporter in the town – Richard Smethurst the textile manufacturer. He was instrumental in the building of the first chapel, close to Market Street (later renamed Chapel Street). The chapel, capable of holding 500 worshippers, served from 1792 until 1842,, when its role was taken by Park Road Wesleyan Methodist Chapel. After 1847 the old chapel became the first Roman Catholic chapel in the town centre. It later became a Mechanics Institution and finally served as 'a common music hall.'

Park Road Chapel was one of the confident Victorian Methodist chapels, a handsome stone building in a classical style, built for £2,300 to seat 700 people. The Sunday school met in the basement until 1867, when an extension was provided for the purpose.

A circuit was created based on Chorley in 1858, embracing Chorley, Whittle, Brinscall, Wheelton, Withnell Fold, Coppull, Adlington and Euxton. Demand for new chapels kept pace with growth of the town; Trinity Chapel in Rawcliffe Road dates from 1895 and was funded generously by Mr T. W. Rice. He also backed Market Street Wesleyan

School, a fine example of the emphasis given to education by the denomination. The school opened its doors in 1859, and was enlarged in 1863, serving as both school and chapel. Its achievements were of a high standard, so much so that 100 children were refused admission as day scholars in 1882 for lack of places. A year earlier the average daily attendance was 386. An outlying chapel was established at the south end of Eaves Lane in 1868. This developed from a meeting in the nearby home of John Moss.

The Primitive Methodists made no impact until 1820, when Thomas Batty preached in Water Street near the Britannia Inn. Encouraged by his reception he preached again on Sunday 12 May at the Market Cross, to a large, well-behaved audience. On his second visit he held a meeting in Gillett's Yard, using an upstairs room while a travelling circus's band tuned up in the room below. Growth in support was slow but a circuit began in 1846 and a chapel was built in West Street in 1859. A schism occurred, and one group built the Cunliffe Street Chapel in 1866 while a secessionist group of sixty became the United Free Methodists. They met in rooms in Queen Street, in the Co-operative Hall, and at the Railway Street Chapel after 1866. William Tootell the diarist worshipped here at the end of his life. The Moor Road Primitive Methodist Chapel opened its doors in 1876; Heapey Road Chapel in 1884, and the Lyons Lane Independent Methodist Chapel in 1899.

Congregationalism

Although there are some references to Presbyterian beliefs in seventeenth century Chorley, the real history of the local movement begins in 1783, when two preachers – Mr Johnson from the Countess of Huntingdon's Connection Chapel at Wigan, and a Mr Redmayne from Horwich – came to the town. Johnson, preaching in the street, was attacked by a fanatic throwing stones; the assailant drummed up miners to heckle the minister, yet Johnson's preaching is said to have swayed the colliers who then locked up the assailant. The message took hold and meetings were held regularly in a house in St Thomas's Square for eight years. Land was acquired for a chapel in Hollinshead Street, and this opened in 1792. Revd James Wraith was the first minister at the chapel, which was said to be a branch of the Anglican Church until 1805 when a new minister emphasized the Congregational spirit.

Hollinshead Street's Presbyterian Chapel, now a United Reformed Church Chapel, celebrated its bicentenary in 1992. [Lancashire County Library]

The movement flourished until 1834 when, following Rev Jones' departure for America, two candidates struggled for the vacant ministry. An astonishing series of acrimonious episodes followed – in one a group sang hymns to drown out the opposition in the pulpit – and there were bitter rows. The rest of Chorley gathered to enjoy the spectacle and Mr Fazakerley turned out, as a magistrate, to read the Riot Act in a chapel! One group seceded to the Baptists; a separate contingent founded a chapel in St Georges Street. Hollinshead Street's school was built in 1836: in 1882 it had 190 Sunday scholars.

The next Congregational chapel was built in Eaves Lane in 1905, under the auspices of St George's Street Chapel. Chorley's Congregationalists went out to carry their message to neighbouring villages, preaching in Whittle, Clayton-le-Woods, White Coppice and as far away as Blackrod.

Baptists

Baptist congregations in Chorley were always small. One group, founded before 1802, met at Back Mount, where Edward Morris of West Cottage was the manager: it had no more than fifty worshippers. The second group began in 1821 at Holborn (off Market Street), later moving to Anderton Street. Numbers were increased in 1838 when a group seceded from Hollinshead Street Chapel. A chapel was built for the Particular Baptists in Chapel Street (the building is now *Malcolm's Musicland*). In 1851 there were sittings for 100, a Sunday school and day school, although the congregation hardly exceeded thirty. By the 1880s ministers generally came from nearby towns. The chapel was sold in 1950.

The Salvation Army

The Salvation Army, formally established in 1877, spread rapidly. By 1888 there was a small unit in Chorley with its headquarters in an upper room of the Co-operative Store at one corner of the Market Place. In that year five members of the army, led by Captain Whiteley, fell foul of the corporation by holding a meeting on the market one Tuesday evening in July. A crowd of 200 curious onlookers gathered, to listen to the service, and the market's inspector called the police. There had, it seems, been friction as the inspector had threatened to charge the army a toll if they sold the *War Cry* on the square. The case came before the magistrates who found the party guilty of obstruction but dismissed the case on payment of costs. In their best tradition the Salvation Army stood their ground: only one paid, and the other three went to Preston House of Correction for seven days. When they returned home they were feted as heroes, paraded and cheered for cocking a snook at the authorities. The great man himself, General Bramwell Booth, came to Chorley in August 1907. He was greeted, appropriately for his Methodist background, at Cunliffe Street Primitive Methodist Chapel by Alderman Sharples. Perhaps Chorley had come to terms with the 'Sally Army' at last!

Some customs and traditions

New Year's Day, 1863, fell at a time of hardship with more than the usual chill of winter. The Cotton Famine was still starving the mills, and Chorley's celebration of the New Year festival had a muted ring. Churches and chapels held their customary midnight services, then, as the bells rang out the old year, bands paraded the street. A journalist for the *Preston Herald* felt that the festivities were less numerous than in previous years.

Easter brought pace-egging and 'lifting'. The latter had an ancient pedigree: it was meant to symbolise the resurrection of our Lord and on Easter Monday women were lifted by men, with a team of four 'lifters', women repeating the practice for men on the Tuesday following Easter. Baines, writing of the 1830s condemned it as 'a rude, indecent and dangerous diversion, practised chiefly by the lower classes of people . . . it subsists at the lower end of the town and the women have of late converted it into a money job'.

May Day events were more likely to be blessed with fine weather. In the 1880s processions were followed by a show of horse teams, with prizes for the best turnouts. A decade earlier the town's carters had marked May Day with decorated carts.

Walking Day has been celebrated in May for many centuries, its origins linking with Whitsun celebrations and with the old parish custom of walking the bounds. It was the practice in some periods to separate the denominations into different days for their walks; in 1827 the Revd Thomas published his protest at the mixed procession which incurred his anger, because it gave the Catholic walkers what he saw as undue prominence. This episode apart, Walking Days usually brought out the new, best frocks and the most attractive hats, while banners flashed colour in the spring sunshine and there was a promise of refreshments at the end of a long walk.

Chorley's 'Big Lamp' was erected in 1864 and taken down in 1948, but stays alive in local folklore to the extent that it is used as a place-name for the junction of Market Street, Bolton Street and Pall Mall. [Lancashire County Library]

In July the Henpecked Husbands Club went on the march: there were similar tongue-in-cheek gatherings in Egerton and Rochdale. It was centred on Bolton Street and Chorley Moor, where a procession of men went from pub to pub, with a band of old tins, frying pans and kitchen tools followed by a man carrying a clothes prop with a crinoline nailed to the top, while other men carried two poles with a bed sheet stretched between. July was also the

A Walking Day procession *c.* 1910. This print by Luke Berry shows the contingent from St Mary's ready to set out from near the Albion in Bolton Street. [Author]

month for Club Day, held on the first Saturday in July. The different Friendly Societies processed through the town from the pubs where their meetings were held. Despite the apparent exclusiveness of the day it also included the rest of the community – Market Street was decorated with flags and bunting and it is possible that this was the direct ancestor of the Wakes Weeks.

Many of the old traditions died out in the Victorian era, perhaps because of the new larger communities made up of families new in the area. In the 1870s, however, 'bidding to the funeral' was still practised. When someone died one member of the family was sent round to bid friends and relatives to attend the funeral. As they arrived at the house each would take a drink from a large pot of ale on the table. The pewter pot bore either a black or white ribbon, supplied by the pub landlord. Another custom at funerals was for the men to wear a sprig of box in their lapels; the sprig of box was thrown into the grave. One correspondent to the *Chorley Standard* in 1866 deplored the old custom of heavy drinking as part of christening, wedding and funeral ceremonies. Corpses were often kept waiting for burial until Sunday, when family members could travel without losing pay.

William Moss went against the grain of opinion in 1864, arguing that Guy Fawkes Night should not be kept. Burning an effigy of Guy Fawkes, shooting off firearms and lighting bonfires all expressed a mood of anti-Catholic feeling and Moss argued that one should 'live peaceably with all men.'

At Christmas the shops in Market Street vied to put on the best and most alluring displays of their wares. Huge quantities of livestock were slaughtered to feed the Christmas table. A report for Christmas of 1874 said the yule-log, wassail bowl and mummers had given place to modern fancies such as the Christmas box and Christmas tree, ideas imported from Germany by Prince Albert. Shoppers could, nevertheless, enjoy the cakes and confectionery of the Misses Corbett, renowned for the quality of their Chorley cakes.

Rivington Pike holds a special place in the affections of townspeople from Chorley, Horwich and Bolton. Whenever the nation was in danger of foreign invasion the beacon on its summit was prepared in readiness to carry the message from hill top to hill top. A hundred years after Elizabeth's reign local Nonconformists made the steep climb to a natural hollow below the pike where services could be held in secret and free from oppression. Two centuries later the pike appealed to more secular but no less deep-rooted feelings, for Whitsuntide marked the start of Rivington Pike Fair, comparable with the modern Good Friday congregations on the pike.

In the 1870s hundreds of people, most of them young, climbed to the top, looking out from the beacon to the west as countless numbers have done since. Stalls sold nuts and gingerbread, and there was more refreshment and liquid fare at the Black Lad Inn in Rivington village. A cluster of stalls at the inn sold oysters, nuts and oranges. For those hardy souls who got to the top it was a break in routine from the tedium of mill life, a chance to wear your best clothes, have a bit of fun and get closer to heaven.

Food and drink

Chorley's location, within easy reach of productive farmlands, gave the weekly markets a variety of produce. It is not easy to discover, however, what people ate. In 1401 a complaint was brought by William Wolston against Henry and John de Asshehowe. The two had attacked him in Chorley, and destroyed many of his crops at Heath Charnock; these included corn, fine wheat, barley, beans, peas and oats. His livestock comprised horses, bullocks, oxen, cows, pigs and sheep. A Charnock inventory for Astley two centuries later is very similar. Church dues payable at Astley give payments for cattle, hay and calves, plus a penny for each beehive and fourpence for each pigeon house, pigeons being the traditional source of fresh meat in some months. Chorley Hall had a pigeon house in the fourteenth century and its fishpond was to be seen until the 1950s.

Documents relating to the Anderton Feud of the fifteenth century mention pasties and a posset, while pobbies (made from milk and potatoes) was popular in the 1800s. Oats, the ever reliable crop in the damp climate, appears in every century, oatcake porridge and buttermilk being a staple for poor families. Alderman Mangnall, who recalled growing-up in the 1830s, said that jannock was normal fare in his home, while white bread was a treat twice yearly.

There was a dispute in 1866 between the Improvement Commission and the Chorley Pig Keepers Association. Many households kept pigs in the backyard, and there was a suspicion that cholera was caused by this 'farming'.

Queen Victoria's Diamond Jubilee of 1897 was celebrated in style in all parts of the town. Anderton Street, seen here, was recorded with its bunting and crowds eagerly waiting the big parade. [Lancashire County Library]

Largely because their records have survived the diet of the better off is readily pictured. The Gillibrands at Astley had a variety of fruit trees at Astley Hall in the 1710s and James Talbot's Bagganley farm was able to supply a succulent table of fresh food. The Leigh family, who lived at Union Street in the 1760s, dined on a wealth of local produce and paid for specialities too. The coach brought 3½ pounds of tea from London at £1 14s. 4d; the market and local shops provided veal, oysters, legs of pork, mutton, pigeons, ducks and geese, tongue, cheeses, raspberries, a cask of beer, 30 pounds of beef (for 7s. 6d.), and spirits from Mr Threlfall. Likewise Lord Willoughby wrote to his steward in the 1750s to order Alpine strawberry roots for delivery to his London home.

In 1801 oats, wheat and barley were important cereal crops locally, while potatoes, beans and turnips were grown mostly for home consumption, the many small garden plots to be found attached to cottages before the Industrial Revolution regimented workers into the terraced properties.

Music

There must always have been music of a kind in past centuries. A few accounts mention pipes in late medieval records, and Mr Blundell's diary talks of Miss Wastley playing on the virginals at Astley Hall in the 1710s. Later on a love of music is found among the working people of the town, fostered by the need for choral music in church and chapel. The south door to St Laurence's was at one time flanked by a stone staircase to give musicians access to the church. In 1884 John Bannister wrote about musical worthies, especially John Warburton and Robert Mather who were singing teachers, two Robert Blackburns (at Smethursts End and Duke End), William Catterall, Thomas Gillett the artist, and James Mather who emigrated to the USA.

Bannister began his musical instruction at St George's in the late 1840s. Robert Mather, a small determined figure, was his tutor. His small house in Pall Mall, crowded with a large family, was a musical haven, Mather had a leading part in the choir of the Primitive Methodist Chapel in West Street. He and his colleagues were not restricted to plain hymn music but expanded their repertoire to include Handel's Messiah and Judas Maccabaeus. His advice to Bannister was, 'Neer mind . . . it dusund matther whad tha coes um [the names of the notes] . . . so us ua giv um reet saands'.

Arthur G. Leigh, later an alderman, taught music and published sheet music, as did Harry Chester Wilcocks, and the *Chorley Tune Book* includes pieces with familiar local names. Added to these were the brass band concerts, and the formal parade bands of the volunteers, together with the musical concerts which formed the fare of many winter evenings: Chorley's musical life in Victorian times was richly varied.

Flags, bunting, banners and processions fill Market Street from end to end, in celebration of the coronation of Edward VII in 1902. Among the onlookers a striking contrast of clothing can be seen. [Lancashire County Library]

The cotton masters

Most of the leading mill owners in Chorley in the 1800s were not natives. Three families in particular warrant special attention: the Smethursts, Lawrences and Browns. The Smethursts migrated from Bolton in the eighteenth century. Richard Smethurst, born at Darcy Lever in 1756, died in Chorley in 1822. His son, Richard (1790–1857) laid the foundations of the dynasty which ran North Street Mills. So powerful was their influence that the area around the mill was known as 'Smethurst's End'. They built the Old Mill at Preston Street in 1824, and the New Mill in 1834. Tower Mill followed in 1851. In the early period both George Brown and William Lawrence, later to be masters in their own right, worked here. John Waring, who began at North Street at the age of seven, worked for four hours, with two hours of schooling and then 'play for the rest of the day' in the 1830s. Smethurst's mill suffered a fire in 1835 but was saved by the fire engine from nearby Waterloo Mill.

There are no derogatory accounts of the Smethursts: rather the contrary, for during the Cotton Famine the family worked at a personal loss rather than break with their workers, winning esteem and affection as a result. The family survived this crisis well enough. In 1866 they opened a large new weaving shed, which in June that year was turned into an impromptu restaurant, when two sittings of 1,200 employees sat down to celebrate the wedding of the master's son, Augustus W. Smethurst.

The 2,400 guests munched through 1,400 lb of beef and mutton, 800 lb of plum pudding, 1,500 lb of potatoes, 300 Melton Mowbray pies, 2,400 oranges, 150 lb of nuts, and downed 36 gallons of cider with 6 loads of ale. The young master became one of Chorley's favourite characters. Born in 1830, he was educated at Rossall before working in the mill. He was the first mayor (1881 to 1883); the portrait of him in civic robes shows a large, portly man, gazing off camera, perhaps dwelling on business. He was said to be a plain, blunt speaker, with a 'mellifluous voice'. Many accounts describe a genial, loveable man who had time to spare for any worker – his name was shortened in common use to 'Gustus' Smethurst. Politically a Liberal, he was a member of the Anglican church and is commemorated for posterity with a memorial in the parish church. He preferred to live near his works and built Rookwood (where Chorley hospital now stands) in 1865 for £8,000. At this date the mills were valued at £250,000, with 1,000 looms, 120,000 spindles, producing jacconets and fancy goods. The mills were sold in 1887 to the Chorley Cotton Spinning Company.

The Lawrence and Brown dynasties had later starts. William Lawrence, born in Preston in 1787, was sent to work from the age of six at Moor Lane Mill. He toiled from 4 a.m. to 9 p.m. for 1s. 6d. weekly. In 1810 he came to Chorley to work at Water Street Mill. In directories for 1841 and 1851 he is listed as a farmer (at Lloyds Farm in Hollinshead

Street) and manufacturer. In 1851 he set up in partnership with George Brown, to build a weaving shed for powerlooms in East Street. They later quarrelled and Lawrence built a new mill on Lyons Lane. Around the mills he built rows of houses at economical rents for his workers, in Derby Street and Buchanan Street. The Lawrences went in for both weaving and spinning, whereas the Smethursts had concentrated on spinning. The firm had four mills in Lyons Lane as well as Cowling Mill. The family home was at Moss Cottage on Eaves Lane. The younger William Lawrence (one of twenty-two children) was a good businessman and in time an alderman. When his son Edward reached the age of twenty-one in 1899 the event was a jamboree for all the extended 'family'. The workers bought him a mahogany desk, a present on his return from the latter-day Grand Tour of Europe. The firm laid on a trip to Blackpool as a treat for the workforce, with free entry to the Winter Gardens and the Tower. Luke Berry's photographs show the mills decorated with bunting, looms stopped, eerily silent. Lawrence kept going through the Cotton Famine by speculating in cotton to ensure raw cotton for Lyons Lane.

Bread, the staple of life, was a powerful image in local politics. James Lawrence's campaign in 1903 argued that Liberal Free Trade policies would put the 'Big Loaf' on every family's table. [Lancashire County Library]

George Brown was the third of the cotton masters. His is a 'rags to riches' story. He was born at Euxton, in 1811, where he learned handloom weaving from his father, a hard taskmaster who would fling the paste brush in his face if the child fell asleep at work. In 1829 he left home and set out for Chorley, where he was helped by the owner of Weir Mill. At Hollinshead Street Sunday School he learned to read and write. He next took the step which was to enable him to make the transition to mill owner. Using a dog-cart he began to 'put-out' to weavers in Eccleston and Bretherton, selling the cloth to Goodiers of Preston.

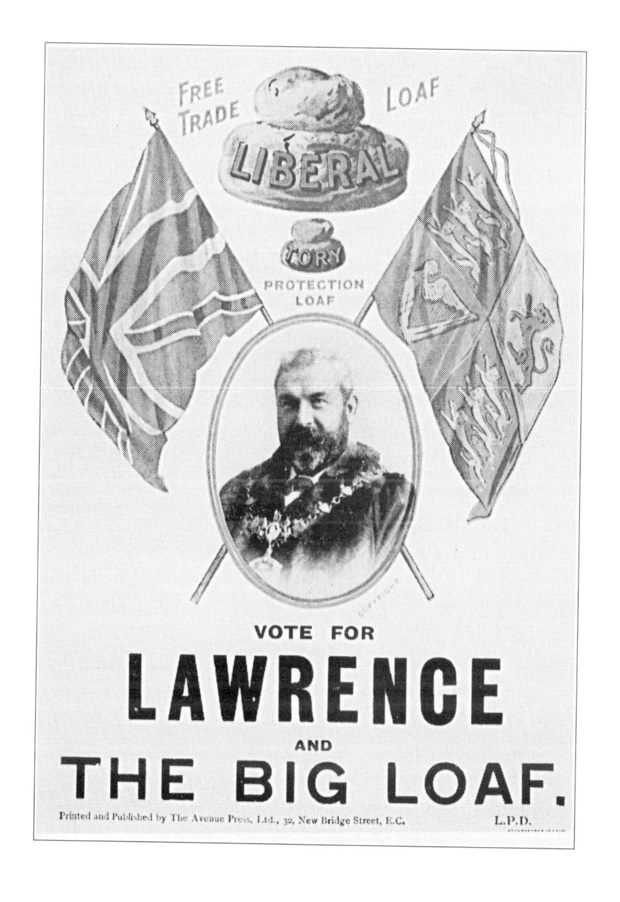

There he came in contact with a merchant named Jones, who was so impressed with Brown that he advanced him an unsecured loan of £100. That working capital was his boon. He took over a building in Parker Street as a small works, using dandy looms from 1851. Soon afterwards he went into business with William Lawrence, but working in his own right he developed the site around East Street and Friday Street where the Albert Mills were constructed. Only yards away from the mill, Brown built a house, East View.

Lawrence's Lyons Lane Mills, Townley Street, gaily decorated for the coming-of-age of Mr Edward Lawrence, the proprietor's son, in 1899. [Lancashire County Library]

Brown's Primrose Mill (1861–6), with Albert Mills, ran 992 looms. He served as an Improvement Commissioner and was on the town council from 1881. George Brown fits the archetypal image of a cotton master. He was a frugal man, who walked to the station when on his way to the Manchester Cotton Exchange. As the other mill owners entered their first class carriage Brown would invariably choose third class. Why, he was asked, did he travel third? 'Because there isn't a fourth!' he is credited with replying. He was a gritty, determined man, but capable of open-handed generosity to old friends.

He had a large family and was succeeded by his son George Thomas Brown in 1884. Sadly the various claimants to the estate of George senior squabbled in the courts over his will.

The Cotton Famine, 1861–5

The issue which dominated the lives of ordinary people in the town during the 1860s was the Cotton Famine. In the years that followed this event the widespread hardship which it caused was etched vividly in the memory of a generation, just as memories of the First World War and the Blitz have been in this century. The phrase 'Cotton Famine' was coined at the time to describe the drying up of supplies of cotton to feed the hungry mills, as a result of the civil war in America, from 1861 to 1865. It had a grimmer, more personal, meaning to thousands of people whose livelihoods dried up with the supply of cotton, bringing to them the reality of starvation.

It was predominantly a Lancashire experience, felt in every town and village where cotton was a major employer of labour. Other parts of Britain and even France were affected but nowhere was the disaster so badly felt as in Lancashire, the cotton industry heartland.

Ironically, the start of the 1860s was hopeful for the cotton industry. In spite of the periodic boom and slump of the 1850s, the decade had witnessed phases of new mill construction, with several examples in Chorley itself. Heyworth's Redan Mill at Cowling dates from 1851, Brown's Friday Street Mill from the same year, Rice and Hall's Moor Mill was built in 1852 and Lightoller's Victoria Mill in the same period. Lawrence's First Mill went up in 1857, Smethurst's Tower Mill in 1851 and the Primrose Mill in 1861.

In that year Chorley had twelve weaving sheds, a printworks and twelve other cotton factories. Out of a population of 18,027 (8,798 males and 9,229 females), over 6,000 people made their living employed in cotton. Across Lancashire 500,000 people, in two thousand factories, with 300,000 power looms, 2½ million spindles, worked to convert 1,390 million pounds of raw cotton into finished cloth.

Later, one observer noted that in 1860, 'the Lancashire workers . . . were at the head of the English working class. They had the highest wages, and were, of all workers, the most intelligent and best organised'.[16]

In 1861 the USA exported 1,261,400,000 pounds of cotton; twelve months later, curtailed by the Union blockade, only 533,100,000 pounds left the eastern ports; the prewar levels were not again reached until 1871.

At the outbreak of the civil war in April 1861, Britain's warehouses held large stocks of cotton, and it was said that problems would have arisen anyway in 1861 from over-production. For some weeks these stocks cushioned the effects of the dwindling exports and it was not until October that mills were forced to go on short time. In that month the poor law guardians began to see the first trickle of what was later to become a flood of applicants for relief. By the month of January 1862 claims were 70% in excess of normal for the month, and February saw a rise to 105%.

As news of the crisis spread, a remarkable thing happened. From various quarters relief organisations sprang up, dedicated to raising money for the worst-hit areas. Some were purely local schemes, others national and at least one international. In Chorley a Relief Committee sat from 12 February 1862 to 21 April 1865. The committee was headed by the rector, Revd Canon Master, together with Mr A. W. Smethurst, Revd A. A. O'Neill, Mr G. H. Lightoller, John Cheetham, J. G. Welch and others. During those three years the committee distributed £14,446. By the end of 1864 £1,750 had been spent on bread, £579 on flour, £358 on coffee and sugar, £234 on clogs, £197 on school fees, £2,006 on clothing and £5,825 on the tickets issued to be redeemed against goods (a widely copied system of relief which, with the exception of a riot at Stalybridge, worked well). One account of the system used in Chorley is given in the *Preston Herald* for 1 February 1862.

> We have pleasure in noticing the noble and self denying spirit in which the operatives of Messrs Smethurst's and Mr Lawrence's Mills (which are at present running full time), have come forward to the relief of their fellow operatives, 300 of whom have been entirely unemployed . . . since October last. The following is the result of the unsolicited and consequently purely voluntary contribution sent in from these mills contributed in two weeks £19 12s. 7d. which has been carefully distributed by the committee in the shape of tickets of order for provisions. Those shopkeepers being favoured with the orders were suffering most from the state of the trade. The tickets were of value from 1s. to 6s. and were distributed according to the number of the family and the urgency of the case. Those who had the distribution of these tickets were followed by number of persons begging them to come and see this case and other cases of distress.

The number of people in receipt of help peaked at 3,908 in February 1863, while October 1864 saw the weekly level drop as low as thirty-four. All of these people would have been familiar with the tithe-barn at the parish church where food was given out under the system described above. A soup kitchen was opened up in Back Street (on the site of the Normid store), just as in an earlier crisis in 1842. Clothing was given out from a depot in High Street; the twin spectres of hunger and lack of clothing haunted the children of that period.

The relief networks did the best they could, but hardship was widespread. One doctor said that 'insufficient and innutritious diet' caused disease to increase alarmingly. 'Measles were very prevalent in Ashton, Blackburn, Bury, Chorley and Manchester, whooping cough in Chorley, Manchester, Oldham and Stockport.' In Standish Street alone there were five deaths from measles late in 1862. Some young women were forced to turn to prostitution in order to survive, while the rate of illegitimate births grew; nevertheless, contemporary observers commented that in spite of all those ills, crime did not increase and public disorder was very low.

Inevitably, the collapse of trade ruined many cotton manufacturers. Best known in Chorley was the case of Isaac Hibbert, father of the future Sir Henry Hibbert. In October 1864 his stock was sold off by auction: it included 1500 lbs of cotton, yarn, handlooms, frames, healds and jacquards. Young Henry left school in that year and threw himself into learning the cotton trade, by day at the Crosse Hall works and by night at Mr Brown's science classes.

Others turned the vicissitudes of fortune to their advantage. William

Worden, a cotton weaver in Preston prior to the Cotton Famine, was soon without work. He hit on the plan of buying baskets of herring in Preston and walking to Chorley to sell them in the Market Place. His trade increased, he began to sell fruit and vegetables, and the name M. Worden & Sons is still present on Chorley Market Place.

In another way, which could not have been anticipated, Chorley benefitted from the Cotton Famine. Robert Rawlinson, one of the town's most distinguished citizens, was instrumental in devising a scheme of public works in Lancashire. The aim of his scheme was to give useful paid employment to able-bodied men thrown out of work, by using them as unskilled labour on projects for the public good. In Chorley the scheme used men, whose skills normally lay in spinning and weaving cotton, as construction gangs for new roads under the supervision of Mr Derham, the town's surveyor. Ackhurst Lane, or Southport Road as it is now better known, was formally adopted by the Improvement Commission in 1866, having been built along an old footpath to give a more direct route to Euxton than in the past. John Waring, in his eighties, recalled in 1916 that he had spent part of his time on relief work in planting trees at the Chorley Cemetery. A similar scheme built a new road through Butterworth Brow and in both cases the usefulness of these new highways was quickly established. At Mealhouse Lane, for example, a number of thatched cottages were demolished in 1866 to allow wider passage for carts and wagons.

One curious feature of the Cotton Famine was that a new phase of building began, cashing in on depressed rates of labour and cost of machinery. Lightoller's opened up their large mill again in April 1863, after an eighteen months closure and putting 350 workpeople back to work. By this time an alterative supply of Surat cotton from India was being used, although the quality of the fibre was inferior. There were also specially chartered blockade runners which fetched American cotton.

Since the 1860s there has been a widely held belief that the cotton workers passionately supported the anti-slavery cause, in spite of the suffering caused to them by the loss of cotton imports. This is not, however, entirely accurate. In June 1863 the Chorley public were entertained at the Mechanics' Institute by Mr & Mrs Fredericks in a series of dramatic sketches. After the performance Mr Fredericks gave a spirited defence of the Southern States, saying that slavery was poorly understood in England, for the negro slave in his experience was well cared for. Like many of his Confederate countrymen he hoped that Britain would throw her weight behind their cause from self-interest, but it was not to be. According to one report published in 1869 one emigrant from Chorley fought for the Union during the civil war, was promoted to officer status and retired to ranching in Texas when the war ended.

The conflict ended in April 1865. In England the cotton industry began to rebuild, especially with new mills. The New Mill for Smethurst's was altered and extended in 1866 by 66 feet to a length of 100 feet. There was a new warehouse, as well as a weaving shed for 384 looms. In 1867 a tribute was paid by the press to the working people of Chorley who had earned a measure of respect by their conduct in the face of the Cotton Famine. It is not surprising that the seventy and eighty-year-olds of the 1920s remembered the grim years of their youth.

CHAPTER EIGHT

Climax and Catastrophe

The Volunteers go to war

The Chorley Rifle Volunteers took over their new barracks in Devonshire Road in December 1895. More correctly known as the 1st Volunteer Battalion, Loyal North Lancashire Regiment, they were already well-established in Chorley by this date. Their scarlet uniforms (adopted in 1868) were a regular sight for bystanders. The officers came from Chorley's elite: Lawrence, Widdows and Gillett from the mill owners. The NCOs were usually time-served regulars, like Colour Sergeant Brady, and they were a professional backbone to the unit while the rank and file came from all walks of life. All were bound together in a spirit of Victorian patriotism, loyalty to the Queen and a keenness to serve, though service rarely meant active service.

Things changed rapidly in 1899. The regular 1st Battalion was serving in South Africa when trouble with the Boers intensified – the Loyals 2nd Battalion of regulars sailed to join them in time for the outbreak of war in October 1899. A besieging Boer army soon took on the Loyals and townsfolk in the town of Kimberley. The defence was relieved in February 1900.

At home, meanwhile, there was a scramble to join in. Twenty reservists were called up in November in Chorley and they received a resounding farewell. Nine of the men were treated to a dinner at the Royal Oak, with toasts, tributes, and the invocation of the ghosts of Waterloo, Wellington and Nelson to recall England's past glories. Crowds of people, thousands strong, cheered them to the station.

The Boers proved a hard nut to crack; the British military next called up the militia and volunteer units to swell the ranks. This call was received enthusiastically in Chorley. All the Chorley corps, made up of 250 men from Chorley and 50 from Horwich, volunteered for active service. From the four companies available, the Loyals were to send one abroad – their colleagues in Chorley's Artillery Corps also volunteered for action. The Loyals chosen to serve were selected by their height and chest measurements, shooting ability and status. They were unmarried men with no responsibilities. At the end of January 1900 a mixed contingent from Horwich and Chorley left for Fulwood Barracks, to become regulars.

The local press published letters written home by soldiers, their

VOLUNTEERS' HOME-COMING.

SPECIAL

OF THE

Chorley Standard

37th YEAR OF PUBLICATION. AND DISTRICT ADVERTISER.

WEDNESDAY, MAY 22, 1901.

A special edition of the *Chorley Standard* was printed for Wednesday, 22 May 1901, when Chorley's volunteer soldiers from the Loyals returned home from South Africa after twelve months' service fighting the Boers. [Lancashire County Library]

accounts shifting from the previous jingoistic fervour to the reality of action. John Hindle of the RAMC was at Colenso, while Private J. Hall, Coldstream Guards, fought at Magersfontein. He wrote that 'The place where the enemy are is like their being at the top of Rivington Pike, we being at the bottom. The bullets are continually flying past our heads like stones'.

At home everyone wanted to help. It was suggested that female weavers could serve as nurses once they had had a month's training at the Cottage Hospital. News came home of local men wounded or killed in mighty battles. Private Cowell wrote home to a friend: 'It is an awful sight to see the dying and wounded around you. Bob, stop where you are if you can'. Long before peace was agreed in 1902 the Loyals' Active Service Company came home, in May 1901, to an even bigger celebration than the farewell they received two years earlier.

Their return was eagerly prepared, as soon as they docked at Southampton on the *Idaho*. By the time they arrived at the railway station on a May evening thousands upon thousands were out to welcome them, the streets were decorated, with bands playing and flags waving. Their comrades from the Loyals, in their scarlet tunics, lined Chapel Street. The returning heroes, clad in khaki, were fêted all the way to the barracks, via the cattle market and Market Street. Lieutenant Stowell said the company had marched 1500 miles in twelve months, fought seventeen engagements and learned to live with the climate of the veldt.

For Chorley the Boer War was a glorious interlude. For the volunteers it sent abroad it was a short, sharp war with few casualties and a victory of sorts. The veterans talked of battles in faraway places: Mafeking, Bloemfontein, Ladysmith, Spion Kop and Modder River. As the years rolled on they recalled friends left on Spion Kop or a dozen other battlefields. Thirteen years later the spirit which had carried these men from their homes to the Transvaal was evoked for the Kaiser's War. Some re-enlisted, many people remembered how relatively painless it had been and the enthusiasm of the Loyals was rekindled in the Pals' Battalion.

Sir Henry Tate (1819–1899)

Most would agree that Chorley's most celebrated son is Sir Henry Tate. The reasons for this are not hard to discern: the Tate Gallery which he endowed has international renown, while the article which made his fortune is an ingredient of daily life under its brand name of Tate & Lyle, sugar and sugar products. His father, William Tate, was born in Newcastle. William was successively a Methodist lay preacher, a Baptist and, after his marriage in 1797, a Unitarian. Two years later he was invited to Chorley to serve as minister to the Park Street Chapel. Caleb Ashworth Tate, brother to Henry, went into trade and set up a business in Liverpool which afterwards became the training ground for young Henry in 1832.

Henry Tate was born in Chorley on 11 March 1819. Where he was born has puzzled generations of local historians, although the evidence which survives confirms the conclusion reached by R. H. Blackburn, Tate's biographer, in 1940.[1] For several years prior to 1819 Revd Tate lived at Terrace Mount, Jane Dawson and Revd Henry Brierley being his neighbours. These houses were owned by Abraham Crompton, who acted as patron to the Unitarian Chapel. Tate used some outbuildings here as a private school to supplement his stipend. The poor rate book for 1821 shows that the three properties at Terrace Mount were occupied by the individuals named above, but a pencil note alongside in a contemporary hand says 'Pulled Down', the entry being scored through, presumably corrected by the poor rate collector.

The survey made for the turnpike diversion of 1822 and the schedule dealing with the road show that properties across from the parish church were in the intended path of the new highway and its embankment over the Chor. This seems to prove that Tate's birthplace was removed not long after his birth. In 1824 the work carried out on the manse to Park Street Chapel was completed, allowing the Tates to move house. Some accounts maintain that the manse was already in place, the 1823–4 building work being an extension and refurbishment. According to the rate books Tate's home for a short period prior to the return to the manse was no. 12 Water Street not far from the chapel.

William Tate died in 1836, having served thirty-seven years as minister, and was buried in the chapel's graveyard. By this date Henry was already a grocery apprentice. He acquired his first shop in Liverpool in 1839, and others followed. He married Jane Wignall at Aughton in 1841 and moved into the wholesale trade in grocery. From grocery he moved to sugar refining, a long-established Liverpool speciality, based largely on the city's trading links. It was to be the making of Tate's fortune. By the 1880s he was a wealthy man, and after his death on 5 December 1899 his wealth was shared out in the way which made him famous. He gave £42,000 to the University of London, and bequeathed the Tate Gallery to the nation, including sixty-five of his own private collection of paintings.

Henry Tate's fame rests on his fabulous wealth, his generosity and his passion for art. Many causes, including public libraries, benefitted from his kindness. The Chorley Public Library received a gift of £500 from him in its fledgling days, one of the rare contacts he seems to have made with his birthplace. No other man or woman native to Chorley achieved so much in one lifetime.

Mr Sante's Grand Theatre

During this century the cinema, radio and television have brought regular, cheap and affordable entertainment to every town and village in the country. In the past public entertainment was an occasional and long-awaited landmark in the calendar. The seasonal fairs held in market towns like Chorley were not solely for business but were also opportunities for travelling players to entertain gatherings of people from outlying areas. One seventeenth-century traveller to Chorley recorded in his diary that he saw a religious play at the fair – perhaps in the style of everyman plays.

> Friday, being Bartholomew Day, I hired a horse and went with Thomas Leech to Croston . . . we went to Chorley . . . it was the faire . . . we went to see a show concerning the lives of man from his infancie to old age.

The fair which was held on 4, 5 and 6 September was traditionally a pleasure fair right up to this century, while the fairs held in March, May and August were trading events. Early in the last century William Tootell's diary records visits to Chorley by several groups of players – Mr Thornhill's for example – but Tootell omits to say what plays they performed and (equally important) where they could be seen. We know from some years later that the assembly room of the Royal Oak Inn was used to hold major events, such as charity balls and soirées for fashionable society, so it may be that it served as a theatre too. By the 1830s there was a theatre of sorts in Chorley, for a rare surviving playbill from 1838 advertises a series of performances of a play called *The Bride of Astley Hall, or the Outlaws of Chorley Moor*. This period piece, written and performed by a group of amateur players, has a list of characters including Sir Edward Anglezark (privately leading the outlaws), the good Sir Reginald Charnock of Astley, Oscar of Heapy (an outlaw chief) and Old Margery of Darwen (a supposed witch). The bill also describes some of the painted scenery as scenes of Astley Hall, Wheelton Old Tower and the cavern of the outlaws on Chorley Moor.

Mr C. H. Duval opened a theatre in Hill Street in 1865. The opening play was *Green Hills of the Far West*, with Shakespeare's *Othello* in the following week. In 1877 Duval built a wooden theatre on the cattle market naming it the Theatre Royal. Measuring 110 feet long by 50 feet wide, the Royal was designed to seat 1,500 people, with a dress circle and side boxes. For this theatre Duval put on as the opening piece a comedy called *Extremes*, a humorous play about Lancashire life and men.[2]

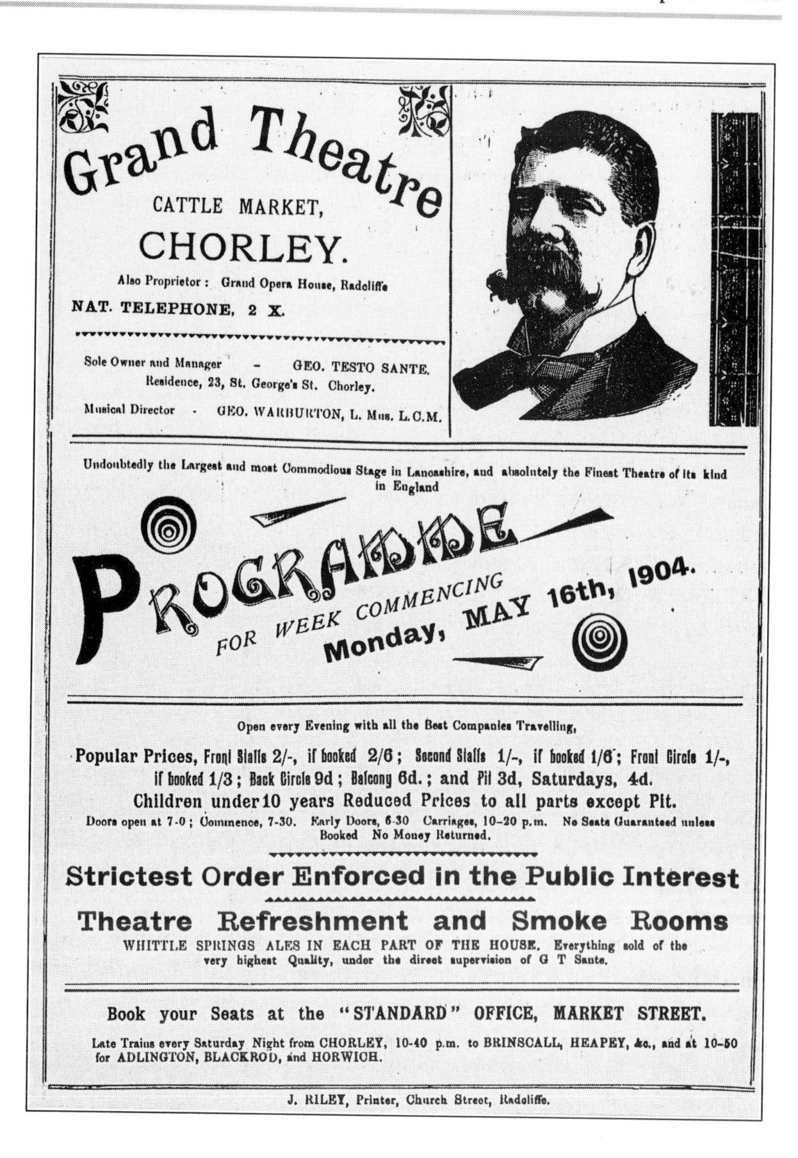

Grand Theatre
CATTLE MARKET,
CHORLEY.
Also Proprietor: Grand Opera House, Radcliffe
NAT. TELEPHONE, 2 X.

Sole Owner and Manager - GEO. TESTO SANTE.
Residence, 23, St. George's St. Chorley.
Musical Director - GEO. WARBURTON, L. Mus. L.C.M.

Undoubtedly the Largest and most Commodious Stage in Lancashire, and absolutely the Finest Theatre of its kind in England

PROGRAMME
FOR WEEK COMMENCING
Monday, MAY 16th, 1904.

Open every Evening with all the Best Companies Travelling,
Popular Prices, Front Stalls 2/-, if booked 2/6; Second Stalls 1/-, if booked 1/6; Front Circle 1/-, if booked 1/3; Back Circle 9d; Balcony 6d.; and Pit 3d, Saturdays, 4d.
Children under 10 years Reduced Prices to all parts except Pit.
Doors open at 7-0; Commence, 7-30. Early Doors, 6-30 Carriages, 10-20 p.m. No Seats Guaranteed unless Booked No Money Returned.

Strictest Order Enforced in the Public Interest

Theatre Refreshment and Smoke Rooms
WHITTLE SPRINGS ALES IN EACH PART OF THE HOUSE. Everything sold of the very highest Quality, under the direct supervision of G T Sante.

Book your Seats at the "STANDARD" OFFICE, MARKET STREET.
Late Trains every Saturday Night from CHORLEY, 10-40 p.m. to BRINSCALL, HEAPEY, &c., and at 10-50 for ADLINGTON, BLACKROD, and HORWICH.

J. RILEY, Printer, Church Street, Radcliffe.

Programmes for Sante's Grand Theatre are very rare. This example from 1904 features a drawing of the strongman himself. [Lancashire County Library]

Throughout the Victorian period the town attracted varied forms of entertainment; travelling circuses, especially Sanger's and Buffalo Bill's, brought memorable, exotic shows; the Mechanics' Institute held programmes of readings and theatre; after 1879 the new town hall had large rooms suitable for dramatic performances, and increased leisure time and higher living standards gave people a taste for more. In 1893 Mr Mortimer built a wooden circus on the cattle market facing Cleveland Street; one account described it as 'admirably arranged and first class entertainment given, it was well patronised for a time until the novelty wore off'. Following Mortimer's death the lease was taken by Mr Myers, who staged Myers American Circus, which featured equestrian acts and catered for the vogue for Wild West shows. In January 1894, however, the *Chorley*

Standard reported a different kind of performance. The pantomime *Cinderella* was staged and Myers used fifty local children as a whole range of characters. 'Guest' characters included Mr and Mrs John Bull, famous soldiers and statesmen and Queen Victoria herself: 'The Clarkonians continued their marvellous exhibition on the flying trapeze, whilst the clever and extraordinary equestrian feats of Mr James Washington Myers are always witnessed with deserving admiration'. The same programme included a contest of skill under the patronage of Chorley Football Club, the competitors having to kick a football through a ring 4 feet in diameter. The event was won by Heyes, the St George's goalkeeper.

Myers' premises were referred to about this time as a temperance theatre of varieties, or music hall as we would now describe it; however, the theatre's decline in popularity was attributed in the end to its lack of variety in fare. The 1890s were a golden age for the music hall, with no real competition. Myers' theatre closed in 1894 but later in that year the lease was taken over by a man whose name became a byword for the best in popular theatre, first in Chorley and then in Radcliffe and Whitefield.

He had the magnificent name of George Testo Sante, and in appearance he was said to be equally striking; blonde, with curly moustaches and the physique of a circus strongman. Sante was larger than life. His name was purely a stage device, for he was really called George Mulhall, but one and all knew him as Sante. At one time he was billed as the 'Man with the Iron Head', or the 'Strongman', but best of all he gloried as 'Sante the Showman', a name which he lived to the full.

The facts of his early life are sparse and Sante himself was reticent about his birthplace. From his own evidence he was born in 1856, possibly in America, as his first job is stated to have been as a ticket seller in an American circus in 1867. Twelve months later he was a member of a circus travelling through the former Confederate States; in the same year he was touring the West Indies, Cuba and Jamaica. In 1873 he was in Vera Cruz but took French leave, getting free passage on an English steamer to New Orleans where he enlisted in the American navy in expectation of a war with Cuba. Once this episode was behind him Sante went into a roller skating act and came to England in 1876. During this time he went on tour with the famous Sanger Brothers Circus, 'tenting' in the phrase of that era. Whatever apprenticeship he had served before the Cuban War, Sante developed and extended in the 1870s. About this period he acquired his stage name, and he married, his wife also being from a theatrical mould. They were jointly billed as Testo and Onri, in an act displaying gymnastic skills. Twenty years later the pair could still perform amazing feats of strength. Their later stage shows featured stunts which were spectacular for that time and gave clear evidence of Sante's background as a circus strongman. One feat involved Sante pitting his strength against the pulling power of two heavy horses on stage. In another act, Mrs Sante would pull a cannon across the stage, attached to her hair. In 1904 Sante, with the aid of Charles Darrell, wrote *The Showman*, which enabled him to display all of his talents to the utmost.

The Santes toured the whole of Britain, much of Europe and parts of North America in the 1880s; by 1887 he had bought the lease of the Victoria Theatre in Glasgow but suffered a loss of £3,000 when the venture failed. His next project took him to Ireland, where his share in a circus proved successful. He found a taste for theatre management which he satisfied in two more ventures in Wales.

When the theatre in Chorley became available Sante ran it for a season and finding his efforts rewarded spent £700 on remodelling the interior. The Grand Theatre was opened on 16 September 1895. The press advertisement billed the Grand as the finest wooden theatre in England. The *Chorley Standard's* reporter seems to have agreed, writing that it was one of the prettiest and cosiest theatres in the land. The trade press was equally enthusiastic about the Grand. Contrary to the normal practice of having painted Alpine scenes on the act-drop, Sante had his act-drop painted in the form of a Jubilee sovereign with portraits of the Queen and the royal family; he also invested in up-to-date stage lighting and plush seating.

In later years Sante's style of theatre made its mark; on a visit to England in 1987, Mr A. Green of New Jersey, USA, recalled the kind of play he had seen as a boy in 1912. A typical play at the Grand was a melodrama, featuring stock characters such as the hero, a young heroine and her baby, 'and a villain with curled mustaches and a look of the Devil.' Mr Green remembered that during one of these dramas the story had reached a harrowing point, where the villain was doing his worst; unable to stand this any longer one old lady leaped from her seat in the pit and screamed at the villain, 'Tha'rt a reight bad lot!' Young Green at the time worked for Sante's rival, Mark Lorne, who ran the Theatre Royal in Market Street.

Some of the success of Sante's theatre management lay in booking the best travelling companies. Their shows ranged from the Wild West, to Ireland and homely Lancashire mill life, with a trip to Blackpool and plenty of dialect. He did, however, vary the programme, including Shakespearean drama, opera and special appearances of well-known actors of the day such as T. P. Sullivan from the USA and Hanco, the renowned prison breaker, whose act had echoes of Harry Houdini. The audience of the Grand would be as likely to see *East Lynne*, *Hamlet* or *School for Scandal* as a popular melodrama. In 1899 the Chorley Town Council heard that the Grand Theatre was patronised by 150,000 people each year.

Sante recognized the potential of cinema. He built the Pavilion in Clarence Street in 1909, seating two thousand people, as a theatre in the traditional mould; like many others he presented a mixed programme which relegated the films to second feature after the live acts. In the same year he opened the Winter Gardens, a roller skating rink converted from the old drill hall. He hired Professor William Chivers, a skating champion who had worked for P. T. Barnum in the States. At Sante's Hippodrome cinema he took special care in the summer months to provide adequate ventilation for the comfort of his customers. Live theatre, however, was at the core of the Showman's success for many years, a thriving business founded on Sante's conviction that he knew public taste and how to cater for it.

With one final tragic event the Grand passed into local folklore. On the night of Monday, 16 March 1914, the evening show, a pantomime of *Jack Horner*, ended at 10.30 and Frank, George Sante's son, locked up the theatre shortly after 11 p.m. All seemed normal until two patrolling policemen, constables Turner and Baxter, found the theatre on fire not long after 1 a.m. Within five minutes the Chorley Fire Brigade was on the scene, playing jets of water on the blaze, which appeared to have started at the stage end near the bar and rapidly spread to the roof: 'The efforts of the Fire Brigade were futile, the great roof, which was of tarred asphalt and corrugated iron, falling in about half an hour after the outbreak'.

In the light of dawn all that was left of the Grand was the timber frontage, marked with gaping holes. The rest of the theatre was no more than a smouldering ruin. Sante lost £5,000 through the blaze, very little of the fabric being covered by insurance. The pantomime company's thirty-six artistes lost everything – personal belongings, props, scenery, equipment – in the fire. At the end of March a charity event was held in Chorley Town Hall to help them. Sante himself was in the South of England at the time of the fire. His health deteriorated and his death came in November 1916 in Paignton, Devon. He left a widow, Fanny and two sons, one of whom was in South Africa.[3]

George Testo Sante, or Mulhall if you wish, was a marvellous character of his time – a successful businessman, he was primarily the showman he craved to be, supplying the kind of entertainment the public enjoyed, and yet in the 1890s he also undertook a charity scheme which he called the Poor Folks Christmas Dinner Fund. For more than eleven years his charity performance was used to aid the needy in the festive season. Sante made his mark in the ways he knew best.

Leisure pursuits

The game was advertised as a 'first' for Lancashire – a floodlit match to be played between Chorley and Swinton on 24 October 1878. Elaborate preparations were made for the lighting, and 8,000 spectators came from miles around by carriage, rail and on foot to see the electric light illuminate the Dole Lane ground for a game of rugby. They were to be disappointed: the lighting was inadequate, and a torrential rainstorm drenched the crowd. Realising how the restive crowd might turn ugly Henry Hibbert and Mr Ditchfield carried the £70 gate money to the Rose and Crown, where it stayed hidden under the landlady's bed. Several days later a successful replay was held: the goal areas were well lit, though not the whole ground, and the ball was painted white to aid visibility. It was an inauspicious start to floodlit matches!

Until the 1870s football was simply a children's game. It might even meet with the disapproval of the authorities – in 1826 children were brought before the magistrates for playing the game on Sunday. The schoolmaster at Weld Bank had kicked the ball out to encourage the boys and Father Thompson, together with another adult, pleaded in defence that the game might be contrary to the law of man, but not of God.

Rugby football came via Wigan, where John Lawrence was a player for Wigan R. C. His friends were keen and at the Anchor Inn on 15 October 1875 a meeting held to form a Chorley club: the first local players were gentlemen amateurs.

Their strip was dark blue jersey and stockings and, so one story says, they were called the Chorley Bulldogs. Their greatest success came in March 1879, when they beat Rossendale at Blackpool to take the North of England Rugby Challenge Cup.

Elsewhere Association Football was growing. In 1881 elements of Chorley RFC favoured a change and left to play soccer for Birkacre, leaving a weakened rugby side to play on. They too transferred to 'football' in 1883, from which time Chorley town's club has eschewed rugby. The familiar black and white striped shirts soon appeared, hence the Chorley 'Magpies'. They played in the Lancashire League from the 1894–5 season, still at Dole Lane, across the site of the later Coronation Recreation Ground. In September 1901 they moved to St George's Park on the Rangletts, and played here until after the First World War. The club began playing at Victory Park in September 1920. There was a disastrous fire in November 1945, when a grandstand was destroyed and much of the history of the club was lost.

Crowds were normally good-natured and loud in their support; sometimes they were too partisan. A letter to the *Standard* in 1877 complained

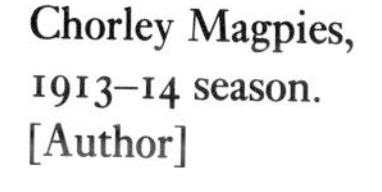
Chorley Magpies, 1913–14 season. [Author]

that youngsters were welcome, but not when they booed the opposing side. The correspondent complained that they threw mud, rotten oranges and brickbats at two visiting sides. In November 1895, a travelling side of lady footballers played an exhibition game at Dole Lane, with two sides of ten players each and a loaned goalkeeper from Chorley F.C. The ladies wore bloomers, red and white or blue, put on a first-class show, and ended the day as guests of Mr Sante at the Grand.

The gentleman's game of the Victorian era was cricket, formal fixtures beginning in the 1860s. The Chorley team played home games on their pitch at Chorley Moor, behind Willow House. Here, too, gentlemen made up most of the side – three of the Widdows family, one Lightoller and Mr Part, possibly Mr Part of Astley Hall. This team must have been the Chorley West End side which amalgamated with the Chorley Amateurs (who played at Yarrow Bridge) in 1905 to form Chorley Town. After this they played at Windsor Park.

The common man's game seems to have been bowls. Richard and William Buckley, labourers, from Charnock Richard, with Richard Sharrock, a butcher from Heath Charnock, were caught playing bowls on a Sunday during worship in 1592. Much later Nicholas Blundell's diary tells us that he bowled at the Yarrow Bridge in the 1710s. He might also have played on the green which used to be behind Dickinson's store in Market Street. After 1829 the Fazakerley Arms had a green, and the Robin Hood and the Parkers Arms in Park Road had greens before the 1840s. The game grew in popularity at all levels. The Chorley Subscription Bowling Green dates from 1852, its green being off Windsor Road. Working mens' clubs developed their own bowling greens as recreational attractions, and by 1902 there were at least a dozen bowling clubs. Adjacent to the old Red Lion was the Skittle Alley, which seems to have dated from the early eighteenth century. A review of 1901 described how long bowling was once popular in local pubs, the aim being to throw bowls furthest in the fewest throws.

At the turn of the century the other sport with wide appeal was pigeon-flying. There were reported to be ten thousand pigeons racing for four homing societies in Chorley in 1902. Cockfighting was much older. In 1758, 'a main of cocks' was advertised at Ormskirk between William Scarisbrick and Henry Leigh of Chorley, the fights to take

12

SPECIAL ENGAGEMENT OF THE

New Bi-unial Combination Matagraph

(THE CINEMATAGRAPH LIVING PICTURES.)

ALSO OF . . . MR. HARRY GERRARD, of LEIGH,

DRAWING ROOM ENTERTAINER,

In the TOWN HALL, on TUESDAY, MAY 8th.

PROGRAMME.

1 **The Sentinel and the Bear**
2 **Fire Call**—Turn out of Belfast's Smart Brigade.
3 **Blackpool**—An interesting and lively view of the sea front.
4 **Joke on Boy—Fishing**
5 **Dragoons Swimming their Horses Across a River**—A very fine water scene.
6 **Irish Jig**
7 **Scotch Reel**
8 **Chokee Bill as a Nurse, or "The Bobby's Flirtation"**
9 **Kissing in the Dark**—Very novel and Amusing.
10 **Forth Bridge**—Magnificent view of the Forth Bridge, showing an express passing within a few feet of camera.
11 **The Launch**—The launching of the magnificent liner "Braemer Castle."
12 **Embarking**—Passengers embarking at Southampton for the Cape.
13 **Military View**—March past of Scots Greys.
14 **Tarantelle**—A lively dance in fancy and picturesque costumes.
15 **Queensbury Tunnel**—A most popular and successful picture.
16 **The Quarrelsome Neighbours**—Very comic.
17 **The Housemaid**—A pretty housemaid flirting with a sweep.
18 **Greasy Pole**—A most amusing picture shown backwards.
19 **Children Plaiting the Maypole**
20 **Tramp and Artist**—A very lively picture.

Also several of the latest pictures from South Africa, and a selection of high-class Dioramic Views.

At intervals, Mr. HARRY GERRARD will render the following items :—

Humorous Song .. .. "The Glorious Days to come"
Humorous Song .. .. "No"
Humorous Scena .. .. "The Serial Story"

DOORS OPEN AT 7-0, TO COMMENCE AT 7-30.

ADMISSION - - 6d. and 3d. CHILDREN - - 1d.

This programme for the 'Matagraph' comes from 1900 when the patrons could see twenty short films and early newsreel pictures of the Boer War in South Africa. [Lancashire County Library]

The Theatre Royal in Market Street, 1911. Mark Lorne, the theatre's flamboyant manager, boasted the motto 'Read, Mark, Lorne'. [Lancashire County Library]

place over four days. In 1824, though, the select vestry ruled that any pauper keeping dogs or game cocks would not be eligible for relief. Some years later a Chorley blacksmith had premises at the bottom of High Street where the birds were hidden under the hearth. At this period cockfighting was prohibited on penalty of a £5 fine.

Hunting for game and its shady equivalent, poaching, were as old as the town's existence. Old men living about 1900 could remember hunting rabbits in the Dingle (the site of the cattle market) in their youth. James Talbot several times refers in his diary to hunting, once for hares at Hartwood Green with hounds, and may too have hunted with the crossbow he loaned to Mr Wilkinson in 1824. John Heyes of Quarter Greys, tenant to Thomas Cross, had to keep a hound, beagle or greyhound for his master as part of his tenancy. With large expanses of moorland and old woodland within easy reach Chorley had much to offer to the hunter.

Getting into the countryside for recreational pursuits became popular in Victorian times: rambling clubs sprang up, and cycling clubs ventured further afield, but less organised activities predominated. In the 1880s and again in 1897 public trespass on Healey Nab raised the issue of public rights of way which conflicted with the demands of owners of shooting rights. Allen Clarke, Bolton's famous dialect writer, married a Chorley woman and in one story from 1916 Clarke described a walk through Crosse Hall, through Bagganley to the top of the Nab on a balmy, summers day in 1916. Small boys in the 1920s made a days outing to the Nab, fortified with a billy can of bread and lard. Walking produced a few 'oddball' events – Mr Mitchell's attempt to walk one thousand miles in one thousand hours in a field behind the Yarrow Bridge in 1869 was one.

Athletics events started to appear in the 1880s, and boxing in several clubs in the years after the First World War, when Chorley produced some talented boxers. In the early nineteenth century Bob Gregson of Heskin was all-England champion, and bare-knuckle fights continued locally for decades. In 1867, for example, the police broke up a prize fight at Standish, after James Bentham had challenged James Roberts by

Sept 3 1815

CHORLEY RACES, 1815.

TO BE RUN FOR, ON CHORLEY RACE GROUND,

On MONDAY, September 4th, 1815,

A VALUABLE

Saddle and Bridle,

By any Horse, Mare, or Gelding, that never started for the Value of 50 Pounds Matches and Sweepstakes excepted ——*Second Best to have the Bridle.*

Mr. *H*——'s bay f. 4 years old, by Syntax, black & red. | Mr. N——'s bay h. aged, by Fly, purple & red.
Mr. S——'s g. f. aged, by Tett, blue & green. | Mr. *H*——'s bay h. aged, by Sweep, red & green.

And on TUESDAY, SEPTEMBER 5th,

A VALUABLE

SADDLE AND BRIDLE,

By any Horse, Mare, or Gelding that never started for the value of 50 Pounds, Matches and Sweepstakes excepted.——Second best to have the Bridle.

(*Horses*—the same as entered for Monday.)

And on WEDNESDAY the 7th of SEPTEMBER,

A HANDSOME

PURSE of GOLD,

By any Horse, Mare, or Gelding, that never started for the Value of 50 Pounds, Matches and Sweepstakes excepted

Mr. W——'s black g. 3 years old, by Skyrocket, black & red | Mr. T. W——'s b f. Moggy Lowther, blk. & g.
Mr. R——'s c. c. 4 yrs. old, by Spanking Roger, pur & red. | Mr. S——'s b. f. Maid of Lodi, by Tim Bobbin.

Two or more Horses to start each Day or no Race.

A MAIN OF COCKS,

Will be fought during the Races.

PLAYS and ASSEMBLIES as usual.

N. B. It is particularly required that all Pigs shall be kep up during the Races,

GEORGE BARNES,
JOHN AINSWORTH, } *Stewards.*

(PARKER PRINTER.) Mr. SCHOFIELD, Clerk of the Course

The Chorley Races were an annual event held on the Stump racecourse. Several of these advertisements survive from the early years of the last century. News accounts describe these race meetings as lively, colourful and boisterous social events. [Lancashire County Library]

As the Victorian era drew to a close working people generally enjoyed greater freedom for leisure pursuits. For those able to afford a bicycle, cycling provided a means to travel further afield. As this photograph shows it was not solely a male preserve. [Lancashire County Library]

throwing down a sovereign. Four rounds were fought in front of two hundred onlookers.

What should have been the more sedate activity of dancing was occasionally censured. Mr Hodgkinson warned the Improvement Commission in 1865 of the evils of dancing: 'He knew . . . that young men who held respectable positions in the town, were in the habit of frequenting those places, and dancing in clogs with factory girls, just for the purpose of creating a noise and disturbance'. These raucous affairs were held near the Big Lamp. Twenty years later the rector protested from the pulpit about the dances held in the town hall, which were associated with licentiousness and drunken revelry. Nevertheless, scores of dances were held to raise charitable funds or for pure fun.

Sante's Grand Theatre was well known in Chorley, and there were other entertainments of this kind. Music hall was held in the old chapel in Chapel Street, and the Theatre Royal opened in Market Street in 1911. Townspeople could see travelling waxworks, numerous menageries, Sanger's Circus, Wombwell's Circus and could enjoy regular visits from Buffalo Bill's Wild West Shows. In 1904, for example, the huge show came in by train, and set up its arena on Millers Field at Weld Bank Lane. Two shows daily featured a recreation of *Custer's Last Stand*.

From 1800 to mid-century Chorley was in transition from a rural market town to a thriving and growing industrial centre. During this phase old customs died. One example was the loss of the Chorley Races, held annually, to coincide with the September Fair. They survived until at least 1842. In some years four days were given to the races, in others no more than two, but one day was devoted to foot races. Although the posters refer to Chorley Race Ground no permanent fixture was used. Chorley Moor is often said to have been the race course, though the more likely site is Stump Fields. Starting from the old town hall or the Royal Oak the race lasted over 1½ miles. There were handsome prizes – a purse of gold (in 1814) or a saddle and bridle.[4] In 1842, when the races were held late in September to avoid a clash with Preston Guild, the steward's purse was £7.

The last day of each fair was given over to entertainment with foot races, sack races and novelty events. A favourite and regular race was 'A Foot Race, for Half-a-Guinea, or a New Pair of Shoes, By men in Wooden Clogs, from opposite the Royal Oak . . . to the Joiners Arms and back; each clog to contain six pease – NB The pease to be counted upon their return, and no boiling allowed'. One race had men running with false wooden legs, another was for old women (not less than forty years);

cockfighting, circuses, side stalls, theatre, provided every ingredient for a lively autumn fair. After 1842, though, the races seem to be less evident and it is possible that the new railway line, by cutting through the race course, led to their abandonment.

The advent of cinema has already been mentioned. As well as George Sante's Pavilion (1909) there was the Hippodrome in Gillibrand Street, opened in 1909. This remained a cinema only until 1946, and in 1948 became the Tudor Ballroom. The Public Hall Picture Palace in Dole Lane was renamed the Empire Electric Theatre in 1910, closed in 1958 and since 1959 has been the home of CADOS, or 'Little Theatre'. The Theatre Royal, opened by Mark Lorne in 1911 in Market Street, was converted to a cinema in 1931. It closed in 1955 to put on stage shows once more, was demolished in 1960 and Lennons Supermarket was built on the site. Two super-cinemas appeared in the 1930s; Bolton Street's Plaza opened in March 1937, while the Odeon was part of the group of buildings on the site of the old Royal Oak, opened in February 1938.

Books for the people

Before 1800 the few libraries in the town were in private hands. A newsroom was opened at the Black Bull Inn in 1789, but it was solely for the use of patrons who paid a guinea each year for privileged access to regional and national newspapers brought to Chorley by the speedy new mail coaches. The newsroom moved to the Royal Oak some time later and

Jolly and Buckley's drawing of the Chorley Free Library in Avondale Road. The project began in 1897, the year of Victoria's Jubilee and opened to the public in 1899. The sketch shows that a large niche over the entrance would have housed a statue of the Queen. [Lancashire County Library]

Councillor John Wareing was one of the champions of the free library movement in the town, though each move to adopt the Public Libraries Acts was rejected by the town council between 1881 and 1897. [Lancashire County Library]

then in 1833 to the Red Lion Inn. The venture folded in 1846 and in 1852 the Mount Pleasant News Room began with non-sectarian principles and subscriptions low enough to attract working men. It was said that anyone using these newsrooms would be pestered for snippets of news by those who were unable to pay or illiterate.

In about 1798 a Chorley bookseller-cum-draper named William Bibby issued a catalogue of his wares, including popular chap books. He offered to buy parcels of books and libraries, but also advertised a circulating library. Charles Robinson kept a bookshop in Market Street from the 1820s onwards. Robinson was also a printer, bookbinder, stationer and circulating library owner who advertised 'a London parcel twice a month'. Very little of his printing work survives, apart from his *History and Directory of Chorley* (1835), and a number of playbills and posters. The *History*, which derives in part from Baines (1824), displayed his local knowledge and included a directory which was not bettered for many years. The Union Library, a subscription library, opened in Back Mount in 1814. Subscribers paid twelve shillings per annum for membership.

The next library was part of the Mechanics Institute in Chapel Street (the old Methodist Chapel), in 1844. The clientele were chiefly working men who could also attend classes in a night school and enjoy the lectures on popular themes. John Hallam later acknowledged his debt to the classes, where he first learned to read at the age of twenty-one. The Institute moved to the town hall in 1851 and soon had a good library of nine hundred volumes but the enterprise came to an end in 1880.

In 1868 Union Street's Music Warehouse had a stock of ten thousand popular sheet music scores, forming a special circulating library. In the same year Chorley Co-operative Society's Education Department Library advertised five hundred 'new' books for its members and their families. Some churches had libraries, as did political clubs such as the Reform. Good as these were they were bound to reflect a limited religious or political viewpoint, though their very existence was enough to persuade local politicians that a public library would be unnecessary.

Chorley was slow to adopt the Public Libraries Acts, which had promoted town, free or public libraries from the 1850s. Each time the idea was proposed it was rejected on the grounds of cost, though from 1882 Councillor John Wareing championed a Chorley free library. His pleas, though persuasive and soundly based, were thrown out. In 1883 a committee was set up from among enthusiasts in the town, with the public voice of Edwin Crew, editor of the *Chorley Weasel*. Like Wareing an outsider, he knew the benefits of libraries for working people.

In 1891 and 1895 Alderman Hibbert proposed that the town council should adopt the Acts, but each time was defeated. The public library eventually came into being as a commemoration of the Diamond Jubilee of Queen Victoria in 1897. H. T. Parke provided the cost of the building and the Whittle family gave a plot of land in Avondale Road, although public opinion favoured a site on the Market Place or in Market Street. On 13 December 1899 the library was opened. The first librarian was Edward McKnight. Considerable progress was made in the next quarter century, including the provision of a school library service in 1922.[5]

A branch library at Eaves Lane opened in 1965 and a major extension was made to the reference library in 1972. On the reorganisation of local government in 1974 the library service was amalgamated into the Lancashire County Library.

Votes for Women

The Reform Acts of 1867 and 1884 greatly increased the number of men who had the vote, but the voting rights of women were delayed considerably longer and were only achieved after a determined campaign. Chorley was not untouched by the battle which was being waged. For instance, during the election of 1913 an unknown Irish mill girl lectured a crowd of people, estimated at one thousand strong, in St George's Street. A local song went,

> Put me on an island where the girls are few
> Put me among the most ferocious lions in the zoo;
> Put me on a treadmill and I'll never fret,
> But for pity's sake don't put me near a Suffragette.[6]

The opponents of women's suffrage conjured up a whole catalogue of fears; one fear traded on the numerical inferiority of men against women in the population – men would face the 'tyranny of petticoat government'. Another maintained that all women were basically uninterested in political affairs – dozens of accounts in newspapers of the day prove the assertion to be false. In the course of the 1900 election, for example, a fight broke out at the Ellerbeck Colliery pithead, when a young miner wearing the Conservative colours in his cap got into a scrap over an election dispute with a pitbrow lass named Catherine Burns. Although knocked to the ground by him and kicked she gave as good as she got and moreover acted as her own counsel in court.

As the Women's Social and Political Union movement grew, branches sprang up all over the country. The idea took hold relatively early in Lancashire, where women always made up a sizeable section of the working population. One of the earliest pro-suffrage meetings in Chorley was held on 11 January 1910, when the town hall assembly room was the venue: 'Long before the time announced for commencing the meeting the Assembly Room was absolutely packed to the doors. The aisles were crowded with a serried mass of young life, and from the disposition of a large section of the audience it was evident at an early stage that the meeting would be of a turbulent character'.[7]

The room filled up so rapidly that an overflow meeting was held outside, and addressed in its own right by a Miss Farquharson. In their speeches the ladies argued passionately that Britain's stance on suffrage lagged behind that of progressive countries, and that taxation (which affected and was paid by women just as much as by men) should be matched by representation. The speakers were booed, heckled, interrupted and almost drowned out by catcalls and interruptions from rowdy young men. And yet they continued, setting out reasoned arguments, backed up by statistics and telling examples to prove their point. Eventually the audience warmed to the spirit of the young women on the platform, at one point cheering loudly when one speaker stated that 'She had heard it said that an angry woman with a frying pan was equal to any man with his fists'.

A meeting to be addressed by Mrs Pankhurst in March 1910 was cancelled, but locally the movement remained active. Progress was slow: feathers were ruffled in 1912 when, at a meeting of the town council, Councillor Sharples moved that 'this Council, believing that the question of Women's Suffrage is ripe for solution urges Parliament to take the earliest possible opportunity of passing some measure for the enfranchisement of women'. A counter-motion, to prevent the discussion of the issue was carried. Within a week Miss Edith Eskrigge, writing on behalf of the Suffragists of the North-West, launched a broadside against the council – she pointed out that in recent months one hundred and fifty other councils had tackled the issue, regardless of party politics.[8] One of her colleagues, Miss Cicely Leadley Brown, wrote to the press to contrast their work with the Anti-Suffragist campaign which was actively growing at the same time.

The death of Lord Crawford in 1910 led to a series of events which put Chorley in the national spotlight, highlighting among other issues the question of women's suffrage. Crawford's demise elevated his son, Lord Balcarres, to the House of Lords and he, as the sitting MP for the Chorley Division since 1895, was forced to resign his seat in the Commons. A by-election was called, arousing all kinds of press interest. Balcarres, a Conservative, had had a majority of 2,000 at the previous election and thus all looked rosy for Sir Henry Hibbert, the Conservative

NATIONAL UNION OF WOMEN'S SUFFRAGE SOCIETIES

Law-Abiding AND Non-Party

Final Rally ON CATTLE MARKET,

Tuesday, Feb. 18th,

AT 7-0 P.M.

Printed and Published by A. Hill, Livesey Street, Chorley.

Chorley's by-election of 1913 focused local attention on the issue of Votes for Women, as this hand bill shows. [Lancashire County Library]

On the land women and young girls such as these shared manual labour but were excluded from social and political equality. [Lancashire County Library]

candidate. His background was ideal: locally born and bred, from a cotton background, with town and county council experience, he was sure to appeal to the electors. His opponent, the Liberal candidate, was John Peter Todd Jackson, a Wheelton man, from the same industrial background as Hibbert.

Jackson's election address focused on several points: Free Trade, Tariff Reform, religious education, the policy of the Liberal government and votes for women. Sir Henry's platform excluded any support for the latter: as a Tory he would not endorse the extension of the franchise.

In the course of the campaign the National Union of Women's Suffrage Society set up their offices at 17 Crown Street. The workers spoke at different meetings up and down the division: one speaker, Miss Helga Gill (from Norway) addressed an audience of five hundred people at Coppull on the morning of the 13 February, before going on to speak to a second meeting at Cowling during the mill's lunch break. One group of Suffragists held an evening meeting on the cattle market, their audience listening attentively for an hour. The next day one party hired Greatorex's coach to drive them out to the Talbot Mills at Bagganley; their audience of mill girls listened carefully, but were of course non-voters. The trip was spoiled when they came 'under fire' from a gang of youths who had watched from a grassy bank and ripped up sods to be used as missiles. Greatorex later recalled how the ladies escaped in a hurry from a rain of soil and stones.

On the 14 February a great crowd gathered near the Reform Club in St George's Street, where rival Home Rule and Conservative speakers vied for their attention.

> Adjoining Home Rule and Conservative meetings started simultaneously, but where as speakers from the former platform had an attentive audience and a peaceful hearing, the Conservatives underwent severe heckling. Mill girls provided most of the fun. "Three cheers for Mr Jackson" cried one when the din was at its height, and the crowd responded lustily. "What about Bonar Law?" queried another of the girls. A storm of booing followed.[9]

Though Jackson made a spirited fight of it, the 1913 election was a comfortable win for Hibbert, keeping Chorley in the Conservative camp. Nevertheless, votes for women was not defeated; in fact it seems to have grown in strength. In March 1913 Miss Todd was the Chorley delegate to the National Union of Women's Suffrage Society. Towards the end of that year Shepherds Hall in Chapel Street was the venue for the N.U.W.S.S. when several speakers once again argued for a resolution of the problem. Councillor Sharples posed a question to his audience.

> Was the man who occupied a slum dwelling and had only a table and an orange box, who had the right to vote and would exercise it probably either way for the price of a pint of beer, as capable as the woman who slaved from morning till night?[10]

In 1918 women over thirty were given the vote, which they had hoped would be won by persuasive argument. Ten years later all men and women aged twenty-one and over were given the right to vote.

The First World War

For months before the outbreak of war in August 1914 the local papers kept people informed of the move to conflict. During August local Territorials were in training at Kirkby Lonsdale. They were recalled in haste, the Loyals (the 4th Battalion, Loyal North Lancashire Regiment) called on men from the special reserve, ex-soldiers and former volunteers.

'Pals' battalions saw friends and neighbours serving together. Here the 11th [Service] Battalion, East Lancashire Regiment's Chorley 'Pals' parade at the Drill Hall in Devonshire Road in February 1915. [Lancashire County Library]

Photographs of the Loyals, parading at the Drill Hall in Devonshire Road, show ranks of erstwhile civilians and some still in working clothes. They were all in uniform soon enough and sent into action across the Channel. The mood of the time reminded many of the departure for the Boer War; some individuals were even veterans of 1900. Their officers were usually local men, such as Major Hindle, son of Chorley's mayor; Captain Hibbert, son of Sir Henry; Captain Whitfield; and Lieutenants Brindle and Reynard. Kitchener called for ten thousand volunteers and the mood of patriotic fervour and supreme confidence fired an active recruiting campaign. One recruiting station, at 17 Bolton Street, was early off the mark and the practice began of printing the names of volunteers. For the Loyals three companies recruited – F. Coy from Horwich, G. and H. from Chorley. A recruiting office opened at the bottom of Peter Wink in Market Street. By 12 September 1914 five hundred Chorley men had enlisted.

Another response to Kitchener's call was made on behalf of the East Lancashire Regiment. Across the land 'Pals' battalions were formed, units of men who volunteered in their locality, and trained and served in action under strong local affiliations. The Chorley 'Pals', never sufficient to form a separate battalion, became part of the Accrington 'Pals' which owed much to Councillor Harwood, Accrington's mayor who had family ties with Chorley. The Chorley area had the Chorley Pals, Croston Pals and (on the strength of one photograph) the Charnock Pals. Captain J. C. Milton, a local solicitor, had no trouble enlisting men; 196 were recruited. In December 1914 they were issued with their Melton uniform, of blue serge and blue caps with red piping. Other recruiting in the town moved briskly: 1,000 men were wanted, 1,040 volunteered. Everyone expected a short duration to the war.

The Pals lacked training and experience, though both would come in time. Training began locally, then in camp at Caernarfon and Rugeley in 1915. Local pride ran high, so the battalion, parades and ceremonial had an extra interest. In August 1915 they were paraded through Chorley and inspected on the cattle market. In December they embarked for Egypt, to guard the Suez Canal and remained until March 1916 when they took ship to Marseilles and the Western Front. They were to be part of the offensive on the Somme planned for the summer of 1916.

Early in the morning of 1 July, a warm, perfect summers day, the Pals climbed from their trenches to assault the German lines at Serre. Heavily laden with equipment their pace was slow. The enemy, with heavy machine guns ready, engaged in a slaughter along the whole British lines on a level unprecedented even by the scale of horror the war already knew. The Pals fared badly: 700 men left the trenches; 235 were killed and 350 wounded within minutes. First-hand accounts trickled home, and the towns where the Pals recruited held their breath. There were sixty thousand casualties on the British side in one day, and though the battalion served to the end of the war the spirit of 1914 was never recovered.

The Loyals had also seen extensive action by this time, going into action at Festubert at 6 p.m. on 15 June 1915. Losses here were heavy; twenty six killed, including Captain Hibbert, 266 wounded, 110 missing. They went on to take part in Ypres, Delville Wood and Givenchy. Their C. O., Lieutenant Colonel Hindle, son of Alderman Hindle, was killed in November 1917; the war's victims were from all walks of life. Other Chorley men fought in France, at Gallipoli, and in Mesopotamia. Some fought at sea, others in the R. F. C.

The War Memorial in Astley Park is a faithful copy of the market cross which had stood on the town's green for centuries. [Author]

When the end came it had been inevitable for months that the war would wear itself out. Gone was the buoyant mood of 1914: relief was the dominant theme of November 1918. There was a United Service of Thanksgiving at the town hall and then the reckoning. In December 1918 the *Chorley Guardian* featured two columns of names of servicemen decorated for valour; there had long been pages of photographs with brief details of casualties of countless actions. The mourning was both personal and across the community: nothing would ever be the same again. And then something remarkable happened.

Mr Reginald Arthur Tatton wrote to the mayor, Alderman Wilson, in February 1919 with an offer to give Astley Hall to the town as a war memorial. The War Memorial Committee accepted, and Astley Hall and park moved into public ownership.

The arch from Gillibrand Hall's entrance in Letchworth Drive was removed to make a new entrance for Astley Park in Park Road. A cenotaph was made near the park entrance. Chorley is unique in having such a distinctive memorial to the dead. Inside the hall a room was set aside as a room of remembrance; it includes the three books which Miss S. M. Knight made to record the names of the dead from Chorley and district. She had begun in April 1919 to appeal to relatives for names and details, all to be recorded in Miss Knight's 'Golden Book'.

On the home front things changed subtly. As men went away to war, many women joined the Women's Army as land girls, or acted as nurses. Cuerden Hall and the two hospitals, Chorley and Eaves Lane, catered for many wounded servicemen. Gillibrand Hall was home to Belgian refugees from 1914. Rationing began and poor families faced even more hardship. The war ended officially on 11 November 1918; its consequences remained for decades among the families of those who took part in it.

Conclusion

THE decade which followed the First World War ushered in a new period of change. Distant, worldwide economic forces battered on the local factory door, bringing a slump in trade, increased unemployment and the gradual but inexorable long-term decline of the cotton industry. In 1914, however, a newly-built weaving shed in Grime Street was given over to one wing of the fledging Leyland Motors, forging Chorley's link with the motor trade lasting for most of this century. Likewise, the 1930s saw yet another key player in the area's economy emerge with the construction of the Royal Ordnance Factory at Euxton in a time when unemployment was high.

The decline of cotton in this century is too complex to summarise here, Chorley's story is at least similar to many cotton towns in this respect. Yet it must be said that much of this book has been an attempt to chart the processes of change in Chorley's history by looking at specific topics. Generally, such changes have no clear landmarks in time, though some, such as the sale of the Gillibrand estates in 1880, began a process which developed major areas west of Market Street and Pall Mall for domestic housing up to about 1910. Many other changes, however, have no precise origins. They came about gradually over a span of years, recorded in the recollections of older people. It seems no accident then that the newspapers of the 1910s and 1920s contain so many accounts of how life used to be. These early forms of oral history are valuable indicators of change, even if they dwell on nostalgia and wistfulness. John Waring, for example, interviewed in 1916, recalled how much Market Street was altered from the days of his youth in the 1830s. The first shops came about in this way.

> Residents first began to display goods for sale in their house windows and as time passed on windows were enlarged and the places were transformed into regular shops.

The process of change has no end. A new century is drawing near with unknown changes in store. It is to be hoped that those qualities which have characterised Chorley until now, adaptability, resilience, hard work and a keen sense of humour will continue to serve the town in the twenty-first century.

References

Chapter One

1. Sidney Campion, *Sunlight on the Foothills* (Rich & Cowan, 1941), p. 80.
2. Richard Crossman, *Diaries of a Cabinet Minister*, vol. 1: Minister of Housing, 1964–66 (Hamish Hamilton, 1975), p. 171.
3. *Chorley Guardian*, 9 February 1924, p. 5.
4. *Country Life*, 8 July 1922, p. 14.
5. Lancashire County Council, *Lancashire's Woodland Heritage: an Introduction Based on the County Woodland Survey* (Lancashire County Council, 1986), p. 5.
6. *Chorley and District Archaeological Society Quarterly Bulletin*, vol. 1, no. 2, June (1959), pp. 1–2.
7. John Hallam, *The Surviving Past: Archaeology Finds and Excavations in Central Lancashire* (Countryside, 1985), pp. 33–8.
8. C. Robinson, *An Historical and Descriptive Account of the Parish of Chorley . . .* (1835, reprinted Chapter One, 1988), p. 11.

Chapter Two

1. T. C. Porteus, Notes on the Charnock family, Lancashire Record Office, LRO, DDX 985.
2. William Farrer and L. Brownbill, (eds), *The Victoria History of the County of Lancaster* (*VCH*), vol. 6 (Constable, 1911), p. 129.
3. Chorley deeds of Leagram Hall, no. 73, Local Studies Collection, Chorley Library.
4. Bond, 100 Marks of Silver, Alexander of Clayton and John of Clayton of Quhytehill to James of Standysh of Dokysbury, 31 May 1434, LRO, DP 397/4/5.
5. *VCH*, vol. 2, p. 199.
6. G. H. Tupling, *South Lancashire in the Reign of Edward II*, vol. 1, 3rd series (Chetham Society, 1949), p. 93.
7. T. C. Porteus, Lords in the Manor of Chorley (1931), p. 6. Manuscript notes in the Local Studies Collection in Chorley Library.
8. William Farrer, (ed.), *Lancashire Inquests, Extents and Feudal Dues, part 2: AD 1310–AD 1333*, vol. 54 (Record Society of Lancashire and Cheshire, 1907), p. 185.

9. Ibid, p. 185.
10. Hawkshead-Talbot papers, LRO, DDHK.
11. G. A. Birtill, Highways and Byways, *Chorley Guardian*, 12 January 1968, p. 16.
12. M. Beresford, *New Towns of the Middle Ages: Town Plantation in England, Wales and Gascony* (Lutterworth, 1967), pp. 80–1.
13. Farrer, *Lancashire Inquests*, p. 207.
14. T. C. Porteus, *The Hundred of Leyland in Lancashire*, new series, vol. 90 (Chetham Society, 1931), p. 72.
15. *Universal British Directory* (E. P., 1793), pp. 667–72.
16. Hallam, *The Surviving Past*, p. 64.
17. 'The Chorley Survey', in R. D. Radcliffe, *Miscellanies relating to Lancashire and Cheshire, volume the third*, vol. 33 (Record Society of Lancashire and Cheshire, 1896), pp. 1–60.
18. Grant by Richard the Marshall, clerk, to James of the Bonk, of Chorley, fletcher, 24 March 1417/8, LRO, DDX 5/4.
19. M. A. Atkin, Some settlement patterns in Lancashire, in D. Hooke (ed.), *Medieval Villages: a Review of Current Work* (Oxford University Committee for Archaeology, 1985), pp. 171–85.
20. British Library (BL), Harleian MS 2042 fol. 239.
21. An Act for Separating the Chapels of Chorley . . . 33 Geo. 3, 24, 1793.

Chapter Three

1. E. M. Hance and T. N. Morton, 'The Burgess Rolls of Liverpool During the Sixteenth Century', *H.S.L.C.*, vol. 35 (1883), pp. 147–86.
2. *Univeral British Directory*, pp. 667–72.
3. M. A. Brigg, 'Walmseleys of Dunkenhalgh: a Family of Blackburn Hundred in the Elizabethan and Stuart Periods', *Transactions of the Lancashire and Cheshire Antiquarian Society* (*L.C.A.S.*), vols 75 & 76 (1965–6), p. 97.
4. A number of books and articles have dealt with the contentious question of Myles Standish's birthplace, among them the three following titles which summarise the different arguments:
T. C. Porteus, *Captain Myles Standish: His Lost Lands and Lancashire Connections: a New Investigation* (Longman Green, Manchester U.P., 1920); G. V. C. Young, *Pilgrim Myles Standish: First Manx American* (Mansk-Svenska, 1984); L. Hill, *Gentlemen of Courage Forward: a History of the Standish Family, Lancashire from the Norman Conquest in 1066* A.D. *Within the Context of English History* (Magnolia, 1987).
5. G. A. Fallon, *Roman Catholics in Standish* (Standish Local History Society, 1976), p. 19.
6. T. C. Porteus, Brooke estates, LRO, DDX 985.
7. G. Ormerod, *Tracts Relating to Military Proceedings in Lancashire During the Great Civil War*, old series, vol. 2 (Chetham Society, 1844), p. 279.

8. Rental of Chorley, Public Record Office (PRO), 10 Henry IV 1408, Norris Papers B. M. Add. MSS 36924, vol. i, fol. 131d, 132.
9. Examination of witnesses taken at Chorley Manor Court concerning Astley and 'the Ackers' especially as to right of way, 7 November 1670, LRO, DDTa 244

Chapter Four

1. E. Robinson, *A Discourse of the Warr in Lancashire*, edited by W. Beamont, old series, vol. 62., (Chetham Society, 1864), p. 4.
2. J. J. Bagley, *A History of Lancashire*, 4th edn (Finlayson, 1967), p. 45.
3. Rigby Lieutenancy Book, 1627–40, LRO, DDHK.
4. Robinson, *Discourse.*
5. Letter from Thomas Gillibrand to John Warde, 1643, LRO, DDX 258/61.
6. E. Calamy, *The Nonconformist's Memorial: Being an Account of the Ministers Who Were Ejected or Silenced After the Restoration . . .*, vol. 2 (Harris, 1775), p. 88.
7. Great Britain Royal Commission on Historic Manuscripts, *Manuscripts of Lord Kenyon* (HMSO, 1894), p. 174.
8. C. L'Estrange Ewen, *Witchcraft and Demonianism: a Concise Account Derived from Sworn Depositions and Confessions . . .* (Heath Cranton, 1933), pp. 411–12.

Chapter Five

1. Wicker survey . . . 1716, PRO, FEC 1/227.
2. R. Sharpe France (ed.), *The Registers of Estates of Lancashire Papists, 1717–1788*, vol. 2, 1717 (Record Society of Lancashire and Cheshire 1960), pp. 45–50.
3. *Chorley Weasel*, 1881, pp. 412–13.
4. Letter from the Bishop of Chester, 1778: draft with notes. Local Studies Collection, Chorley Library.
5. Township papers, 1737. LRO, DDHK.
6. An Act for Dividing and Inclosing Several Commons . . . Chorley 7 Geo. 3, 13, 1767.
7. Healey enclosure, c1760, LRO, DDX 985.
8. *Manchester Mercury*, 5–12 April 1757, p. 3.
9. *Preston Guardian*, 26 April 1884, p. 9.
10. T. C. Gillett, *Story of Weld Bank* (Author, 1974), pp. 50–3.
11. Wedgwood MSS, 18929–26 in T. C. Porteus, *A History of the Parish of Standish, Lancashire* (Starr, 1927), pp. 41–2.
12. Home Office papers, PRO, W01/1003/183.
13. Home Office papers, PRO, W01/1003/5, Oct. 1779.
14. Ibid.
15. *Chorley Standard*, 29 April 1865, p. 1.
16. Quarter Sessions Order Book, 1780, LRO, QSO/2/149.

17. Annual Register, 27 June 1780, p. 926.
18. Quarter Sessions Court of Enquiry . . . 1779. LRO.

Chapter Six

1. *Chorley Standard*, 13 May 1865, p. 1.
2. A. P. Wadsworth and J. P. Mann, *The Cotton Trade and Industrial Lancashire* (Manchester U.P., 1931), pp. 95–6.
3. *Chorley Guardian*, 30 September 1933 (Supplement, Withnell and Brinscall), p. 3.
4. A. Burton, *The Canal Builders* (Eyre Methuen, 1972), p. 184.
5. N. Blundell, *The Great Diurnal of Nicholas Blundell of Little Crosby, Lancashire*, 3 vols: vols 110, 112, 114 (Record Society, 1968, 1970, 1972).
6. *Chorley Echo*, 26 May 1883, p. 80.
7. M. Roberts, Standishes of Duxbury and Miles Standish: news-cuttings in the Local Studies Collection, Accrington Library.
8. Standish pedigree, 1842. Local Studies Collection, Chorley Library.
9. T. C. Porteus, *Queer Stories of Old Chorley* (Chorley News Co., n.d.), p. 12.
10. James Talbot, The Baggenley Hall day book, microfilm in Local Studies Collection, Chorley Library.
11. Chorley Vestry Town Book, 1781–1823, MSS in Local Studies Collection, Chorley Library.
12. *Preston Pilot*, 29 April 1826, p. 2.
13. *Chorley Standard*, 13 May 1865, p. 1.
14. *Blackburn Mail*, 17 May 1826, p. 3.
15. Campion, *Sunlight*, p. 80.
16. *Preston Pilot*, 22 July 1848, p. 8.

Chapter Seven

1. *Chorley Standard*, 1 July 1865, p. 4.
2. *Chorley Standard*, 31 May 1873, p. 2.
3. Robinson, *Historical and Descriptive Account*, p. 11.
4. *Chorley Weekly News*, 2 August 1924, p. 8.
5. Township papers, LRO, DDHK.
6. Robinson, *Historical and Descriptive Account*, p. 13.
7. Thomas Hawkshead's book, MSS in Local Studies Collection, Chorley Library.
8. R. Kuerden, 'A Lancashire Itinerary', *Local Gleanings Relating To Lancashire and Cheshire*, vol. 1 (1876), p. 211.
9. W. Bolton, Chorley Past and Present in *St Mary's Bazaar Gazette* (1907), p. 23.
10. Chorley Vestry Town's Book, 1781–1823, 11 April 1803 in Local Studies Collection, Chorley Library.

11. R. Rawlinson, *Report to the General Board of Health on . . . Chorley in the County of Lancaster* (HMSO, 1853), pp. 21 *et seq.*
12. R. Rawlinson, *Report on the Sewerage and Drainage . . . Chorley* (Lawson, 1857), pp. 1–16.
13. *Blackburn Mail,* 18 November 1795, p. 2.
14. *Chorley Weekly News*, 23 February 1924, p. 5.
15. G. B. Census, 1851, RG 9/3120.
16. A. Tougan-Baranowsky, *Les Crises Industrielles en Angleterre* (1913), pp. 398–9.

Chapter Eight

1. R. H. Blackburn, *Sir Henry Tate* (Chorley Guardian, 1940), p. 19.
2. *Chorley Standard*, 17 March 1877, p. 3.
3. *Chorley Weekly News*, 1 April 1916, p. 7.
4. Chorley Races, 1814. Poster. Local Studies Collection, Chorley Library.
5. *Chorley Public Library Annual Report*, 1900, pp. 3–10.
6. *Chorley Weekly News*, 12 February 1913, p. 5.
7. *Chorley Weekly News*, 15 January 1910, p. 5.
8. *Chorley Weekly News*, 15 February 1912, p. 8.
9. Chorley by-election scrapbook, 1913. Local Studies Collection, Chorley Library.
10. *Chorley Weekly News*, 4 October 1913, p. 5.

Bibliography

Aspin, Chris, *The Cotton Industry* (Shire, 1981).

Bagley, J. J., *A History of Lancashire*, 4th edn (Darwen Finalyson, 1967).

Berry, Luke & Sons, *Chorley and Neighbourhood* (Berry, Luke & Sons, 1900).

Birtill, G. A., *The Church on the Brow: St Laurence's, Chorley* (Chorley Guardian, 1968).

Birtill, G. A., *The Field of Churls* (Chorley Guardian, 1970).

Birtill, G. A., *Follow any Stream* (Nelson, Bros., 1968).

Birtill, G. A., *The War and After* (Chorley Guardian, 1976).

Birtill, G. A., *What Mean these Stones?* (Chorley Guardian, 1965).

Blackburn, R. H., *Borough of Chorley, 1881–1981 . . . Jubilee Souvenir* (Chorley Corporation, 1931).

Blundell, F. O., *Old Catholic Lancashire*. 3 vols. (Burns & Oates, 1938) especially vol. 2.

Cescinsky, Herbert, *Astley Hall, Chorley, Lancashire: a Report on the Hall and Its Contents* (Chorley Guardian, 1923).

Chorley Borough, *Astley Hall, Chorley: Illustrated souvenir* (Chorley Borough, c. 1930).

Chorley Borough, *Opening of Chorley Park . . . 31st May 1924* (Chorley Borough, 1924).

Cornish, E. M. J., *The Story of the Parish of St George, Chorley* (British Publishing, n.d.).

Farrer, William and Brownhill, J., eds., *The Victoria History of the County of Lancaster* (Constable, 1911) especially Vol. 6.

The Flat Iron: a Newsletter for Local History (Lancashire County Library, No. 1. 1987 to date).

Freethy, Ron, *Turnpikes and Toll Houses of Lancashire* (Countryside, 1986).

Gillett, Tom C., *Magpie Parade: Chorley Football Club, 1875–1946* (Author, 1946).

Gillett, Tom C., *The Story of Weld Bank* (Nelson Bros., 1974).

Gillett, Tom C., *Tales of Old Chorley* (Author, 1981).

Grayson, Robin F. and Williamson, Iain A., eds., *Geological Routes around Wigan* (Wigan & District Geological Society, 1977).

Hall, William, *Vindication of the Chorley Spinners* (Leigh, 1826).

Haward, W. I., *Secret Rooms of North West England* (Dalesman, 1964).

Haworth, Gordon, *Astley Hall, Official Guide* (Chorley Borough, 1981).

Headley, Horace, *History of St Peter's, Chorley* (Sandiford, 1901).

Heyes, James, *Album of Old Chorley: a Collection of Photographs* (Lancashire County Council, 1978).

Hills, R. L., *Cotton Spinning* (North Western Museum of Science & Industry, 1977).

Hodkinson, Kenneth, *Old Chorley: 'In the Footsteps of Wilson'* (C.K.D., 1988).

Porteus, Thomas C., *Astley Hall, Chorley, Lancashire* (Sandiford, 1923).

Porteus, Thomas C., *A Chapter of Beginnings in the History of Chorley* (Preston Guardian, 1923).

Porteus, Thomas C., *A History of the Parish of Standish* (J. Starr & Sons, 1927).

Porteus, Thomas C., *The Hundred of Leyland in Lancashire*, new series, vol. 90 (Chetham Society, 1931).

Registers of the Parish Church of Chorley in the County of Lancaster, 1548–1653, transcribed by . . . Edward McKnight, vol. 38. (L.P.R.S., 1910).

Robinson, C., *An Historical and Descriptive Account of the Parish of Chorley* . . . (1835, reprinted Chapter One, 1988).

Turner, William, *Pals: the 11th (Service) Battalion (Accrington) East Lancashire Regiment* (Wharnecliffe, 1987).

Walker, F., *Historical Geography of Southwest Lancashire before the Industrial Revolution*, new series, vol. 103 (Chetham Society, 1939).

Wilson, John, *Chorley Church* (Author, 1914).

Wilson, John, *Verses and Notes* (Hill, 1903).

Appendix

A table of key dates in the cotton industry, Chorley 1770–1914

Date	*Name of mill*	*Location*	*Associated with*	*Type/notes*
1777	Birkacre	R. Yarrow	Rd. Arkwright	Spinning (water)
1780	Astley Park	R. Chor	Townley-Parker	Carding engine
1785	Crosse Hall	Black Brook	James Duxbury	Printworks
1786	Tootell Street	– do –	Richard Salisbury	Spinning (Jennies, etc.)
1788	Water Street	– do –	Robert Lightoller	Spinning; Trig Hall
1788	Petition to Parliament from the spinners of cotton yarns and manufacturers of calicoes and muslins.			
1789	–	Hollinshead Street	John Ryding	Thomas Hindle
1790	Heapey Mill	Printing		
1791	Lower Burgh	– do –	John Parkinson	Spinning; fire 1791
1793	Cowling Bridge	– do –	Birch Rees & Evans	Printworks
1795	–	Hollinshead Street	Joseph Pilkington	Bankruptcy 1795
1802	Old Mill	Standish Street	Robert Lightoller	Spinning
1804	–	Water Street	Hilton & Sale	Boulton & Watt steam engine
1815	Waterloo Mill	Water Street	James Anderton	
1819	–	Standish Street	Robert Lightoller	Gas lighting introduced
1820	'The Factory'	Town's Green	Thomas Brown	Sales 1817 and 1820
1824	Cowling Mill	Cowling	Hole & Wilkinson	Calico printing
1824	Old Mill	Preston Street	Richard Smethurst	Spinning
1826	Water Street	– do –	Hilton	Spinning
1834	New Mill	North Street	Richard Smethurst	Spinning
1838	Crosse Hall	Cowling	Richard Cobden	Printing
1840	Sherbourne	Lyons Lane	Lawrence Anyon	Fire 1873
1842	Stump	Stump Lane	Messrs Wallwork	Spinning; renamed Fosterfield 1855
1851	Tower Mill	North Street	Richard Smethurst	Destroyed by fire 1911
1851	Redan Mill	Cowling	Heyworth	

1851	Friday Street	Friday Street	George Brown	Power looms introduced
1851	Castle Mill	Albion Street	Foster	Wilson & Gornall 1858
1852	Moor Mill	Pall Mall	Rice and Hall	Muslin goods
	Croft Mill	–	Rice & Co.	
1852	Victoria Mill	Lyons Lane	Lightoller	Fire 1909
1857–8	Lawrence's	Lyons Lane	William Lawrence	First mill
1856	Canal	Botany Bay	William Widdows	originally built for R. Smethurst
1857	Dole Lane	Dole Lane	William Atherton	Jacconets
1861	Primrose	Friday Street	George Brown	
1861	Greenfield	Steeley Lane	Brindle (1903)	Sale: 1880: 547 looms
1861	Weld Bank	Saville Street	Rice – 1861	Weaving
1866	Lawrence's	Lyons Lane	William Lawrence	Second mill
1866	Primrose Shed	Friday Street	George Brown	Weaving
1872	Heapey Bleachworks	Heapey	Rylands & Co.	1871–2 Old Works demolished
1874	Brook Street	Tatton Street	James Fletcher	
1886	Progress Mill	Seymour Street	Thomas Howarth	over 200 looms
1887	Jubilee Mill	Pall Mall	Jolly	weaving
1888	Public meeting 3 November to petition restrictions on steaming in weaving sheds			
1897	Weldbank Printworks	Plock Estate	Barton Kershaw	Calico bleaching and printing
1897–1900	Diamond Mill	Railway Road	George Edge	
1902	Weavers Institute	Chapel Street	Chorley Weavers Association	
1903	Hope Mill	Lucas Street		Cotton and Muslin
1905	Fosterfield	Eaves Lane	Fosterfield Mill Co. Ltd	Cotton goods
1906	Talbot	Bagganley	Talbot Spinning & Weaving Co.	
1906	Cowling Mill	Cowling	Cowling Spinning Co. Ltd	Spinning
1910	Yarrow Mill	Yarrow Road	Downs, Coulter & Co.	
1914	Park Mills	Deighton Road	Joseph Blackledge & Sons	Extended 1959
1914	Weaving Shed	Grime Street	Ash & Livesey	Leyland Motors (1914)

Index